Locks, Tides - and French Brie

in which a Circumnavigation of France by boat is achieved . . .

Don Wark

authorHOUSE®

AuthorHouse™ UK Ltd.
500 Avebury Boulevard
Central Milton Keynes, MK9 2BE
www.authorhouse.co.uk
Phone: 08001974150

First published by AuthorHouse 9/12/2011

ISBN: 978-1-4520-9436-6 (sc)

See book WEB Site and forum:
www.locksandtides.com

This book is printed on acid-free paper.

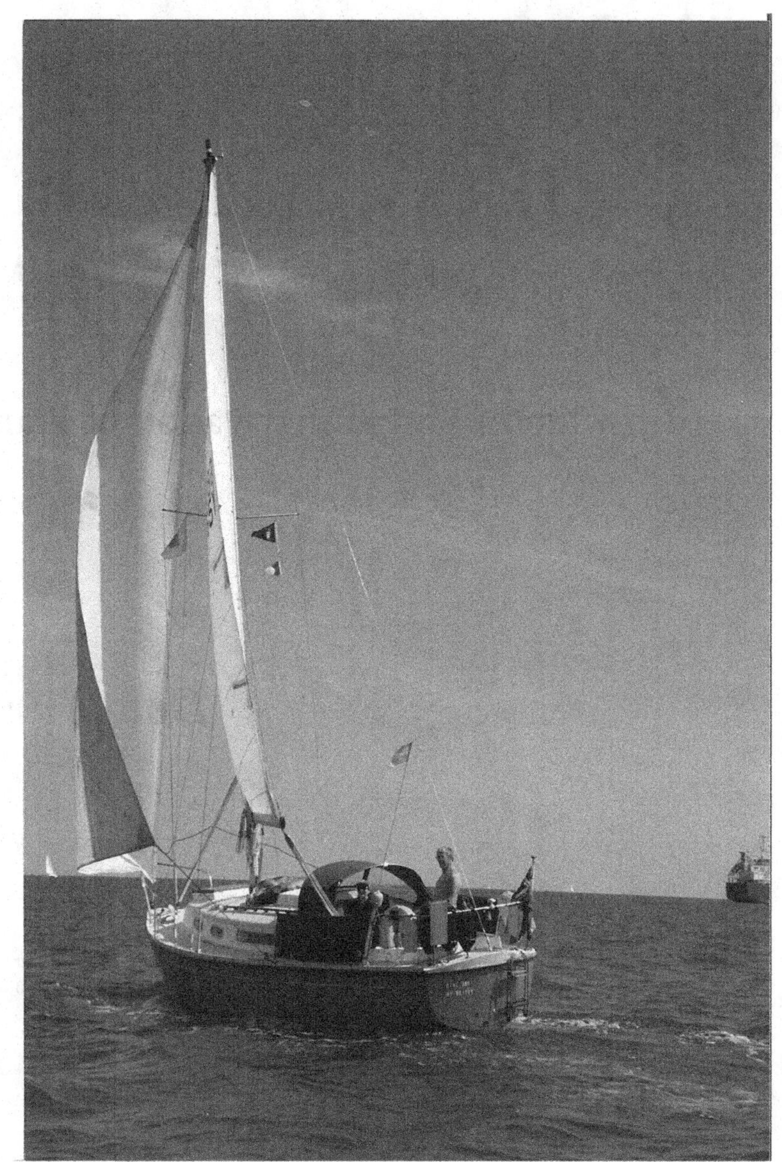

‘Locks, Tides - and French Brie’

In which three veterans set out on their own ‘Yellow Brick Road’; in fact to circumnavigate France by boat. The heroine being the long suffering ‘*Wise One*’.

Front cover photo: Don’s reaction to the Pouilly Tunnel entrance.

[PS Please show this book to your friends; but don’t lend; it might not come back and anyway spoils the sales……]

Contents

Acknowledgements

'*Sailing Today'* who have published a number of accounts of these travels through the French waterways.

'The Wizard of Oz' and L. Frank Baum who provided a theme and a setting for our own adventures.

'Goodbye Yellow Brick Road' and Elton John who (unknowingly) provided the background music to the writing.

Dorset County Council, Archaeological Unit, with whom I corresponded on the issue of Celtic movements to Britain.

Cloisters Museum, New York for advice on matters to do with C16th tapestries.

Helena Drysdale and *The Writers' Workshop for* advice and encouragement.

Janet Murphy of *Adlard Coles Nautical* for her invaluable advice and encouragement.

'The Battle of Quiberon Bay, 1759' by Nicholas Tracy.

Margaret Hackett and Dick Cole for proof reading and steering me away from some howlers.

Mentor Jacky for her memory, photos and endless patience.

The Prologue

It had been a hot autumn day with a clear blue sky and gentle wind. We sat in the cockpit with our feet up and a well deserved cold glass in hand. The river was quiet with a few modest yachts at moorings, nosing the slightly ebbing current. A touch of mist was just perceptible up-stream where heron stood carved in stone on the water's edge. The wooded banks of the Vilaine River curved away westwards towards La Roche Bernard and the sea. Eastwards the land opened up to allow the river to wind across the flattened plain to distant Redon. For us, little mattered except the slow golden approach of autumn, the shortening evenings and the nearby little restaurant with promise of 'moule' (or better). Tomorrow a large crane would shatter this idyll as we returned to what is laughingly called 'the real world'.

But how did we get to be here? Well, with a bit of extra time on our hands we were aware that

'When men in black gowns are doing their rounds
They bind with briars our hopes and desires.'

We certainly didn't want any of that. In the past we have sailed in our old friend *Wise One* as far as Belle Ile off the South Brittany coast. Perhaps there was a quite different way of getting there and at the same time achieving a sort of circumnavigation of France. That could be our claim, anyway.

I guess we were a both a bit 'blown away' by our many options and therefore (Frank Baum would understand) we needed the *'Yellow Brick Road'* to get us there and home again – and at the same time to be the wiser for it. Certainly on the way we will meet strange beasts in Paris, giants on the Rhone, Tin men in Carcassonne, witches, wizards, heroes, villains and monsters. There will be blood and guts by the bucket; burning bodies and cross eyed Popes. There may be some strange stories on the way (who knows?). Jacky, of course, plays the part of Dorothy and myself the Scarecrow (straw brains and sartorial inelegance included). So – off to the land of the Munchkins and to the Emerald City (wherever that is).

It's a story worth telling (well I think so anyway). Dear reader, what do you think? Come and talk to us on www.locksandtides.com and we'd love to hear from you.

Part 1
Summer 2005 Southampton to the Med.

In which we make a fair start, lots of friends, meet strange beasts in Paris; and break into the Med (by the uphill route).

A l'eau; c'est l'heure.....

(Hint: say this again and keep saying it until the English mysteriously emerges…)

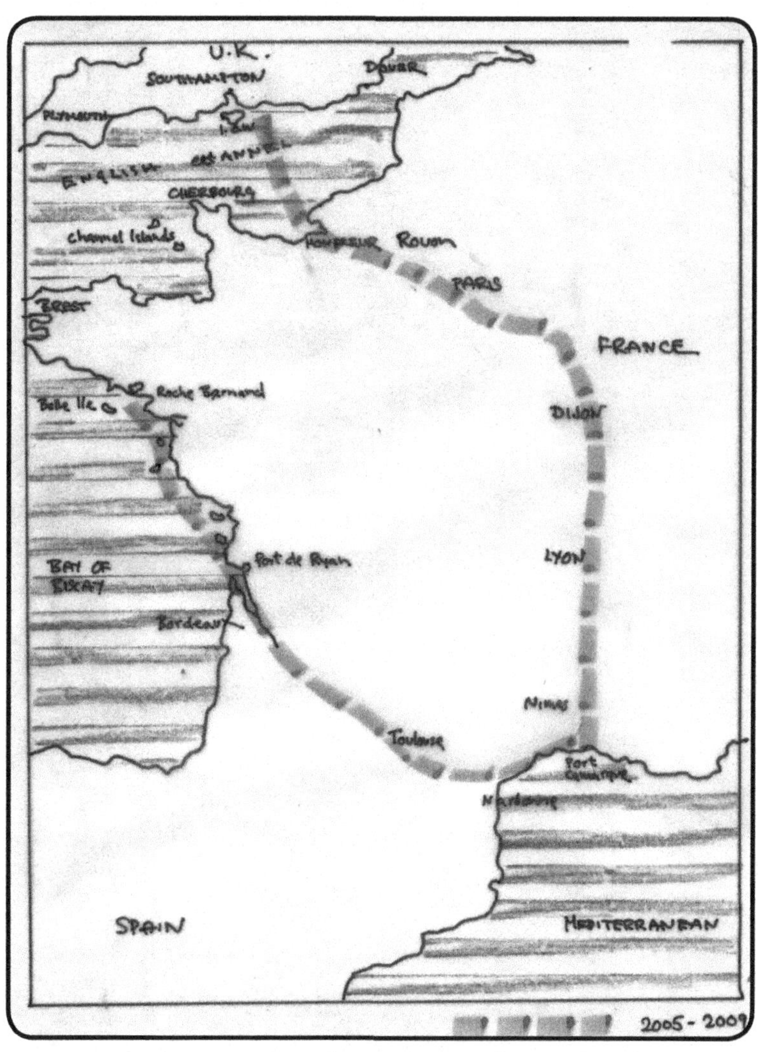

Map 1 Southampton to the Med.

Chapter 1

The Channel Leap

OK, let's just begin at the beginning with a few introductions. Jacky and I met when we were both in college in Leicester and old Leicester friends will occur during this tale. Jacky had graduated from an Air force Service up-bringing to study textile design. I was then in my fourth year of an architectural course. The '60s were a wild time; or so I'm told. Anyway, life was quite busy really and crowded with demanding rugby twice a week proceeded by essential training and succeeded by even more essential post-match analysis.

But there was time to rescue Jacky from the clutches of her senior tutor and life was pretty good. She saw herself through the Basic Design Course and on to the textile bit while I completed mine and had a (working-as-an-architect) year in South Africa, much of which I saw by motorbike. When I returned we were married in my home-town Lincoln. Jacky set up a design partnership with several graduated friends and I took an architectural job in Leicester. If you want somebody for your quiz team, (or go to the opera with) or just to get something done, I guess you would choose Jacky not me.

So far no boats although we had both sailed in our 'teens. However a long standing (academic) ambition of mine was realised when we moved to Edinburgh for Jacky to lecture for a couple of years while I did a post-grad in Town planning. I was closeted day-time in George Square for a couple of years but we did find time to make friends and do other things. We got in a bit of sailing on the Firth of Forth with student friends. Other old Edinburgh friends will re-emerge during this story. Time passed (as it does) and jobs took us to Merseyside where Jacky went back to college on a teacher training course. We lived initially in New Brighton and there we bought our first boat.

For over fifty years we have both sailed although to begin with not together. That first boat was *Delta*, a 16'6" converted ship's lifeboat, gunter rigged, red sails, two berths and a bucket. A tallow–armed weight on the end of a line was our depth sounder and our steering compass sat in an old wooden box in the corner of the cockpit. Speed and distance were deduced by a box of used matches which could be chucked over the side (one by one) and average speed calculated She looked (and sailed) like a heavy-weight mirror dinghy and was moored on the entrance to the River Mersey in the mud and sand of the Dee Estuary. Experienced yachtsman Nigel sailed with me to the Isle of Man and pronounced *Delta* as "quite the slowest sailing vessel I have ever been in." But still that didn't stop Jacky and me from traversing the North Wales coast, through the Menai Straights and the infamous Swellies (leave Wales to port and Anglesey to starboard) to our holiday flat in Port Dinorwic.

Jacky, in those early days, used generally to drive by 'Renault 4' from our home in New

Brighton and, later when we lived in Rainhill, with young Anna and Alex. She would 'phone the coastguards at the Point of Ayre to see if I had gone by yet. Times change. I suppose that, for Jacky, weaving the fabric of life between Rainhill and Port Dinorwic was appropriate for one trained as a textile designer. In Merseyside she split her time between lecturing, designing, sketching, mothering and driving a Renault 4. And with a great deal of good humour she seemed to put up with me too. At that time my jobs lay variously in Liverpool, St Helens and Wigan. Jacky managed this peripatetic employment time by sharing jobs and four small children with friend Jenny to the extent that school staff were confused as to which child belonged to which parents. We thought that amusing at the time but I guess schools now find that quite normal.

It was in Port Dinorwic on the Menai Straights that we fell in with Hazel and bearded-optician Sydney (and young Lizzie and violin-learning-Jonathon) from Leeds. They had the first floor holiday flat below us in Dinorwic and would arrive at two in the morning with a Range Rover, kids, dogs, grannies and gear. We couldn't beat them so we had to do the other.

They commanded the biggest yacht I could possibly imagine and invited us on board their 31'6" Westerly Pentland, *Polly Garter.* Their dinghy *Willy Wee* was, naturally, "tender to Polly". (Nice one). Sidney of course was much older than I. (He could give me a good five years). In between telling unlikely tales, writing and directing plays, he wanted a crew and together (sometimes with others) we sailed between North Wales, the Isles of Tiree and Ardramurchan Point (West coast of Scotland); between Dunmore East in Southern Ireland, the Scillies and Belle Ile in southern Brittany. With *Polly Garter* we became quite committed to sail-cruising.

For Sydney and Hazel the all-important skill was to go with the flood tide to a choice riverside restaurant or bar; enjoy blue cheese and red wine and still find the boat floating on the ebb to carry you back to deep water. Miss the tide and you could sit on your twin keels in the mud for hours. But even that was no great hardship (provided of course that you *had* made it back on board).

Jacky and I left the shallow and tidal waters of the Dee Estuary and deserted beautiful North Wales when a job called in Southampton. We knew we would miss the evening sandbanks at low tide which constricts the mouth of the Dee – and provide an evening basking bed for the mournful seals. Sailing at low tide out to those banks in a late summer evening to be serenaded by the cries of the seals was an irreplaceable experience. So too was the wonderful mountain backdrop as you nose past ancient Conway and head on up the Menai Straits to Bangor past the endless tidal flats of Penmaenmawr and the foothills of Snowdonia. As also were the winter assaults on the Snowdon range from our small place in Dinorwic.

We took with us the proceeds of our holiday flat and the sale of *Delta* and were in the market for our own genuine sail-cruiser. Sadly our pockets were still not deep enough but the problem was solved by partnering with Brian and Kay. Partnerships, of course, share the costs, the worries and the work. But to make it worthwhile, partners have to have the same objectives and pretty much the same pockets.

Although Brian looked much more mature than I, I guess that we were of a similar vintage and both had young families. B and K had both been employed in East Africa; and Brian in the district police service (you could tell) and Kay as a bush nurse. With a great deal of good humour she seemed to put up with Brian. In the Solent he took charge of the renowned Calshot Activities Centre and was always the source of solutions to problems or the names of people who could. As we went into joint boat ownership, Jacky did note the oily handprints on the white plastic-work – and I noted that the engine continued to run. I learnt a lot from Brian (and still Jacky stayed with me).

So, for us, it worked and we bought the largest boat we could together afford: a six year old, Thames Marine Snapdragon 890. She was (and still is) sturdy, competent, six berth, 29 foot, bilge keel, fibreglass sloop. She was built in 1974 in down-stream Thames by the then prolific Thames Marine. As a bilge keeler she was particularly suitable for her home waters in the South East and Thames Estuary where many of her sisters still sail. While not designed to win many cups in the round-the-buoys racing on a Sunday morning, her strength lies in taking the family to a creek or island and returning safely; and doing so in some reasonable comfort. Down below she has a theoretical six berths. One is now dedicated to chart stowage, DIY tools, 'oilies' and life jackets. One berth is created by the collapse of the saloon table to make a comfortable double.

Two berths lie in the fore cabin; generous in width at the shoulder end and a bit minimum for four friendly feet at the foot end. Although the fore cabin double berth requires an athletic head-spring over the pillows to get out, it is our preferred option. Normally, therefore, the main cabin is not decorated by a slumbering person or abandoned bed clothes. Friends, you may deride the fat sterned charter vessel with a free standing full sized double berth flanked by reading lights on occasional bedside tables; but they do have something to recommend them.

Cooking is inevitably Jacky's province (Why? Well tradition dies hard and she's good at it). Our twin camping-gas burner with oven performs well – not by itself, naturally and reinforced by a certain amount of eating out. We have to remind ourselves that the time we now spend on board should not be regarded as a 'holiday' (when, for a limited time, you might eat out most days) but just a change of life style (when you can't afford to eat out as much as you really wish). So on-board eating remains an important part of our lives.

The 'heads' are, for a small boat, reasonably convenient. All new, going-foreign boats should now have holding tanks fitted and we really must get some installed. That requirement in sheltered waters will gradually become mandatory but, of course, must come hand-in-hand with the provision of pumping out stations which at present are rarely available. There is no integrated hot water system on board which would be nice but is not essential. All in all, for a modest twenty-nine footer, she is a generous little cruiser.

That was in 1980. Since then we have often talked about up-grading to something a bit newer, a bit bigger, a bit more 'contemporary' but somehow there never seemed to be enough benefit. A bigger boat can always cope better with fresh conditions and therefore be more efficient and comfortable at sea. It can also cope better with more people and their gear. The downside is that costs also rapidly increase with extra length. Now we sail mostly with just two people (us) over limited distances and I don't think we would do anything very different with a larger vessel. Over the years we have kept up with investment in new rig and equipment although for many years we resisted the proliferation of electronics that now tend to dominate any cruising boat. So our Snapdragon 890 suits us very well. (However, it could be nice if...)

We understood that the name *Wise One* came from the company of first ownership i.e. the boat lift manufacturers 'Wise and Co'. Made sense. We long debated a change of name (the down-side of '*Wise One'* is perhaps obvious) but we simply could not agree. Brian and Kay wanted something with an unpronounceable African combination of the letters NGOX (and a click somewhere) whereas we were looking at something like *'The Dark Lady'* or *'Buds of May'* (unlucky connotations?). So the name never changed.

The two families split holiday long-haul trips ("you go, we come back") and between us *Wise One* sailed for 20 years between Weymouth and Chichester; between the Solent and Channel Islands, between Cherbourg and Flushing; between Falmouth and South Brittany (Belle Ile again). There eventually came the day when Brian and Kay moved away from the Solent and Jacky and I bought out their share. Sad, that. We still keep in touch and Brian, (having quite mellowed), and Kay now split their time between growing a lot of apples and grandchildren. At this stage paid employment for us was beginning to be increasingly optional.

Halcyon days, now work is ending, you may find where 'ere you sail. Tritons all the while attending with a kind of gentle gale.

(Thanks to C C and Anon)

Jacky's previously expressed interest in sailing 'in-land' re-emerged. A plan was hatched.

Several of our sailing friends had gone through the French Inland Waterway system down to the Mediterranean, taking a couple of hard working weeks to deliver their vessel in the shortest possible time. We decided to do it at great leisure and take the whole summer giving us time to explore towns, sketch (Jacky) and drink wine (both). Year Two could perhaps then be spent in the Med. The Western Med however did not seem to me to be a hugely attractive proposition in many ways, including marina congestion, no doubt costs and weather. Turkey, Greece and Croatia hold the cruising skipper prizes, but represented (to us) a long distant commitment of perhaps three or four years and two or three thousand miles. Maybe, for us, those areas are best done by charter and, indeed, that is what we are now doing.

Slowly an alternative emerged achieving a sort of circumnavigation of France via Paris, the central canals, the Mediterranean, the southern canals and the Atlantic coastline to meet up with *Wise One's* previous south Brittany trip to Belle Ile.

The trip seemed to be a bit like Dorothy and the Scarecrow setting out on the Yellow Brick Road of Frank Baum fame. They trusted in the Brick Road to get them to the Emerald City.

We could do something similar; but on water (there's nothing to say you can't). It's true we would have to do a little bit of planning, but no doubt many decisions would also be made as we went along. In fact this first summer would cover some 1000 miles rising about 400 metres above sea level and involve about 230 locks. Give or take a few. But even young innocents (us) have to work out the first bit. The most decisive part of any journey is the first mile.

Route planning from Southampton therefore started with exploring the French port of entry. Is that an obvious statement? Well there are options and we did have to find out where the *Yellow Brick Road* was going to take us. Jacky said:
"What is the problem? Obviously we enter the Seine at le Havre and just head on up to Paris"
"Well. It's not really a problem, but I am a bit puzzled how the Le Havre to Rouen bit works. It seems a bit daunting to me. Besides, we're in no great hurry so let's just explore the longer open water and river option of entry via St. Valery-sur-Somme."
But the problem there was the small 'tidal window' into the Somme after a long Channel crossing from Brighton; and nowhere to go if you miss the window. (Would you want to hang around for seven hours in the Channel waiting for the next tide?). So I conceded the logic and returned our thinking to the River Seine.

The first choice for small boats entering the Seine is the marina in Le Havre. This is big, modern, efficient and no doubt has all support services. However much more attractive to us than Le Havre is its small historic neighbour Honfleur. This delightful town was, at one time, of little use to those continuing up the Seine until the construction of a locked entry and dredged channel into the little port. Since you need to start your journey up-river with the whole flood tide ahead of you, leaving Honfleur near top-of-tide didn't help. Depending on your draft (and my twin keel Snap was OK) the lock is only *not* accessible two hours either side of low water. So Honfleur it was.

Fundamental also was the question of the mast which is too tall for bridges up-stream of Rouen. Most people take it with them, extending over their vessel fore and aft and being a permanent threat to scalps and other boats. Given our leisurely timetable, we opted to leave the mast behind in Honfleur and have it road-hauled to our eventual destination. Expensive but more comfortable. Getting quotations for lifting, storing and transporting was a frustrating process. French contractors don't seem to answer e-mails, letters or return 'phone calls. Rouen is a possible (and last) place for mast removal but none of my many messages were answered, even those to the Tourist Office appealing for help. However not so in Honfleur where the Port responded immediately and so did Monsieur Challe's boatyard with good advice and quotes. (Are you still there Frederic?)

Otherwise preparations were fairly routine. Charts and Pilot books for the whole trip are absolutely essential and a matter of some personal preference. My own preferences are shown in Appendix 4 along with other useful reading matter.

We provided ourselves with three 'luxuries' which are now essentials (always so with luxuries). The first was a magnificent cockpit 'conservatory'. I specified a bimini to provide shelter from the noon-day sun but independent of the existing substantial spray hood. You still need the breeze to blow through. We specified as much transparency as technology could produce, (if only our politicians were the same), so we had a superb additional see-out-all-round cabin when all is put together. Of course the height of the bimini is determined by a man standing at the helm which is the same for a 29 footer as for a 49 footer. The smaller boat may therefore have to accept an enclosed cockpit which looks rather bulky for the boat's size. However it really extends the use and enjoyment of our small live-aboard vessel and is thanks to the expertise of Sanders Sails of Lymington (thank you Peter). You can't sail with any of it up; but then for some time we won't be sailing.

Folding bicycles were further essentials; particularly for canal-side communications, lock management and keeping fit. We did seem to get an awful lot of punctures, possibly down to the tough surfaces we generally cycled over. Should I have my time again (which I probably won't) I would pay a bit more for better quality and more chance of resisting the inevitable deterioration of steel gear always stored in a damp and salty environment.

Final essential detail: although we were not allowed to travel the inland waterways after dark, we still needed to replace the masthead navigation light. We solved this by swapping the varnished ensign staff with an aluminium pole nicked from our swimming pool brush; we jammed in one end of it a solar-powered garden light. The ensign flew just below the light which I think in etiquette terms is OK. We could always find our way back to the boat after closing hours and it must have been effective since we had no after dark collisions.

Wise One in canal mode

Final luxury: communications. To stay in touch with friends, family and business we decided that while in the canals we could not always be looking for internet cafes. Our solution was a blue-tooth connection to a laptop giving us full internet access. It worked beautifully – and cost us! As the trip progressed however we found ourselves increasingly able to access WIFI as most marinas and many cafes now seem to have it on offer. And it's a lot cheaper.

For the crossing to Honfleur I was glad to have my old friend Pete along. We've sailed together before and he makes a great ship-mate. Jacky and Kate were to take Pete and Kate's car over and meet us in Honfleur. Pete and Kate live in Minstead and are near neighbours of ours in the New Forest. They would return with our offshore gear which would not be needed for a couple of seasons.

Pete has spent his life as an electrical engineer keeping our national grid working in all weathers. He just takes a bit of a blow in mid-channel in his stride (and could re-wire your boat at the same time, if you required). If you have a practical problem, Pete's your man from (helping) rebuild your kitchen or bathroom to replacing your drainage system. He could even translate that awkward letter that's just arrived from Spain. He has rebuilt and extended his house over the years and so he has a lot of experience to pass on. He also likes the 'Ring Cycle' but there's no need to hold that against him. My publisher has urged me to tell you more about my friends but that's a problem. There's a lot more I know about Pete but have promised not to tell. Unless of course over a pint sometime… Kate has spent her life teaching, organising people around her and bringing up two off-spring into responsible adulthood, sketching, painting, getting involved with village life; and putting up with Pete. No New Year's Eve is complete without Kate and Pete.

Don and Pete

Navigation was straight forward. We started from Southampton where we enjoy membership of the Royal Southampton Yacht Club. We needed ebb tide help from Ocean Village, down Southampton Water and out of the Solent past Portsmouth. The main channel exits the Solent past the great 19th Century No Mans Fort, designed to keep the French out; and it provided a 1940 ac-ac gun emplacement to engage the Luftwaffe. It's a fierce place is the Solent. Then a straight line open water track of 89 miles delivers us to the mouth of the Seine Estuary. There we would need to organise some flood tide to take us up to Honfleur. (This English Channel sailing is all about tides).

Although we have been sailing these waters for some years, leaving port for a Channel crossing is still a slightly dry-mouth moment. The traditional naval First Officer report to the Captain is: "In all respects ready for sea, SIR". I have always thought that to be a momentous statement. 'In all respects'; i.e. boat, gear, provisions, crew, navigation preps, weather checks, paperwork, coastguard report etc. All ready. Well, we had done it many times before so we were not yet into the unknown. That, dear reader, will come in good time when we will need all the help we can get 'on the other side'. Are you ready?

We left Ocean Village on a fine June afternoon to encouraging farewells from the ladies. We thought we would get into the Seine estuary early the next morning which would be OK with the flood tide. The weather was fine and forecast NE F 4-5; a pretty good angle for this track. And so it turned out. On a beautiful summer's day we slipped gently out of the Solent, past Bembridge and its prominent forts, waved farewell to the distant St Catherine's Point as the Isle of Wight gradually fell astern. A bit like the opening oboe bars of the 'Rites of Spring', at the beginning all is simple and at peace. Later on it clattered up a bit. Now, with some hours of steady daylight-sailing ahead of us we settled into the crossing, putting good miles behind us before the evening light faded.

The crossing was uneventful although the conditions during the night were at times quite fresh and the sea, as the French would say, 'un peu agitee' as was my constitution. Sea sick? Well it was our first serious outing of the season and even Nelson was (we are told). And, yes, I occasionally get sick; but Pete doesn't. It can affect people quite differently. Some are genuinely ill. It doesn't affect me that way fortunately. Particularly if I grab the helm, pull on ropes that don't need pulling on. Sing songs in a loud voice that don't need singing until it sort of goes away. I suppose any song would do, but I recall a single-handed trip across the Channel when I couldn't stop my head singing:

When the wind doth blow, I generally go below
And take what comfort the cabin doth grant
Along with my sisters and my cousins and my aunt.
My sisters and my cousins and my aunt!

The Germans have a nice phrase for any won't-go-away-tune; they call it 'an ear worm'. I suppose it is marginally better than having Jonny Cash on auto-repeat all night through the cockpit speakers.

* * *

Dangerous trip, my friends? Well no, although simple things can go wrong. I could tell you about the exploding loo door; but let me recall instead our last trip with Pete and Kate to the West Country.

Jacky and I invited Kate and Pete to join us in a West Country cruise in Wise One. We had reached Salcombe when it became clear that the weather would deteriorate from the West with a couple of days of rain and strong wind. We decided that we could reach Plymouth before it broke and enjoy the up-stream sheltered waters of the rivers Tamar and Lynher. Friends would meet us and beer could be consumed.

The coastal passage was straight forward. My new Yeoman Plotter, interfaced with the Garmin 128 and its cockpit repeater ensured a careful and controlled navigation plan. Dead reckoning tracks right through to Mayflower Marina were prepared to back up the electronics. As dusk fell we had the Great Mewstone rock in our sights. In the deepening night we rounded the Great Mewstone into Plymouth Sound with the lights of Plymouth spread out in front of us, showing clearly where we had to go. We were home really and sat in the cockpit over coffee in a mood of modest satisfaction. In quiet conditions, clear visibility but no moon, the motor pushed us along without hurry.

But there was work to do. I couldn't actually identify the channel buoys against the confusing backdrop of the city. I went below to put the Plymouth Sound chart on to the Yeoman, get it registered and scan with the mouse to secure a position. Dear God! We appeared to be nosing the Shagstone reef that fingers into the Sound to starboard, marked only with an unlit beacon. I went up the companionway steps as though propelled by a rocket calling to Pete "I say I do believe its time for a course adjustment HARD TO PORT. NOW." Just as Pete was saying "What the hell is that? We're in the middle of rocks...."(or words to that effect). And there they were huge in the night. I swear that we could have fended off with a boat hook.

Pete spun the wheel on to reciprocal and blasted the throttle. I dropped down the companionway yelling "Jackie" at top voice – she was relaxing below on her bunk. Galvanised by my tone she took off up the companionway like a trained athlete off the blocks, grabbing a lifejacket as she went. Knowing (far too late) exactly where we were I quickly ran off a new and safe course and yelled it to Pete. We saw the beacon at the end of the reef go by close to starboard, touching the shore lights one by one as we pushed into clear water.

Skippers all: the message is easy and you are all ahead of me. You can't relax boat management discipline ever. At any time. In nearly forty years of owning, skippering and navigating this is the only time that I have put crew and boat into real danger. You don't have to do it twice. That night we could have lost lives.

* * *

Night time crossings in clear weather can be a pleasure. On-shore the sky is dulled by clouds of urban loom. Off-shore, and on a dark night, the stars all come out in countless billions. Shooting stars and tracking satellites carve through the crowded sky. The sky-high white masthead light prescribes a continuous and restless circle against the pin-prick stars. The faint red glow of the steering compass is consulted only occasionally by the attentive helmsman who, from minute to minute, fixes his course by a star. All the navigation thinking was done long ago and entered into the GPS set below. Now the GPS cockpit repeater, set to night-time low illumination, feeds a silent commentary on course and track. Every two hours the watchman slips below to enter the digital information on to the paper chart and into the ship's log. The work of the vessel continues under the whispering, pulling curve of the working sails and the white flecked heave of the night-time sea. All night the lights of other vessels reveal their track with the two mid-channel separation zones well picked out. Where are they going? Anywhere, really, but many on their endless missions ploughing between Hamburg, Southampton, Rotterdam and the Far East or the Americas. Full containers come from China; empty ones are returned. Well it seems like it anyway.

Crossing the busy separation zones requires care and technique. I have been with a skipper who (daytime) invited me to watch a huge ship change course to respect our sail. In my view: unwise! It can be a bit like crossing the M25 whilst pushing a pram. The assumption has to be that the ship has not seen you (they often have, but don't assume it.) At night the big vessel's heading can be read from his navigation lights. A steady inspection of approaching lights will tell you whether there is a danger of collision. If the vessel has seen you then the officer-of-the-watch will be looking at you and making the same calculation.

Choosing the right moment, you change your heading to a point off the ship's stern and as she passes across your track so you follow her stern round until you are back on course. If the vessel has not seen you, then all is still safe. If she has, then the officer-on-watch has a clear signal from your navigation lights that you are taking avoiding action. On a previous occasion I had been sitting in my cockpit for quite a long time watching a vessel approaching. Just as I had decided that I could stand on for a bit longer, a bright searchlight from the ship's bridge stabbed the darkness lighting me up like day. The ship had been watching me as I watched her and I was clearly being advised that it was time I changed course!

As your 'watch' comes to an end your crew mate down below appears as a shadowy moon-lit face in the companion way offering a coffee before you hit the sack. It's a companionable moment while you share information. ("Weather's fine, wind moderating. Keep her on 104 and call me when you see the fairway buoy. You have two vessels approaching from port and I think there's a crossing vessel astern. Yes, there she is, about on 320.").

Slowly the big Cap de la Heve light (entrance to le Havre) appears, firstly as a distant five second night-time 'loom' and then suddenly the bright, flashing spark itself. Your navigation track is confirmed (or corrected). Later smaller shore lights begin to twinkle (its not just stars that do that) and, in the dim grey of dawn, the misty line between sea and sky shows a suspicion of land. Now an over-night ferry, lit up like a small town, noses past us towards Le Havre. The little yachtsmen share the sea with serious people.

The night sky slowly fades into a blue dome streaked with cloud away to the west as *Wise One* leans to a gentle morning breeze and pushes through an encouraging sea. Channel buoys guide you into the main river and past the busy entrance into Le Havre. Honfleur emerges on the west bank and the locked entrance reveals itself. A text to Jacky confirmed that "The eagle has splashed down" so the ladies knew that all was to plan.

The lock gates at Honfleur were open so in we went. In due course the road bridge barring the inner basin lifted and by late morning we were safely tied alongside in our first French port of the project. It was a good moment. and I felt that our trip had now well and truly started. By early afternoon Jacky and Kate had joined us and our party was complete.

Honfleur is a beautiful old town built around its ancient harbour. It really is one of the most attractive of French harbours for a small boat to enter. It was an important medieval commercial and fishing port from which many French settlers later left for Canada. From the early C19th the huge growth of Le Havre dwarfed little Honfleur. Fortunately for us the core of the town remains today in its C18th form. Boudin was born here in 1824 and during the C19th it became a centre for the Impressionist movement. It does not have a marina in the modern sense, but the inner harbour, once a busy commercial basin, is now laid out with serviced pontoons.

The harbour is lined with five to seven storeys 17th, 18th and 19th Century buildings providing a rich mix of shops, restaurants and apartments. A C17th (I guess) stone wharf-side building provides the Harbour Master's offices. Extended views over the Seine give you a distant prospect of modern, commercial Le Havre and (up stream) a sight of the mighty Tancarville Bridge that we were to pass under within a few days. Honfleur must be one of the most attractive of stops on our total trip and certainly an ideal place from which to start the journey.

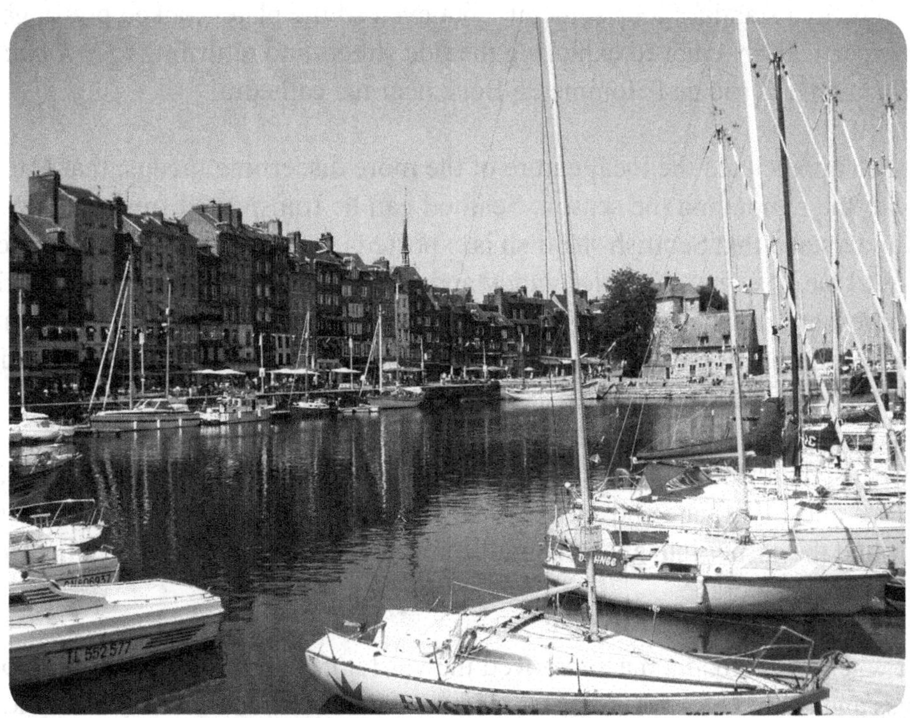

Honfleur Town Centre basin

Honfleur is, of course, a destination for people popping out of the Le Havre conurbation or for longer distance travellers stopping by. In the summer it positively buzzes with activity and waterside eateries and is not, therefore, the quietest place in which to spend a night. Its group of (underused) commercial wet basins, its busy yacht harbour, and its small-scale old-world back streets make it a natural for painters. Clearly a small artists' colony is still established and active. It didn't take Kate and Jacky long to get out their sketch books and start some serious business. Mind you, Kate's primary school teaching background makes sure that we are all scrubbed and shining with crayons well-sharpened and ready for anything….

Up from the central harbour the little streets lead to the 'cathedral'. This alone is worth a visit. Most 12th or 13th century cathedral-churches are well endowed by the wealthy RC Church and are major statements of the power of the local Bishop and of Rome itself. Typically we expect a stone structure of some magnificence using masonry skills and materials, imported from a distance. Modest local churches, however, may display local craft-use of local materials. Often, in areas where boats are built, that boat building craft is evident. Honfleur has a wooden Great Church of St Catherine clearly built by men who knew how to fashion a boat hull. It has a detached oaken bell tower (now part of the Boudin museum) and the whole is of particular interest. For centuries it must have been the ecclesiastical 'poor relation', built from whatever resources the local fishing community could access. Over the years many a local bishop must have longed to rebuild in a more fashionable style and with permanent material. Fortunately for us, no one managed it and now it is a unique local treasure.

And so we four settled into Honfleur for a few days of relaxation and final preparation for our next stage. We ate and drank delightfully in a town that must surely serve more restaurant meals per head of population than any other in the country. Of course the waterside restaurants tend to be to a standard tourist menu – but even so the plates looked pretty good to us. However we particularly enjoyed exploring the side streets and returning to *l'Homme de Bois* and to *la Tortue* in the rue de l'Homme de Bois, near the cathedral

We very much appreciated the local nature of the more discerning menus; that is to say they changed with the region and the season. Seafood can be transported fresh to anywhere; for example I understand that Scottish shellfish is exported in salt water tankers to France (which sounds mad to me). Nevertheless Normandy and north Brittany really seem to cultivate and serve the largest and meatiest moules (amongst other seafood, of course). It's our impression that the further south you go, the smaller the local mussels; but of course Honfleur does offer a wide variety of other eating choice.

However we also had work to do. On our third day we had an appointment with M. Challe's boatyard. Pete and I left Kate and Jacky to explore and sketch while we motored out of our basin and round the corner into another small commercial basin where M. Challe was waiting with his mast-removal crane.

In the past when I have had a mast removed the yard normally preferred me not to be there (owners fuss and get in the way). We were slightly startled to find that M. Challe did not have a team to board, unscrew, detach, un-wire electrics, remove holding bolts, place the lifting strop etc. He simply sat at his crane controls and Pete and I did the rest. Well, no problem and soon the mast, standing and running rigging were placed across several wooden 'horses' and put to bed until next needed. Just as well that I had Pete there, though.

The next job was to prepare *Wise One* for the rigours of the canals. Now if you see a canal boat designed for the job you are impressed by the size and strength of the rubber or timber 'rubbing strakes' around the hull to take the unkind impact of stone walls or other vessels. Our sea-going yacht was deficient in this department but we had a plan! Soon the delicate fibreglass hull was hung with four car tyres sheathed in a rather fetching blue sheeting (two on each side); plus two 4m scaffolding planks bridging the tyres; plus eight normal inflated fenders in their matching blue fender 'socks', all held off the boat's blue topsides by canvas skirting slung down from the scuppers. But make sure the tires are well secured. The French canal authorities don't like escaping tires littering their canal beds. We were ready and Wise *One* was now a canal boat.

One final day was spent relaxing and the ladies sketching the very fine Dutch barge that had taken up the wharf-side by the harbour master's office. Then it was time for more action. Pete and Kate's car was loaded up with our off-shore stuff and headed for home. (Thanks Pete and Kate, we'll see you again later in the trip!). Jacky and I were now ready to go.

Chapter 2

Making sense of the Seine

"..... Thus, the 'Ship of Fools' criss-crossed the sea and canals of Europe with their comic and pathetic cargo of souls. Some of them found pleasure and even a cure in the changing surroundings, in the isolation of being cast off.... The cities and villages which had thus rid themselves of their crazed and crazy, could now take pleasure in watching the exciting side-show when a ship full of foreign lunatics would dock at their harbours......"

(*Foucault's 'Madness and civilisation'*)

So we took off on the '*Yellow Brick Road*' for Rouen and in more ways than one, the unknown. *Wise One* was no longer a yacht but a rather under-powered motorboat with a thirty year-old auxiliary engine. Our canal experience is limited to a couple of trips through the Crinan Canal (west coast of Scotland) and that was many years ago. So we were quite uncertain what to expect. But we will, for sure, find out very soon!

This section had been a mystery to me; 80 km in one tide. There seemed to be nowhere, absolutely nowhere, to stop on the way. The tidal Seine provides a steady counter current and my own cruising speed through the water was about 5 knots max. So how was this supposed to work? Actually it's not too difficult. If you look at the high water time for Honfleur and the equivalent for Rouen you see that Rouen is several hours later. The normal six hour favourable flood simply stays with you for about nine hours as you travel up stream. (Clever, isn't it?)

The Honfleur basin is small, busy and almost enclosed by the tall ranks of C17/18th buildings. Restaurants and people crowd the quays and the feeling is very cosy and friendly. It was all a bit rude to be ejected unceremoniously from the early-morning Honfleur lock into the wide, grey and empty expanse of the lower Seine. We left two hours before bottom tide and initial progress was slow against the last of the ebb. We certainly felt small and exposed. The low-water mud flats encroached either side on to the swirling, brown river, heavy with silt. *Wise One* felt very naked without the comforting support of mast and rigging.

When the tide turned the flood picked up under our keels, we slowly increased speed-over-ground and just kept on going. The sky-high Normandy and Tancarville Bridges were huge markers in the early miles. This is a working river fringed by the busy port of Le Havre with its sprawling docks and access canals. Up stream, the river slowly mellowed and softened but seemed to have few points of great interest to a small boat and stopping seemed greatly discouraged. Although we saw some dinghy activity, you get the impression that leisure craft are not greatly encouraged. As the hours went by and the big river slipped past, so we began to relax into a motor boat routine. The motor thump, thump, thumped; beneath our feet the prop churned and drove; the bow ploughed on through the silted waters; the wake bubbled and spread behind us long and straight. These would keep us company for the next two summers long.

Jacky and the Tancarville Bridge

We arrived in Rouen some 11 hours after departure, having left two hours before low water and plugged a contrary tide for the last hour. Rouen is a place well worth a visit in its own right. It was a city of major importance in the medieval times and much remains of the earlier street pattern and half-timbered buildings. The cathedral of Notre Dame is of great interest and was famously the subject of a series of west-front studies by Claud Monet. The town centre itself is certainly worth a wander and a glass or two.

Rouen has many memories for France – and a few for the English. Joan of Arc is associated by both countries with Rouen, not for her birth (that was in Orléans) but for her trial and death. What's that got to do with us now? If you ask most people about England's continued presence in mainland Europe, they might say "Oh, I think we owned a bit of Calais". True but since William 1's invasion there continued a great deal of ambiguity over the loyalty of very large chunks of France (as we now know it). Very considerable areas of northern France (including Paris) and south-western France lay within Anglo-Duchies with formal loyalties to the English crown. The French throne itself was subject to rival claims as indeed was the English throne in 1066. A substantial objective of the Anglo-French One Hundred Year War was to resolve these issues. England's objective was to achieve a dual monarchy with the English Crown calling the shots and at one point that was very nearly achieved. Initially things went badly for the French forces who became demoralized and defensive.

All was to turn on the unlikely influence of a bright but ill educated peasant girl. Joan was born about 1412. In 1424 she experienced saintly visions in which she was commanded to defeat the invading English and establish French control over the Throne. That all seemed very reasonable so she went to the Royal Court and told the Establishment that they should jolly well stiffen their spines, pull up their socks, put their best feet forward, apply shoulder to the wheel and get those English out.

Perhaps the French High Command were at their wits end in seeking to better the old enemy and were happy to push forward the visionary Joan of Arc as a last ditch attempt to gain military advantage. Certainly young Joan found herself at the head of the army, inspiring the troops and influencing a radical change of strategy. The English fortune were rapidly and fundamentally reversed.

Unfortunately for Joan and after a series of brilliant victories, she was captured by the English, imprisoned in Rouen and tried for heresy. The mechanics of the law at that time were very precise and sophisticated. The proper format of trial and opportunity for defense were clearly laid out. However, and you can well understand this, there was no way that the English were going to allow anything except a guilty verdict, a burning (of course) and a careful disposal of all physical remains. Her execution took place in the Vieux-Marché in Rouen in 1431. But she remains to this day a national symbol of French patriotic independence.

In 1920 she was canonized.

It was in Rouen that at last we found the Government Office that would sell us our permit to enter the Inland Waterway system. This was the only charge for river and canal services that was made and could relate to a limited period (perhaps one month) or to a full year. A sticker on the outside of the boat gave evidence of payment and our identification number.

The 'halte nautique' might be described as minimalist, but had the basics. Here we shared a pontoon with the Anglo-American crewed Dutch Barge from Southampton which we had seen in Honfleur. The beautiful traditional vessel was owned by John, a young American commercial air pilot (and still very much working) who lived on *Vrouwe Antje.* This striking and beautiful vessel was then based on the River Itchen (Southampton) and his plan was to explore the European waterways while living permanently on the barge. He could respond to flying commissions anywhere at short notice.

On board he had Jennie and Mike who have a flat overlooking John's River Itchin mooring. Mike has spent his life in commercial photography, much of that being in the yachting world. Both Mike and Jennie now work for the yacht charter company 'SailingHolidays' and are therefore very knowledgeable about Greece, Turkey and Croatian waters. They had struck up a friendship and, with some significant sailing experience, Jennie and Mike provided the crew element to Skipper John. They all made delightful and knowledgeable travelling companions and were also heading to Paris. They also seemed to enjoy nice food and a glass of something, so we cruised in company and with great pleasure; the first of a number of friendships 'on the move'.

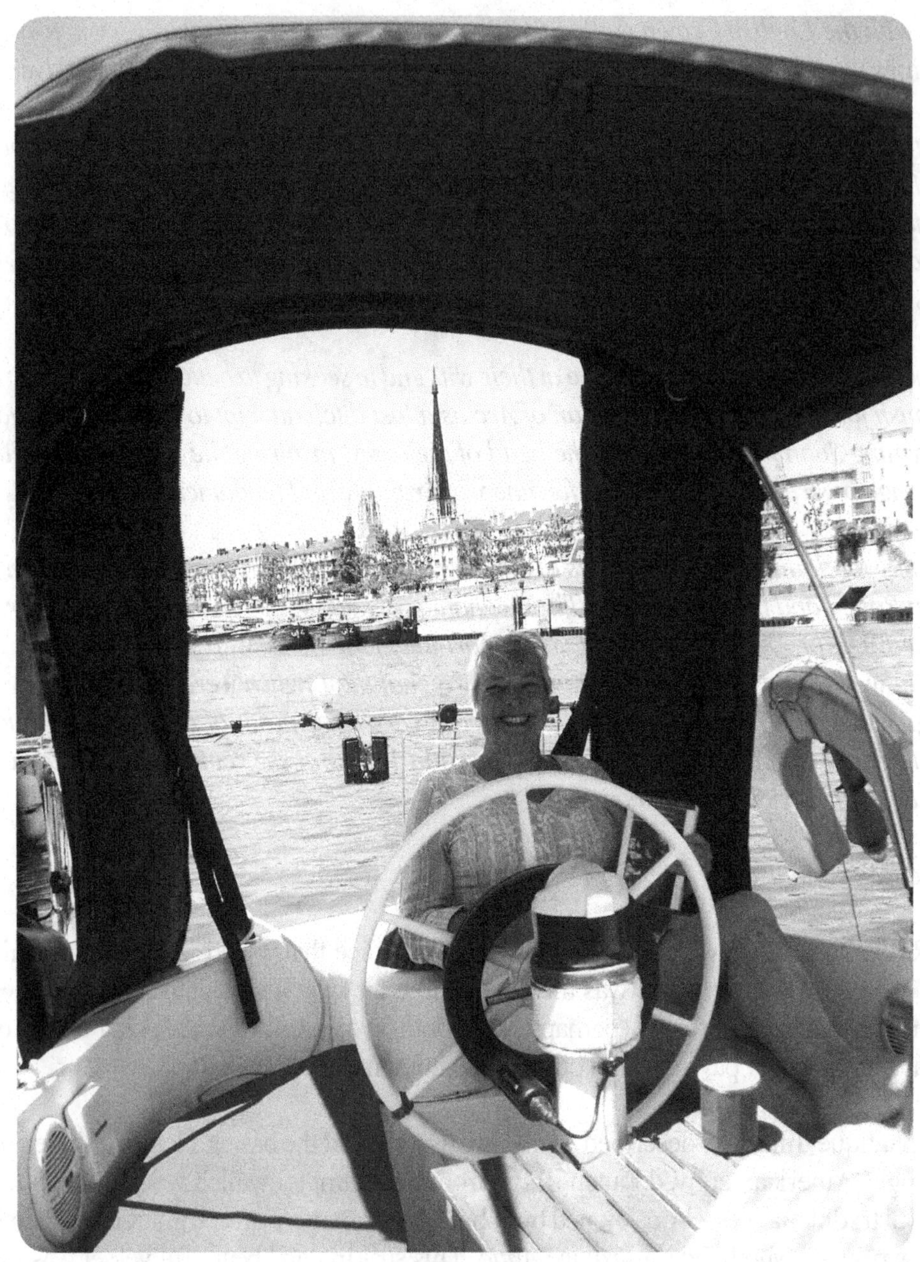

Jacky in Rouen

The Seine is, of course, a serious river. Heavy commercial ‘peniches’ of several thousand tons make a challenging presence and are, by any definition, ‘giants’ on your travels; but quite often they are friendly ones. There still seemed limited leisure movement and leisure provision. Even when immediately above Rouen we still felt that the leisure use of the river was not greatly encouraged.

Just above Rouen lies a fuelling barge, moored outside the navigable channel. You can’t pass up a fuelling opportunity so we fell alongside the steel barge with its heavy wooden strakes to take fuelling boats. What we didn’t foresee was the fast-moving tug punching hard up-stream.

It passed close leaving a heaving, bouncing wash behind and a *Wise One* rolling and crunching against the barge. We fended off with everything we had but nothing could stop our scuppers being rolled under the barge timbers. Our substantial rubbing strake was split and two guard rail stanchions bent and lifted from the deck. And it all just took a minute or two. It was a bit early in our project to start taking damage but at least we got our fuel.

The locks were as serious as the river; the first one at Andresey took us two hours to get through although we were never again to experience that length of delay. The first two rules of the river are that commercial vessels take precedence and the 'Eclusier' (lockmaster) rules.

The third rule is that certain peniche share the lock with nobody, i.e. they carry dangerous cargoes. The peniche is a commercial barge and may be a huge 1000 ton hulk often pushed in triplicate. When empty these vessels tower above us with intimidating black steel sides like rust-streaked cliffs. When full, their decks seemed almost awash so it seemed that it would not take much to sink them totally. The peniches carry bulk dry or liquid goods with the bargee family often on board along with the family laundry, kiddie's toys and the family car hoisted onto the after deck.

The other frequent acquaintance was the hotel boat of extraordinary length and pristine condition. The *'la Belle de Cadix'* for example, is a gleaming, low, 110 m. long and slim 11.4m in beam with 90 double cabins. With an elegant cutter bow she's like a rapier cutting through the waters of the Seine. And she has several sister vessels run by the CroisiEurope Line all designed to make the maximum use of the length of the main river locks. All these craft are earning their living and had our respect as they took priority.

In the case of the Andresey lock, every time we offered ourselves to the lock, another peniche appeared round the river bend behind us and we got our personal red light. Never mind, we got through eventually and, despite damage already sustained, we were glad of our defensive array of tyres, fenders and four-metre planks to see our 'glass' hull through the rigours.

The bargees could often be very helpful, and might offer to take a mooring line so you could lie safely along side the barge as the lock was worked. (A lot easier than sending the only agile member of the crew up a vertical ladder with fore and aft lines firmly gripped in teeth.) At first the big locks could therefore be a bit uncomfortable and challenging. With a small nudge our vast neighbours could crush us against the black and streaming walls or, as they left, could send us bobbing out of control in their thrashing wake. But at least we learnt and we managed.

These main river locks were of an 'intermediate' size; i.e. not as big as the Rhone locks (which we will see later) but rather larger than the older C18/19th canal locks. You enter with care looking for the steel ladder so an agile member of the crew can go up taking the lines with him. If no quayside ladder is available the last option is to seek out the ladder usually bolted to the open loch gates; tricky but it at least gets someone ashore.

Hotel Ship, la Belle de Cadix.

With smaller locks there is sometimes no ladder available and the shore member has to land before the helmsman enters the loch. At that point the (panting) linesman has to be lock-side to take and secure the lines. Whatever else it does, it keeps you slim.

Andresey was our first lock and the eclusier called us to his office and carefully examined all our papers. To go into French waters you need evidence of proven knowledge of continental inland waters regulations, payment of waterway fees, of insurance and of relevant seamanship ability. The RYA International 'Certificate of Competence' meets the latter need and can be obtained through the RYA or your Sailing Club. It is subject to a basic theoretical exam and a practical test on water. To go onto the European inland waterways you also need evidence that you have understood the Waterways Regulations (CEVNI Rules). A careful read of the rules and a simple examination by the RYA soon sorts that out. But you must have the evidence and be able to produce it. This was the only time this happened but we did get the impression that from here on the system knew who we were.

Up stream of Rouen the Seine became more attractive and did now have its attention grabbing 'haltes' at fairly frequent intervals. The first night after Rouen we ducked into the narrow river side 'gut' leading to the little village of Elboef, despite a slightly scary entrance (shallow and narrow), to reach the old wharf. We were not joined by *Vrouwe Antje* who decided that it looked too restrictive for their 60 ft. Port Elboef turned out to be an abandoned old commercial gut cut into the countryside. It was really very pleasant to retreat into such a small waterway, wooded and private. The old wharf was clearly now little used. In the gathering evening we watched bundles of sticks being carried up-stream and dragged on to the bank as busy coypu were engaged in nest building. Fish were rising, moorhen poked amongst the reeds and we saw an occasional flash of kingfisher. Even the croaking of amorous frogs did not disturb the gentle, peaceful and rural evening, away from the pressures of town and big river.

Vrouwe Antje coming up fast

And then there was Les Andelys, a delightful little town where we met again with *Vrauwe Antje* and we both lay to the main river quayside. A cycle trip with our Barge friends to the house and garden of Giverny was a must. Unfortunately in recent years the tour operators have also found it but you can't blame others for enjoying this beautiful and iconic spot.

The day was fine and the cycle ride to the gardens a welcome bit of exercise. Giverny is home to the Museum of Claude Monet, the Impressionist painter who lived here from 1883 until his death in 1926. None of the original paintings are here (you've got to go to Paris) but there are innumerable memorabilia and reproductions. The main reason for the visit, however, has to be the glorious gardens lovingly maintained as Monet knew them. This was a good time for us to visit with wisteria around the famous 'Chinese' bridges and rhododendrons around the water; but there is colour most of the year round to reward the visitor. The gardens were as beautiful as ever with their memorable water lilies and green painted wooden bridges; in fact, you might say, "as pretty as a picture". You've got to go!

The next day La Roche Guyon attracted both vessels for a lunch time stop and an energetic climb up the castle hill. It was a good stiff walk rewarded by long views over the busy river. The delightful restaurant 'Les Bords du Seine' persuaded us to stay the night.

The Seine is now a beautiful river and we shared a number of convivial stops with *Vrouwe*

Antje, often lying alongside. Food and wine were shared and one evening John pulled down a large screen, set up a projector and we watched a couple of films in old fashioned comfort.

Strategic meeting on Vrouwe Antje

The things you can do on a sixty-footer! Other stops included Vernonnet, Meulan, a 'halte' below the Bougival lock and another above the Sureness lock before tackling Paris.

Each one has some memory. At the Bougival halt John suffered unexpected engine failure in mid stream, I returned to effect an alongside 'rescue' (a bit bigger than my elderly 24 HP Volvo was used to), and finally we were helped to the bank by a judicious push from a fire tender where John rapidly resolved an electrical problem. And then there was the public park at Meulan which had no bank-side water supply (but did have a mains electrical point). It did, however, have a drinking fountain which John tapped into for a tank fill. In doing so he lost control temporarily, thoroughly soaking me just as I was in the process of connecting *Wise One* to mains electricity. But in the end, tanks were filled, the drinking fountain was reconnected, and no one was electrocuted. There is a God after all.

Any major city develops gradually as you approach and pass through a slowly increasing scatter of buildings growing gradually into the city itself. Approaching Paris by water is a little different. The banks of the Seine are lined with a few, and then thousands of redundant, steel barges; some derelict, some beautiful homes, some half way between. Nothing better demonstrates the huge change to the European transport systems as bulk goods desert the waterways, even when, unlike the UK, the water transport is on a major commercial scale. Paris seems to provide as few marina facilities for small leisure craft as, perhaps, does London.

There must be other formal marinas (as opposed to just lying alongside the bank) but we were only aware of the Arsenal, adjacent to the Place de la Bastille.

We stopped three times as we progressed through Paris. John had an artist friend who worked in Honfleur and had a converted barge home on the north bank where the Bois de Boulogne meets the Seine. John also had an invitation to lie alongside for a night and we fell comfortably outside him. Our new neighbours were 'at home' and we were all invited aboard. The barge is, of course, just a vast, voluminous, empty steel shell and a designer's real challenge! For our hosts, the daylight and sun streamed through the huge opening cut into the deck lighting up a warm, bright, sculptured space below that surprised and welcomed the visitor. A deck saloon allowed us to enjoy the passing river; a deep and comfortable sitting/dining area allowed us introspective privacy. And all in the best possible taste!

That evening we cycled across Paris to a small recommended restaurant. That was incident-free except me falling off in the middle of a major thoroughfare. (These damn folding bikes are so unstable....). It was a pleasant and unpretentious café. I ordered sardine salad as an entrée thinking of nicely grilled fresh sardines on a green bed. When it came, there was a bed (I had nothing against the bed) but nestling in the middle was an upturned sardine can.... What the hell! I looked around and saw three grinning waiters' faces peering from the kitchen door to see my reaction! I have never been there before in my life; why do strange waiters do these things to me?

Our second city stop was alongside a steel barge (*The Black Pig*) in the shadow of the Eiffel Tower. There seemed to be few actual facilities but this is certainly a distinguished enough location for anyone. Of course we hit the shore with feet working hard to explore this wonderful location. Jacky and I set off for the Eiffel Tower (what else could you do?) to soak up the atmosphere of this extraordinary engineering feat. In the past we have been up the tower and were less than impressed by the organisation and the poor quality experience of this hugely important tourist attraction. ("Come on, Paris, what are you playing at?")

This time we wandered off through the city back streets as heavy clouds gathered over the city. Just in time we dodged into a café as the rain gathered strength. Within a few minutes we were watching a downpour of tropical dimensions, accompanied by monumental thunder, sheet lightening, street floods, floating cars from which once-elegant bedraggled Parisians waded. Water poured through the café ceiling and, just as the storm began to ease, we were all ejected 'for our own safety'. ('Dorothy' and the Scarecrow had now survived floods!). The driest place in Paris was probably our main cabin back on board.

Wise One left *Vrouwe Antje* and moved again up-stream under the bridges of Paris. Leaving the Grand and Petit Palais to port and the Assemblee National and Musee d'Orsey to starboard we safely negotiated seventeen bridges and regally acknowledged friendly waves from people walking the riverside promenades. Notre Dame hove into view and slowly the Ile de la Cité fell behind us.

The first turning on the left was then the well equipped and managed marina at the Arsenal, next to the Place de la Bastille. Entry was through a lock operated after a VHF request in your best French, of course. Access to the extensive canal system running northwards from the city was also via the Arsenal basin and this was *Vrouwe Antje's* next move.

OK, guess where.

We were soon settled in for the night, and a few more, to enjoy Paris. Meanwhile the Dutch barge friends had been joined by John's (decorative and talented) 'significant other', Jane. She had plans to run a company with the barge as a travelling base and WIFI to keep in touch so 'barging' was to be their home activity. The next morning we welcomed them through the lock and into the next canal system running northwards, at which point we waved a final goodbye.

This was June 05, and June was hot! The stone built Arsenal was a furnace. Nonetheless we enjoyed re-acquainting ourselves with the Great City. Revisiting la Saint-Chapelle is always a pleasure and always a new experience. Also new was the meeting with strange, almost unique and certainly fascinating animals of the Paris Jungle. While relaxing over a pavement-side coffee in the Arsenal we became aware of a number of striking passers-by. Very tall and quite stunning looking women hoisted on high spikes or platforms passed singly or in pairs as though on a catwalk. The next coffee table saw our slightly startled looks and explained "le Festivale Gai. Prenez garde !" Our only regret was that the 'ladies' were coming away from the Gay Pride Festival in the Place de la Bastille which was just finishing. Beware where the '*Yellow Brick Road*' might take you....

There were more strange animals to be discovered and our next small project was to search out the White Unicorn Tapestries. These lovely tapestries were the subject of a novel 'The Lady and the Unicorn' by Tracy Chevalier. From the book we learn that the Unicorn Tapestries were woven in the 1500's, probably in Flanders.

The Arsenal Marina, Paris.

In 1841 they were rediscovered in poor condition stored away in a chateau in Boussac. They were purchased by the French Government, restored and placed in the Musee de Cluny (now the Musee National du Moyen-Age). The tapestries represent the five senses: taste, touch, smell, sound and sight. The sixth is known as 'A Mon Seul Desire' which are words woven into it. They are in the period 'Mille Fleur' style and each show a tableau involving an elegant white unicorn and a young noble lady (beautiful, of course). Each tableau naturally reflects its given theme.

Tracy Chevalier weaves her own beautiful tapestry as we read that a nobleman hires an artist to design the six tapestries. The artist takes the opportunity to celebrate his own love for his patron's daughter. It makes an enchanting read and gives additional interest (if fictional) to the tapestries.

The Metropolitan Museum of Art, New York, also has Unicorn Tapestries of the C16, to be seen in the Cloisters Museum, also New York. The style is similar (typically 'Mille Fleur') and are thought to have been woven in Brussels and to be one of several sets. They were lost during the French Revolution but also rediscovered and returned to their rightful French owners in the mid-C19. They were subsequently purchased, restored and donated to the Met. whose WEB site makes no mention of the Cluny collection (or any connection). They look awfully similar to me, both in *mille fleur* style of a similar date and originating from northern France or the Low Countries and featuring white unicorns rampant. It just seems that there must be a link somewhere. However the Met. haven't found one and they comment:

" ....Despite the fact that both sets of tapestries depict unicorns, stylistically they are very different and did not originate from a single source that was dispersed....."

There is a great deal written about them but perhaps there is still a mystery to be solved.

* * *

During the rest of this summer we were still looking forward (with some trepidation) to some 700 more miles and 215 more locks to get to the Med. Ultimately there will be another 1562 miles and 284 locks to Belle Ile *and the Circumnavigation.* We had a little way to go! Are you with us? We'll need all the help we can get!

Chapter 3

Paris to Dijon

'Begin the Bourgogne'

As we left Paris behind, the Seine began to change. It was still very much a commercial river, but imperceptibly it became a little smaller and a little softer. We were continuing east through undulating and well-wooded rural France, but leaving behind the hints of an earlier northern France. At Montreaux the *'Yellow Brick Road'* turned south onto the Yonne. The Yonne still remains a commercial river; but it is a scale down from the Seine. With the Yonne we now enter a river well controlled by locks and wandered through countryside of maturing summer corn and orchards of ripening apples and pears. Somehow the evenings were gentler and – I swear – the sunsets were better with the evening sky painted in deep golds, reds and black.

So far we had negotiated 27 locks in 400 miles; in the next 30 miles we would see a further 17.

Dusk on the Yonne

We began to climb. These locks are generally smaller than those on the Seine at about 93 m in length, 8.3 m in width x 1.8 draught with a rise and fall of about 2 to 3 m. They had one unpleasant characteristic – many had sloping sides. Why, I don't know, but a plastic hull takes unkindly to a rough, masonry slope down (or up) which you rumble trying to fend off with oars or boathooks. (See the Appendix on French Locks.)

At this stage the weather was very hot, well into the 30's. The area produces some excellent wines but we hadn't seen any vineyards yet, only wheat being harvested like mad generating clouds of choking dust; and lots of sunflowers turning from a startling and unreal yellow to a mature brown as we travelled.

Towns and halts went by as the summer progressed; but not without incident. Between Chatrette and Montreau we were progressing in total peace with the world when a commercial barge approached from ahead. I was on the helm and found myself pushed closer to the starboard bank than was comfortable. As the barge approached I noticed the bargee signalling to me to pull out; unfortunately he was occupying the central part of the channel and there was little room to leave the bank. With a massive hull-jarring bang we were stopped dead by a submerged rock (presumably, we never saw it). Such was the impact that my first reaction was to look around for a shallow and accessible bank-side place on which to beach rather than sink in the navigable channel. We slowly headed to a sandy spit, Jacky took the helm whilst I dropped below to check for ingress of water into the bilges. There was no such water. (Relief!).

We continued with caution and slowly returning confidence. Clearly we had hit one of our bilge keels, probably not the hull itself and would discover in due course what damage had been done to the keel. She handled OK and we continued with some care. Later I dived and could find in the murky water nothing to alarm us. When the boat eventually came out of the water the damage was some gel coat lost from the forward edge of the starboard keel and rapidly replaced. Nevertheless the little lesson was there; you never know what's in the canal, particularly near the banks. So on we went to Sens.

Sens is a beautiful old town of ancient history and great interest. We did experience a small problem when we arrived. The river has well serviced bank-side wharfage available to passing leisure vessels. There is fresh water and electricity and no charge is made. The beautiful town centre is a short walk away and so everyone moors just there. 'Everyone' includes long term live-a-boards who occupy the most desirable places for free and never move. This is a frequent problem along the Waterways, but mostly it can be accommodated with minimum irritation. Our choice here was to lie alongside another vessel of appropriate size. We chose a red ensign and started our approach. He saw our intentions and waved us away with fairly impolite and impractical suggestions as to where we might go.

All, however, was not lost as a Frenchman on the bank saw our dilemma. He pointed out his own steel barge further along the bank and invited us alongside. When we arrived he took our lines and invited us aboard. Explaining that we had no chance of picking up electricity from the bank-side power-points since all the terminals were taken by other vessels, he hooked us into his own circuit (which did, of course, come from the free municipal supply). Discourtesy and courtesy can match and cancel and we still enjoyed Sens, thanks to a French bargee.

Sens was an important town during the Roman period. It was fully walled in the 14thC but now there are few fortified remains that we could find. St Etienne cathedral has, however, survived and is (we are told) one of the oldest gothic structures in France. It is famous, amongst other things, for its wealth of C12th statues and stained glass. Alongside the cathedral are the grand Palais Synodal – and the medieval street pattern crowded and overhung with 16th, 17th, and 18th Century buildings. You don't have to do the cultural bit to enjoy old Sens and its restaurants!

At Pont Royal we faced the 'Central Canal Decision'. To go south you are squeezed between the Alps and the Central Massif. There are several canal options and at this point you must make a decision. You have the choices of the long distance Marne, the high Bourgogne, the popular Bourgonnaise or the shallower Nivernaise. We were in no hurry and took the allegedly prettier, certainly higher and possibly slower option of the Bourgogne. As soon as we turned off the Yonne into the canal, life changed. The canal was, of course, built for trade but is no longer commercial. It is 242 km long with 189 locks. The locks are now generally 39m by 5.2m with a rise and fall of about 2 to 2.5m. At its highest it is nearly 400m above sea level. At its summit there is the 3km long Pouilly Tunnel, small in section, one way only and unlit. (Help!) The scale was going down but the work rate going up.

* * *

As a nineteenth century canal system of great ingenuity and beauty, the Bourgogne should have World Heritage status. It is fully maintained and working; locks are all manned, sometimes by small teams of young lock handlers who travel with you for several locks or perhaps all day. It appears that the Regional Departments, (with EU funding) introduce or improve the nautical halts at frequent intervals and then hand them over to town authorities for maintenance. We rarely had to stop without clean water, electricity and sometimes ablutions; generally without charge. We were actually equipped with our own steel mooring stakes and a lump hammer and there was nothing to stop us mooring up anywhere. Generally, however, that might be only for a brief lunch break since there was no reason not to look for an equipped 'halte' for the night. Incidentally if there are no 'ablutions' you are either going to have to wait (which we did) or store. Unfortunately pump-out facilities in the canals are pretty rare. The best place to find one would probably be in a hire vessel base (yes, there are some left) and with the use of a little persuasion …

The investment is huge – and the use minimal. The German and American clientele seem to have deserted the French Canals and the cost of chartering seems to be rivalled by so many more exotic alternatives that the trade is fast diminishing. This was 2005 and things can't have improved since then. Charter fleets were being laid up. On a typical day in July we might see four or five boats going the other way. So where are the boats and how long can the French sustain the cost?

We moved into the canal and on to Jorgny where we fell in with the first of a number of canal friends. Morton and Eva who were a retired Danish couple touring European Inland Waterways in their own motor launch; and Bill and Marie in a chartered motor boat Flambo who were Scots living in Florida and holidaying on the canals. Morton was an ex-policeman and gave us an interesting insight into the experience of a small and liberal country opening its doors to immigrants. ("It's time we closed that damned door!"). The biggest issue seemed to be the reluctance of new-comers to learn Danish. We saw a great deal of these friends over a period of time since we were all moving south towards Dijon at a similar daily rate. They were good company and kept us entertained for several weeks.

Initially, however, the entertainment was at my discomfort. In servicing my 24 HP Volvo diesel, I removed the old oil filter in the traditional fashion, i.e. by sticking a screw driver through it to twist it off rendering it totally incapable of reuse. Only at this stage I discovered that my carefully stored (in an oil filter box) alternative filter was a fuel and not an oil filter. (Who did that?). Morton found this so funny I had to ask Eva to intercede before there was an international incident. Great sense of humour, Morton. We were haunted by the vision of driving to Sweden for a replacement. However a judicious phone call to a mechanic eight miles away produced a compatible filter delivered almost instantly by mechanic M. Didier who was surprised by a big kiss (from me) and a grateful tip.

Medium sized lock in action

And so we proceeded. We travelled most days and typically would cover perhaps seventeen miles and six locks. The chug, chug, chugging of our faithful diesel became just a background to the unfolding panorama of the canal, the hills, crops, woodlands and all changing with the ever moving seasons.

Between Florintin and Tonerre we set a new *Wise One* record of 15 locks, (later beaten by 22 locks and 15 miles). There were often traditional lock-keepers in traditional lock-keepers' cottages. They were often willing to sell you wine and home grown fruit and veg.. But in places this had changed. Now often locks were managed by a couple of student eclusiers on buzz bikes. They were normally very cheerful and chatty although not necessarily very skilled. To some extent speed was important simply because the time absorbed by lock operations really determined the weekly progress through the canal. Best results were therefore achieved if I cycled ahead of *Wise One* to help prepare the next lock. I would then cycle back to meet Jacky and signal either "Press on, the locks open" or "hold back, we're not ready yet". This way Jacky helmed most of the way through central France and I cycled. In fact Jacky generally did (and still does) much of the close quarter helming while I leap about with ropes doing macho and athletic things.

Canal fest

As we proceeded we met up with our new friends at several places. On 14th July we found ourselves in Tonnerre with Morton and Eva plus Bill and Marie and another Danish boat going the other way. Now on Bastille Day the Inland Waterway system closes down. There was nothing at all to do except assemble tables and chairs on the canal bank and load them with everything that goes towards a good feast and booze-up. The town fireworks were magnificent and our BBQ totally unrivalled.

All went according to plan until the fateful 20th July. On cycling back from the next lock to signal to Jacky, I found *Wise One* drifting without power; engine YES, transmission, NO. In short the heavy rubber flexi-coupling which connects the gearbox with the prop shaft had sheered. There had been a 'bump' the previous day which we now believe was a prop strike on submerged timber. A big German launch kindly towed us through the next lock and came aboard to help us lash up a get-you-home connection. In the end that failed and we moored to the bank, waving the rest of the little convoy past.

The eclusier called for help from his canal section manager who arrived in his little white van. He assessed the situation and left us to get a signal on his mobile and call a yard in St Jean-de-Losne. Although Volvo engines had generally been replaced by Japanese engines in the hire fleets, the yard just happened to have an old set of connectors in stock. Bless! He also secured a hire car for the next day for us in the neighbouring small town so we could go some 200 km to fetch it. Then he returned the following morning and drove us to the car hire outlet. What a hero! That day we spent collecting the flexible connection and visiting the wonderful walled medieval town of Semur-en-Auxois. Very well worth a visit.

I fitted the connection and on the third day we rose again and headed gingerly off down the canal. All was absolutely fine; except for a small vibration at higher revs. So we stayed out of higher revs. (Humm).

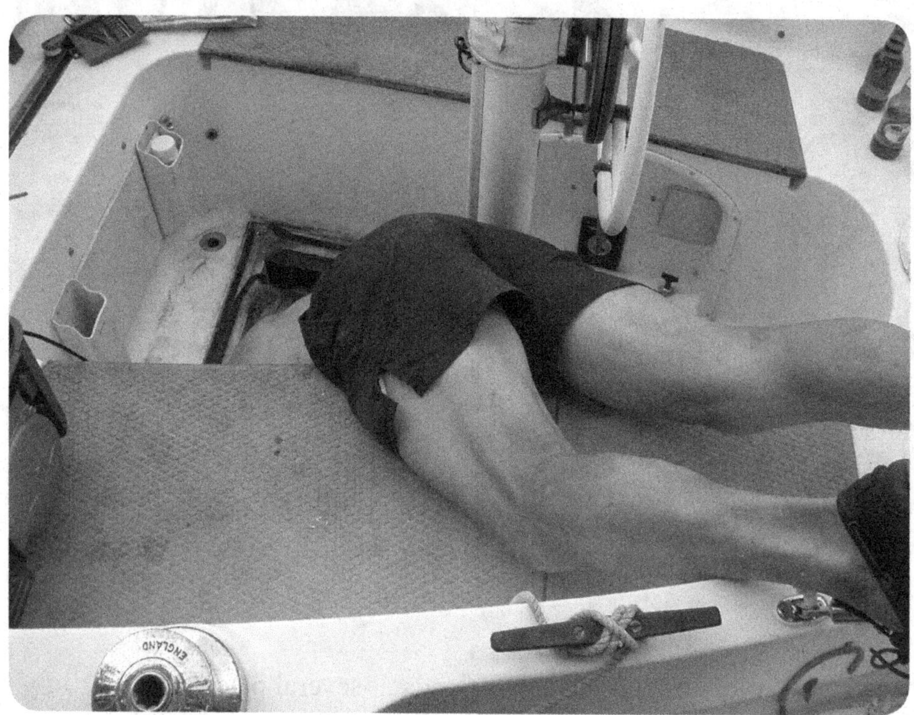

Replacing the broken coupling, not getting wine from the cellar.

So villages, small towns, restaurants and auberges slipped by as we moved steadily upwards and onwards. We had an appointment with old friends from student days. Anna and Harro worked in Germany and live in Mettmann. Nicolas works in Switzerland and lives in Alsace. Anna and Harro were to meet us sometime before the summit tunnel and Nicolas some days later.

These were friends from our old post-grad course in Edinburgh. They are about our age (although some of us have worn better than others). Nicolas has his own architectural practice and Harro has been a director of planning services in several German cities. Anna's legs are just as long and shapely as I had always remembered. She danced professionally and is still busy instructing dancing groups.

I first met Harro in Edinburgh when I persuaded him to buy a poppy for poppy day, (and why not?), which he seemed happy to do. His father had been an admiral in the German U-Boat service during WW2 and at one time could occasionally be seen on the BBC explaining the WW2 from his own perspective. Harro seemed to have a combatative relationship with his father who, in the end, agreed that serious mistakes *had* been made by Hitler; but largely of timing.... Harro and Anna are both very much 'their own people' and debates round a dinner table could be very lively.

I had expected my Edinburgh post-grad period to replicate my undergrad experience with opportunities to show these youngsters how to play rugby or take the chance to learn to fly. What I did find was that 'these youngsters' were generally faster and fitter than I and that our small, international post-graduate group was very much more serious. They had all given up jobs, some had wives and youngsters and all had a lot to gain or lose. As a consequence most of us had little time then for extra curricular activities but we have remained in touch with a number of the crowd. Over the years we have periodically enjoyed Anna, Harro and Nicolas' hospitality and company very much. We were glad they could join us now.

An exchange of text messages with our German friends established that they would find us in the town of Pouilly-en-Auxois on the 24th July from where you enter the Pouilly Tunnel. And so it came to pass that *Wise One* acquired two more crew and a car on the tow path.

The tunnel Crew

The tunnel is 3km long and one way only so you go through by appointment and perhaps in convoy. At one time there was a fixed chain that ran its length, lying on the bottom, and a 'mule' which towed barges through the tunnel. The mule was driven by collecting the chain and hauling it through an onboard drive system. The tunnel is unlit so some competent form of ship's lighting is necessary. Morton and Eva went first with a fairly impressive head light and we followed a little behind. The approach into the tunnel entrance was via a winding and narrow cutting; as the tunnel entry came into view it looked (and is) very small and exceptionally dark. However as adventures go it was not too difficult or frightening; certainly we survived.

We now found ourselves at 380 m above sea level and down hill all the way to the Med. In truth I was looking forward to some favourable current to push us along. From Honfleur we had done 433 km and 149 locks against the prevailing streams. Before we entered the Med we were to do another 900 km and 90 locks. We had down-hill Bourgogne, the Soane and the Rhone before us and the final few miles of southern canals before reaching somewhere to take us for the winter. We were getting there but still with some serious work to do! The part of the Bourgogne Canal so far travelled had been a great experience in all respects (towns, landscapes, friends etc). The downhill half of the Bourgogne was to prove even more attractive than the uphill. Long view over the fields and through the woodlands showed the beautiful C12th Chateauneuf turreted on the hill side. This is an unspoilt and completely fortified little town and well worth a visit.

Chateauneuf

Shortly after the tunnel we were joined by urbane, Swiss Nicholas for a couple of days and proceeded down hill with great enjoyment and increased elegance. In Edinburgh we had shared a house with Nicolas for a short while. We have also kept in touch for some 35 years and visited his lovely home in Alsace. He joined us in Hampshire on one occasion, asking where the nearest airport was. Well there is Heathrow, Gatwick and Southampton. No, no! Into which he could fly his own aircraft – i.e. a two seater cockpit 'micro-light'. So we met him at the Old Sarum sports aerodrome and, as a gesture of appreciation, he took me up for circuits and bumps around Stonehenge country. I could be quite addicted.

Swimming off the boat has to be one of those (perfectly reasonable) dreams that go with hot sun and blue skies. The canals, however, very definitely did not invite swimming. (Except of course for small boys who are immune to harm). An inflated, furry four legged friend stuck in a lock gate reminded us of hazardous life on the water banks. Our German crew warned us of the dangers of rat urine etc etc but they had their own solution. Using our very short hose (cut for the purpose) with shower fitting one end and a cold tap on the other, a refreshing bank-side shower could be achieved. The Germans (but not Swiss) way was to strip off every stitch at the sound of a turning tap. (And why not?).

The discrete alternative for a hot shower was a black shower bag on the deck – but we couldn't hoist it up the mast to get water pressure (as is normal) because we had no mast. Not to worry, we removed the air vent cover in the 'heads' ceiling, fed a pipe through from the bag and had the shower in un-German like privacy.

We still occasionally bumped into Dane, Dutch and Germans on the way and with whom we had already said bibulous farewells. Each day an evening working party was sent by cycle to recover the cars which, in turn, gave us more freedom to roam.

Days slipped easily by as we continued to the city of Dijon and nearly the end of the Bourgogne. Dijon is a major city with a well preserved medieval centre and many half timbered buildings from the 12th to 15th Centuries. A lot seems to happen in Dijon, including musical and gastronomic festivals in the summer (we must go again and give it more time). The cathedral St Benigne de Dijon is well worth a visit as is the $C14^{th}$ Tour des Ducs. The latter has a tower with great views over the city and surrounding countryside and an awful lot of (worn) stone steps to get to the top. The Palais includes the Musee des Beaux Arts. There is of course good cuisine and Burgandy wines. We were happy to taste the Kir which they claimed was invented here. Who were we to disagree?

From Dijon it is a very easy run down to St Jean-de-Losne at the junction of the Bourgogne and the Soane. Here many vessels turn up the Soane and head north again to the Rhine or return north by one of the other central canal routes. Those heading for the Med (in our group, just us) head south down the Soane to join the Rhone at Lyon. St Jean-de-Losne is therefore an important town and a major centre for canal craft and support services of every kind. It was the first real marina that we had seen since Paris. The setting was good – grass, trees, restaurants, eleci and water on tap, facilities and services. Jacky was all for stopping; perhaps for a year or two.

It was here therefore that I sought advice from a marine engineer over our high-rev vibration. After a test drive around the basin he gave his verdict (in French, of course):

"This boat needs to be lifted and the shaft drawn and examined for distortion through impact. But I can't start such a job for two or three weeks. It will then take a week to repair and re-launch". Clearly end of our French project '05.
"What the chances were of getting down to the Med without any further mechanical treatment?" He said, rather thoughtfully:
"Well. You could *probably* make it". So we did.

Canal and river experiences tend to be quite different. Village and towns are often built on river crossings and have been dependent on river transport. Canals, built so much later than the towns, are dependent not on existing communities but on contours, hills and valleys. It is possible to travel some distance by canal without close contact with towns or villages. We can (and do) wax lyrical about the towns and villages we saw; but often there were periods when we saw no town (unless we cycled). Mostly we enjoyed the places we visited but some showed signs of economic distress, some in poor condition, few shops, and fewer people. Of course what stays with us are the good memories, but bits of rural France (as elsewhere) do struggle.

We are left with several abiding memories of this canal section: 1) working the many locks; 2) the beauty, particularly of the downhill section. 3) the friends made from Denmark, Sweden, Holland, Belgium and Germany. 4) the wealth of medieval towns in central France to be discovered. Actually if you want to explore the great wine regions (and this was Chablis country) or whistle stop around the historic towns, the canal is not the way to do it; go by car. But if you want a slow and ever changing perspective on this unique sliver through Europe, then the canals are magical. Whether by car, cycle or boat, do not miss Laroche Migennes, Tonnere, Chateauneuf or the amazing Semur-en-Auxios.

The *Yellow Brick Road* was living up to its great reputation!

Chapter 4

Alone on the Soane and 'Les Cathedrales Engloutie'.

Shortly after Dijon life again became serious as we faced the River Soane leading to the Rhone. All our friends had turned north for the Rhine or the Central Canals. We were left all alone to head south. Fewer locks (but bigger), a river instead of a canal. What had this next section of the *Yellow Brick Road* in store for us? The Rhone certainly has a reputation as a big bully. We'll find out.

Now that we were back in river-mode, we expected to find a richer range of towns and villages accessible to us. We therefore greatly enjoyed Chalon-sur-Soane which had a very pleasant marina based on a great little town. There was a riverside bar with a dance floor at the ready. That night there was to be eating and dancing under the stars (Munchkins at play). This was Burgandy land so that was certainly for us! Dancing did become a little uninhibited involving the chef (for Jacky) and the band leaders wife (for me). She was good and the jive seemed to have no 'house rules' inhibitions. The local ballroom dance group (for whom it was obviously their smart evening) seemed a little surprised.

Tournus gave us a good town centre and a perfect and un-messed-around Romanesque Abbey Church which was itself well worth the visit. And soon we were in the great city of Lyons. Lyons is on the confluence of the Soane and the bigger Rhone which would take us down to the Med. It is a city deep in schizophrenia. We expected a rather grim, modern commercial city with little soul (because we've only seen it from the by-pass). In fact the city centre is a world heritage area. Half is the old medieval town, the other half the nineteenth century merchant city. Moorings are pretty basic, but the city centre is packed with interest and people. It deserved a couple of days before we proceeded into the Rhone and on to Avignon and Arles. All spoiled us with their rich remains of ancient, ecclesiastical and commercial France. But first, the Rhone.

The Rhone has always been an important line of communication. Since it rises in the Swiss Alps, it is subject to major surges. During the spring period of snow-melt the river has always been potentially fierce, if not dangerous. In the 1930's plans were drawn up to tame the river and after the war a string of 12 huge barrages and associated locks were built. Even now when in full spate a small and lightly powered vessel needs to be cautious. Each barrage drove a hydroelectric power plant and they now provide some 7.5% of France's electrical supply. The locks themselves are vast and cathedral like. Whilst intimidating at first, their wall mounted floating bollards are simple to moor to and then slide with you without further rope adjustment. (See the appendix on the French Locks). The Rhone therefore proved to be much more canalised than expected and in August the sea-going current is quite gentle; (dammit).

Leaving Lyons we entered the Rhone through the suitably-massive Pierre- Benito lock. The Pierre-Benito is simply huge but then, it gives access to the massive River Rhone. Well we knew that; but we didn't know it was going to be so large; but there would be others, and bigger. And then downstream to St Vallier (for a night) and Valance and a lunch stop at Tournon. Here we enjoyed again a little historic centre topped off with a castle worth the climb up the old stones. From here you can enjoy the short views over the tumbling red tiled roofs and the long views down the great river winding its way to the horizon.

There were times on the river when we felt a great sense of elevation. As the Rhone found its way between the Alps and the Massif Central we enjoyed long views over valleys to distant hills. The river seemed to be held back giving us unnaturally elevated views – until a trio of massive locks dropped us down to a more natural river level. These three giants of the Rhone were Mondragon, Cateauneuf and Bollene locks, the biggest of which had a drop of 22m.

Bollene Lock

With these Rhone locks you can forget all previous techniques of scrambling up ladders with rope in teeth; or hurling a mooring line to a friendly bystander; or bartering for fruit, veg or wine; or bantering the lock keeper. The eclusier is never seen, communications are by lights or VHF. Going downstream you head into a vast, concrete boat-pen at river level and moor to floating steel bollards on steel rails. As the lock full of water drains out, so you fall for ever (well, about 22m actually) into a gloomy, sun-eclipsed and watery cathedral; as deep as despair. (Debussy would have approved of this 'Cathedrale Egloutie'). The water control within the lock is good. However on departure if you have already cast off, the prop-wash of a giant fellow traveller just in front of you can wreak havoc with your sense of direction. It's not a difficult process but it's certainly quite awe-inspiring. On leaving these giants we would call a VHF thanks and a cheery disembodied acknowledgement would come back.

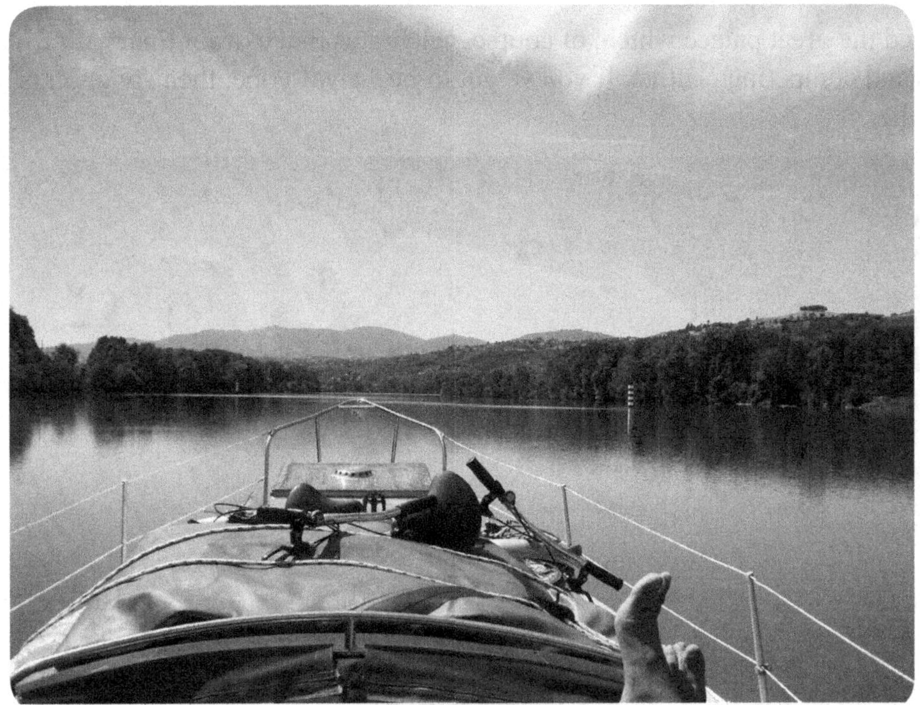

The open Rhone

In Viviers we found ourselves again in a very pleasant medieval town with hospitable pontoons for a couple of days of Repairs and Recreation. The sun-drenched French summer changed and the dreaded Mistral was on us. Northerly gales driving down the Rhone valley periodically whip the Gulf du Lyons into a frenzy and wise off-shore skippers are somewhere safe with a bottle of wine on hand. But the same gale also makes life on the river difficult. A well-found canal boat might manage in a gale in the open waters of the big river; but manoeuvring around the big locks with their accompanying torrential weirs is altogether a different matter. We asked how long this would last and were told that there are three day Mistrals and nine day Mistrals and you don't know until afterwards which one you've got. It was a good time for an oil change. All things have an end, including the Mistral. We moved on to the iconic Avignon.

These old cities are particularly great to enter by boat. We have been to Paris by car or rail on a number of occasions over the years; but gently motoring up the Seine, under the bridges and round Notre Dame is a new perspective on the old place. Lyons by water was a much more civilised experience than battling with road congestion. Avignon by boat was putting the clock back by hundreds of years as the major sights on entry were the old truncated bridge (with people dancing) and of course the Pope's Palace. Comfortable moorings lay almost in the shadow of the great palace. We heard that during the previous winter they had all been swept away by the torrential force of the river in full spate; but that seemed so unreal now that no sleep was disturbed.

We explored the great palace which, of course, celebrates that extraordinary time of competing Popes and competing centres. If you've got to be a rival Pope, then Avignon is not a bad place to settle.

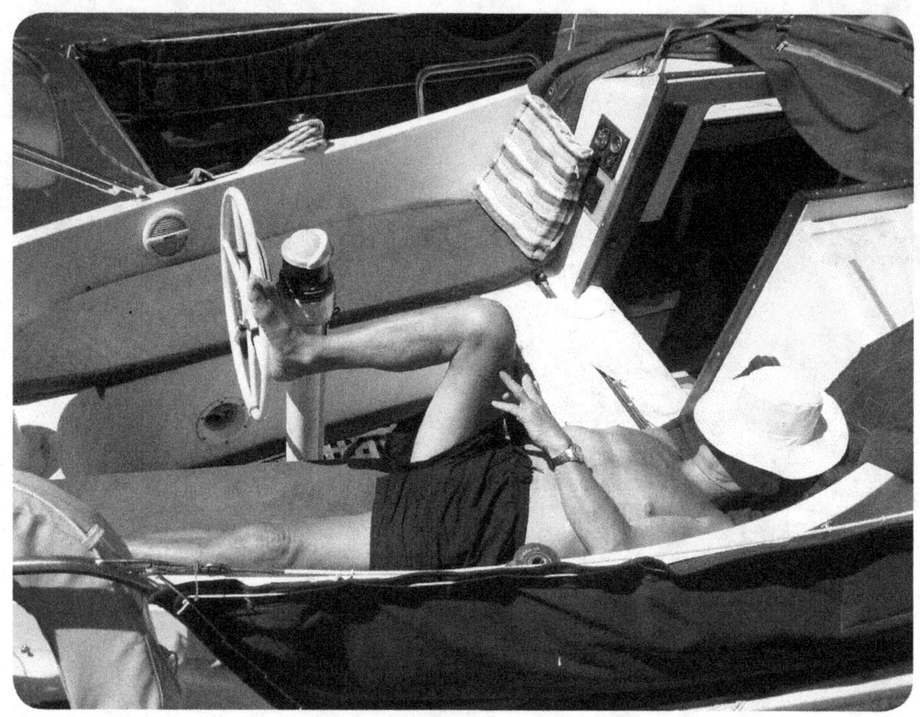

The old Autohelm at work

The period during which the papacy was established in Avignon ran from 1309 to 1379 and lasted for seven successive popes. At that time the secular power of the pope had led to the declaration that they had command over kings and kingdoms and any challenge to Papal authority was declared heretical in the early 14th Century. The French crown could not accept this and the French king even sought to arrest and bring to trial the pope in 1303 on charges of sodomy, simony, sorcery and heresy.

This crisis was followed by the long period called the Babylonian Captivity in which the French Kings exercised close control over the papacy. This started with the appointment of a French pope in 1309 who simply decided not to move to Rome. Instead the Papacy moved to Avignon. The successive six popes were all French and worked closely with the French Crown. However in 1378 there appeared a second and parallel line of Popes which ended in 1417. This period of papal ambiguity was called the Western Schism.

In general the growing secular power of the popes peaked in the 13th century. Southern 'France' in the 13th and 14th centuries still looked to the Holy Roman Empire for their secular authority and had a culture very different to northern 'France'. Inverted commas around 'France' are used because many of the borders of France as we know it were still disputed and the authority of the French Crown, the English Dukedoms and allegiance to the Papacy or to the Holy Roman Empire at times seems quite ambiguous. For example the challenge to the Papacy exercised by the Cathar movement developed in a more free-thinking and independent environment than existed in the more papal-orientated north. Hanging over all these events was the awful appearance of the Black Plague in 1347 which killed an estimated one third of the European population.

So the Babylonian Captivity left a huge legacy in Avignon, most obviously that of the vast and impressive papal palace which dominates the waterfront and must be explored.

During this period and between 1348 and 1350 the Black Death caused appalling losses. In the south of France the population loss is estimated to have been in excess of 50%, particularly amongst the clergy. Pope Clement VI considered he was more useful alive than dead and put himself into quarantine isolation.

We moved on to Arles. Again, a city of huge character with its amazing Roman amphitheatre. It is hard to believe that there is so much of the original structure still remaining. You simply can't go anywhere near Arles and not climb those old stones which pump out so much heat and history. It is easy to re-create in your mind the scene of Roman games and entertainment, the clamour of conflict, the excited and sweaty crowd, the cries of the vendors ("Fried badgers' noses; very cheap!").

Roman amphitheatre, Arles

But this was a further moment of critical choice for us. Autumn would soon be on us and a place had to be found for the winter.

Chapter 5

A winter's tale.

It was now late August, 2005 and at this point our long distant search for a winter berth became more serious by refusals ("sorry, full") and by the damaging prop strike and transmission judder at higher revs which seemed to speak of engine mountings, prop or shaft. And a cheque book. Time to find a secure home and a good contractor. A hired car explored the eastern route down to the Mediterranean coastal Port St Louis. Yes there was space; not surprising, it was bleak and uncomfortable and 40 km in the wrong direction. So a trip to the west and a look at Latte, Aigue Mortes, Ariane (Montpellier) and half a dozen places toward coastal Sète. Only Port Camargue produced a half promise of a two month berth but it does have full management and technical services. It does seem that berths are hard to secure ahead of time; no doubt because travelling yachties are notoriously unreliable. The best (and sometimes only) deal that can be struck is when you have arrived with your boat and can clinch a deal NOW.

Half a promise was the best we had so we left Arles, entered the Petit Rhone and spent two delightful days in Aigue Mortes, the fully walled C13th town built to service the Palestinian Crusades, (more later). Before moving on we walked the top of the walls and enjoyed the views both into the town and away across the marshes to the sea. It was hard to recall that this was built as a port; the sea had certainly retreated a long way.

Grau de Roi

From Aigues Mortes we proceeded to the old fishing port of Grau du Roi. From here with huge rejoicing we at last burst into the open Mediterranean. What a welcome change to escape the canals and rivers for the sea, albeit a brief crossing of the bay and then into the huge marina 'village' of Port Camargue. Port Camargue was built in the 1970's and is said to be the largest marina in Europe. Better described as a marina town, it has some 60 ha. of water, 100 ha. of developed land, 4,500 yacht berths, 175 shops and related services in three shopping centres. (Eat your heart out, MDL). There are all the marine support services that a leisure boat could need. In addition it has an all-tides access to the Med. and is in easy reach of a wide range of land-based activities. Not a bad place to be if you don't mind its sheer size.

Negotiations with le Capitaine started badly: *Winter? Non! Full! Absolutement, mon amis! Who do you think you are? Eh?* So, what next? Bribery? How much? Bathos? Tears? Damaged boat? Family wedding? He gave us six months; I gave him a kiss. The recommended contractor gave us a quote; the insurance company gave us a go ahead. (Thank you, Bishop Skinner).

These first few September days in Port Camargue reminded us of the weather which can occur in this region. For three days storms prowled the Rhone valley and coastline. The skies darkened, the wind gathered itself for a destructive assault and lightening played across the horizon. We sat in the cockpit in the evenings looking at a sky like indigo. The gods now not only chucked bolts of lightening, but fired them from huge battalions of hidden artillery lodged in the massed and heavy clouds. The hurricane eventually fell on us with rain enough to flatten the rising sea and sink a larger boat. It was a theatrical display like no other and every minute appreciated from the cockpit.

The morning revealed that the sandy beach and the beach guards' all-weather hut had been swept away. But the morning sun also brought a rainbow in the west over which, somewhere, there lay the Emerald City.

We celebrated our arrival in the Med., and also celebrated our 40th wedding anniversary. We don't normally make a big fuss, but this was a bit special so a nice meal and a glass or two seemed appropriate. We were however hijacked by French angling/boating neighbours on the pontoon who were drinking to mark the end of their fishing summer. They pressed on us red wine and two very large mackerel ("Have more" they said, "have more!"). What could we do but eat the mackerel? Very tasty and a very economic anniversary. (But I was to pay for it later….).

The French summer finished abruptly with the start of the school term. It has always seemed strange to us; France has weeks more of gentle weather when costs are lower and congestion very much less and yet even those without school age children seemed tied to school dates. As schools go back so the holidaying French vanish, restaurants and cafes close, holiday flats and boats are deserted and the waterfront is left to the foreigners. It is also true that as September progresses the cooler evenings draw in and the small cockpit is less cosy and the cabin becomes somehow smaller.

So that gave us a week of water jousting, bull running, blue brie, red wine and a "*carafe of your best rose, maitre please*". All that was left before going home was sea and sun bathing and plat-de-mer with our very good friend le Capitaine.

So what about our 2005 summer travels? We have talked about the bully Rhone, albeit a pussy cat in August; and the locks in watery cathedral mode or little ones with deadly sloping sides; and the village dancing in Challon. But not the Gaulois-stained voices of the pontoon fisherman overnight. Join me for a drink sometime and we'll yarn a bit more.

Readers’ Notes

Part 2
Summer 2006 Camargue To Royan
Wise One to the Biscay

In which we honour Paul Riquet, join an elevated village feast, face ghosts and demons in Cathar Country, get frightened in Begles and hosed down in Royan.

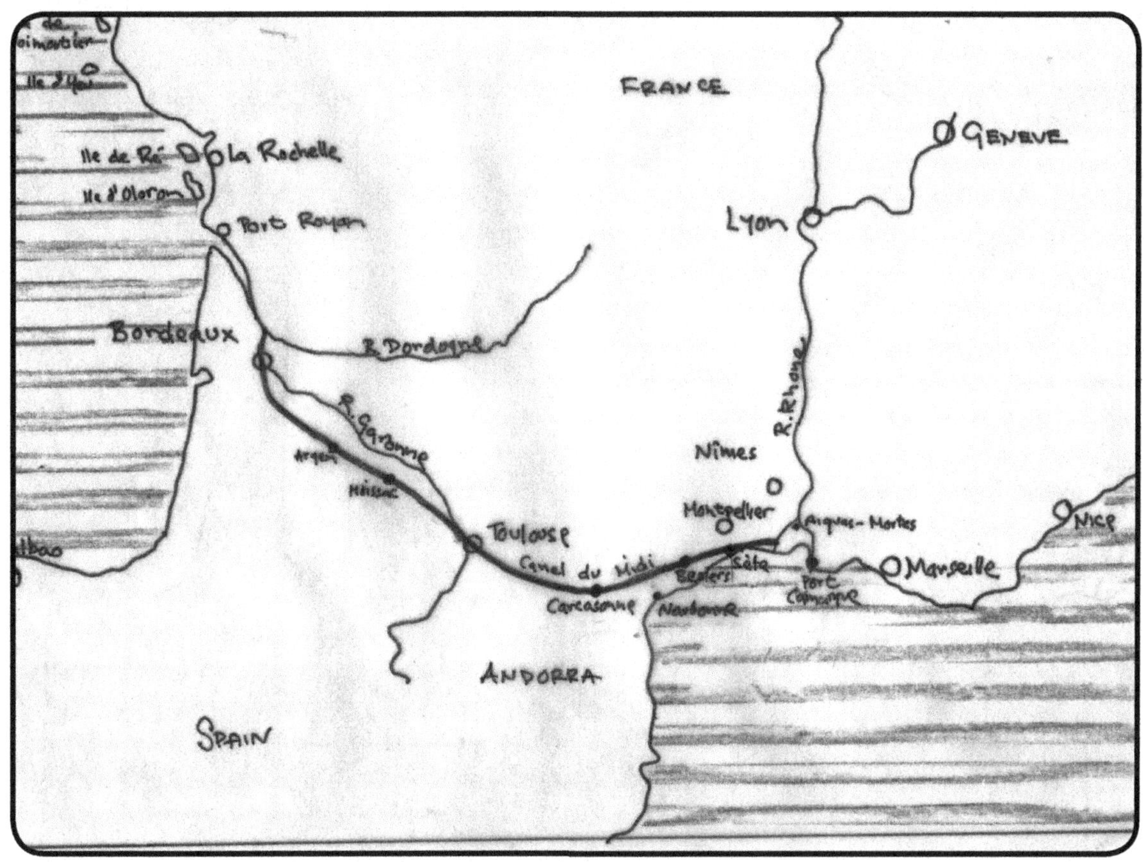

Map 2: Port Camargue to the Biscay.

Chapter 6

Salty Etangs

During the winter of '05 I flew out to Port Camargue to inspect the transmission and stanchion repair work on *Wise One*. The shaft had been drawn, the engine lifted and re-seated, the shaft reinstated and aligned and all seemed good. I approved payment and organised for the mast to be transported by road from Honfleur to Port Camargue. I liked to have all the gear in the same place at least for a short time and it gave me a chance to check and clean the rig.

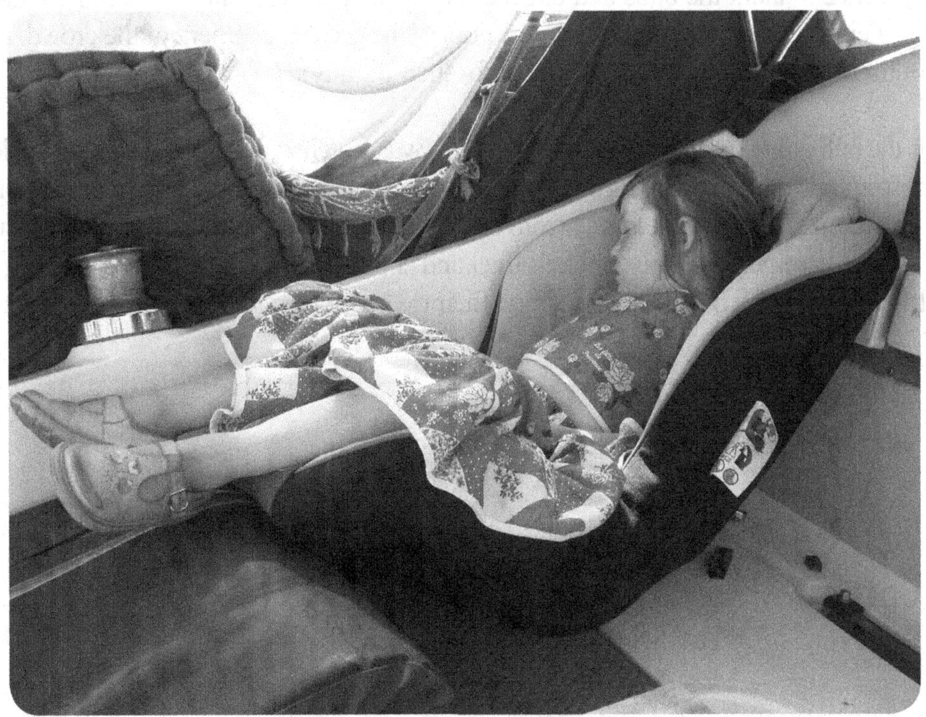

Amelia in Port Camargue

In April '06 we both drove down to Port Camargue taking a load of gear and ensuring land-based mobility. The family joined us for a short while and single-mum Anna (daughter), carefree bachelor Alex (son) and small Amelia (5) camped on board to see how us old folks were faring. Four adults and a small girl were a bit crowded but good fun. Professionally, Anna cares for adults with learning difficulties; she also cares for horses and lives in Oldham. Alex is into global investment consultancy and lives in central London. He is also into kick boxing, football, white collar boxing and works from London. Despite that they get on fine. We had 'always' sailed as a family but they never really caught the bug. A couple of days with the old folk seemed OK before they headed off together for a few days in Spain.

A pleasant beach (reinstated since the gales) is adjacent to the marina as are cafes and restaurants. The car whisked us off to explore Grau-du-Roi and Aigues Mortes and visit relatives in Lunel. Grau-du-Roi is a colourful and lively fishing port through which we would re-enter the canal system from the Mediterranean. It has accommodated the tourist growth of the last few decades, but done so whilst still retaining much of its earlier charm and joi-de-vivre. It still has a significant fishing fleet. The restaurant-lined river banks produce some good food with sea food dominating. The Med. does still yield fish and crustaceans, but if you are offered giant prawns, they have probably come from East Africa. The town is big enough to support a range of other attractions including a cinema, a swimming centre, sports and fitness centres and an arena generally used for bull events.

South-west France does enjoy its bull fighting and, out of curiosity (you've got to try everything once, including Morris dancing) Jacky and I attended the local Big Ring. It was not a fight in the true sense but was entertainment involving a large inflatable paddle pool and a selection of bulls. The local youth were given licence to taunt the bulls and use the pool as a place of escape. When the bulls worked out the ruse, they tended to join the youth in the pool to the great excitement of the crowd. I think no bulls (or youth) were hurt in the process (except for their dignity).

Afterwards the bulls were 'run' through the streets. Crowds watched from behind crush barriers while sunburnt horsemen from the Carmargue in wide black hats led a muscle-charged parade of a dozen bulls. The crowd instinctively edged back from the barrier. Urged on from behind by more horsemen the heavy hooves hammered on the cobbled street and shook the pavement in their passing. All was quite quickly over with the bulls leaving behind their own unique comments on the process.

So, slowly, we settled into a new season.

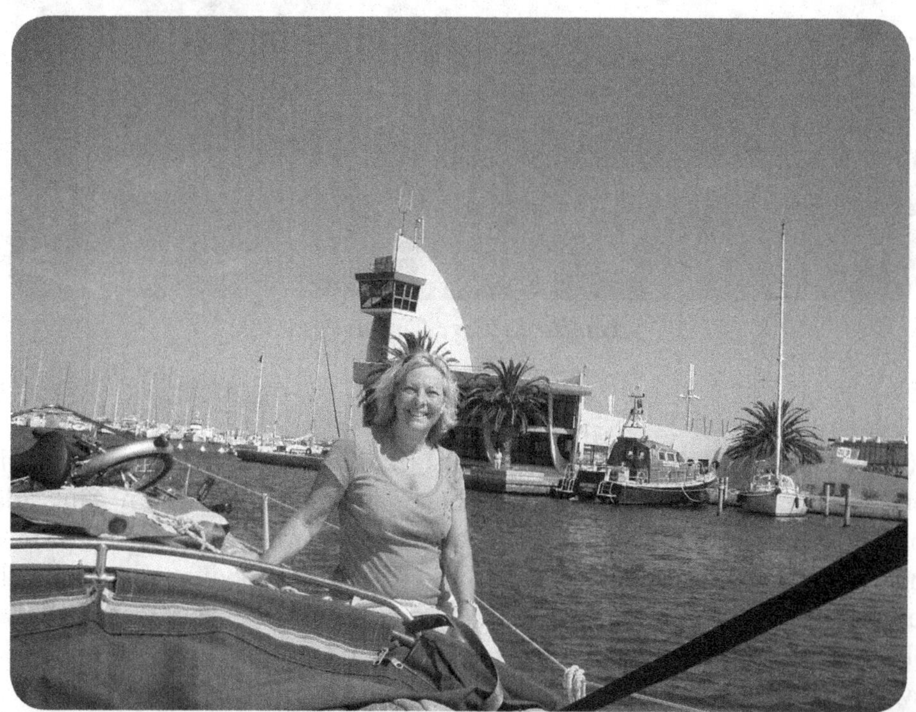

Jacky in Port Camargue

The marina can be quite a social place as we found in the previous autumn. The red ensign was not much in evidence; this was a French place for French people. They generally were local power boats for local angling. Some of the fishing, clearly, was done along the coast. Some of the fishing was done off the end of the pontoon in the harbour. Evidently friends would gather for a midnight fish, a few gaulois and a bottle of Cote de Rhone. New friends and neighbours gradually returned to test our French speaking ability and for a period we simply enjoyed Port Camargue and neighbouring Grau-du-Roi.

After our initial run-in with Chris-the-Capitaine we got to know him better. People ornate the whole of our route and short, square, energetic Chris was both Port Capitain at Carmargue and co-owner of Chris-and-Mary's restaurant on the waterfront. He held our lives in sway having the gift of both moorings and food (well, not free of course). Mary was invisible in the kitchen; King Chris's court was his open restaurant frontage where evenings passed in handshakes and kisses; animated discussions on all topics to do with boating and football; all wreathed in smiles and washed down with something appropriate.

We also frequented the nearby restaurant 'Le Soleau' where the Spanish waiter (we had to christen him Manuel) had incomprehensible French, got all the orders wrong and delivered the bills to the wrong customers. But with hardly a single word in common there was still a continuous stream of jokes and laughter.

Before Anna and Alex moved on we drove off to an evening gig event high in the neighbouring hills featuring nephew Piers and his own songs. All under a warm French night sky and through a haze of local red. Who cares about engine or marina problems?

In due course Anna, Alex and Amelia took off on their Spanish jaunt leaving us to plan the next phase of our own journey. (We'll meet them all again later). The *'Yellow Brick Road'* for summer '06 was to be Port Camargue, Grau-du-Roi (again), Aigues Mortes, Palavas, Sète, Mèze (and the Etang du Thau), Beziers (and my sisters extended family), Narbonne (and old college friends), Carcassonne, Toulouse, Bordeaux and Royan and then (eventually) Belle Ile. Oh, and the bits in between.

* * *

Now a few words about the southern waterways. Let's first look at the historic sequence. The long trip around Portugal and Spain to reach the Mediterranean had always been slow and dangerous (weather and pirates). Trading vessels had always been able to navigate the Gironde Estuary as far as Bordeaux. Small freight barges had been hauled up the River Garonne as far as Toulouse. The missing bit in those early days was between Toulouse and Agde which the Romans had contemplated as a canal link. In 1516 Leonardo da Vinci had surveyed the potential for a canal but the problems of lifting the canal by the required 189 m. and the difficulty of ensuring a reliable water reservoir at the watershed stopped its development until the 17th century.

So what got built? Most people, (but not you, of course), tend to use the title 'Canal du Midi' as shorthand for all those waterways lying between the Rhone and Bordeaux; i.e. the Southern Canals. Not, however, true. At the eastern end is the 120 km Canal du Rhone-a-Sète, completed in 1820. This extends from the Rhone westwards through the low-lying coastal region, much of the way through salt water lakes (Etangs) separated from the sea by sand dunes. The channel generally runs between high banks over which can be seen black fighting bulls, grazing white Camargue horses and flocks of pink flamingos, heads down and trawling for food.

Black Fighting Bull

From Sète the big navigable Etang du Thau carries you 23 km to Agde where the Canal du Midi really starts. From Agde the Canal du Midi runs to Toulouse for 240 km. Everywhere its inceptor, champion, designer, surveyor, and part financier Paul Riquet, (a Wizard if ever there was one) is celebrated. It was put into service in 1681. A hundred years later the Duke of Bridgewater visited and took inspiration from the Canal du Midi to build the first British industrial canal. Paul Riquet got there first and the Midi is now a World Heritage site.

From Toulouse westwards runs the 190-ish km Canal Lateral de la Garonne (completed 1856) which itself stops some 67 km east of Bordeaux. From here to Bordeaux the Garonne is navigable and tidal. From Bordeaux to the sea the River Garonne is joined by the Dordogne and renamed the Gironde which is a widening and swiftly flowing tidal estuary.

A combination of the burgeoning wealth and ambitions of Louis X1V's France and the stamina of Paul Riquet eventually solved all problems. He had help, I am sure, from many talented engineers including the famous Louis X1V military engineer Sabastian Vauban who was involved in the design of the reservoir and a number of bridges. (More of Vaubin later). In total the Canal du Midi is some 240 km. long, contains 91 locks and rises to 189 m above sea level and enters the sea at Sète which was built as its eastern terminal.

These water systems therefore display an ever changing range of temperament that unfolds slowly with your 4 knot progress. Fifty years ago the eastern, Mediterranean section of the route was characterised by marsh, lagoon and mosquitoes. Only small local fishing populations could tolerate the summer humid heat and insect assaults. Post war economic planning in the '50s was followed by a programme of insect control; much land was drained and in the '60s the infrastructure for holiday development was built. This resulted in the huge, planned coastal developments of Port Camargue, Grau-du-Roi, Carnon, Palavas, la Grande Motte, Port Ariane (Montpellier) and Cap d'Agde. Some old fishing communities have managed to hang on to traces of an earlier architectural and community presence. But much is characterised by the developments of the 1970's and 80's.

Our first call after Port Camargue was back across our small corner of the Med, into the canal at Grau-du-Roi and on to the completely walled medieval town of Aigues Mortes. This may well be a very ancient location for a settlement. However it also formed the location for a new-built, heavily fortified port from which the seventh and eighth Crusades departed in the 13th Century. At that time France's southern borders had not been established and this was the only serious access France had to the Mediterranean.

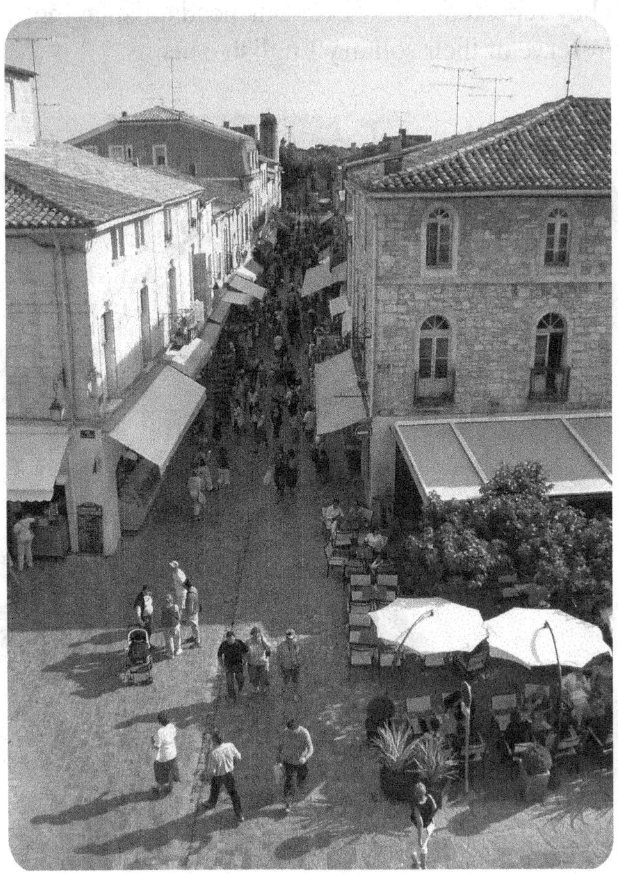

Aigues Mortes

The scale of its (complete) city walls and the impregnable Constance Tower at the main entrance suggests that even a garrison town could not presume its safety. Perhaps it often had a skeleton garrison while the provisions for the next crusade were being assembled and stored. One imagines that the local War Lords of these southern Bad Lands were capable of raiding such valuable treasures. Provisions for war clearly had to be stored behind impressive walls faced up by an impregnable entrance tower. The town in the C13th must therefore have contained both warehouses and small town palaces to house the very important Commanders and their retinues.

It was replaced as a major sea port by Marsailles in the 15th Century after which Aigue Mortes had a limited role in life. Its huge C13 walls and fortified main entry are substantially and impressively complete. However there is now no sign of the C13th buildings and most of what you see date from the C17-C18th. and is of modest scale. This seems to tell us that as the town retained its walls it continued at a modest level of local importance. In fact we are told that **in** the 16th and 17th Centuries it was one of the few safe havens granted to Protestants during the period of their repression; (and references to non-conformist repression reoccur later in this story). The walls, I am sure, were much restored in the 19th Century but are no less impressive for that.

There is a canal basin within the shadow of the walls now devoted to small leisure craft; it was a good spot to spend a couple of days before seriously getting on the move once more. From Aigues Mortes we moved on, turning towards Sète and all points west. Between there and Palavas-les-Flots we ran through a short canal section populated by a *cloud* of (what really seemed to be) kingfishers (honest!). They repeatedly flew over our heads displaying their colours – nothing like the water hugging reserve of their solitary English cousins.

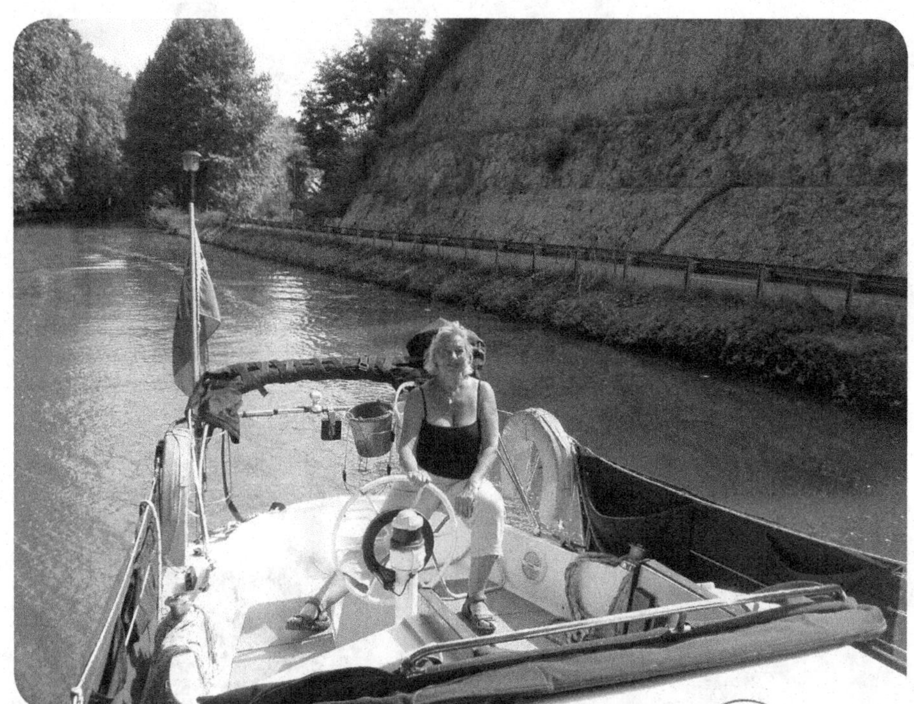

Jacky in charge

We stayed a short time in Palavas which has two marinas. We preferred the smaller, less formal 'Paul Riquet Marina' where we lay to a grassy embankment. We had a mystifying and occasional over-heating problem with the engine and advice was sought, unsuccessfully, on this occasion.

Although much changed by the huge growth of the holiday trade, the town is still a place of some character. It grew around the fishing port and that trade still exists. Inevitably the waterfront is now well devoted to restaurants, bistros and cafes. It has a good beach front to the Med and sea swimming was irresistible.

After Palavas we visited the 'island' 12/13th Century cathedral of Maguelonne. It lies just to the west outside the town and surrounded by salt marshes. If you are lucky you could catch one of their fairly frequent music evenings. A magic experience!

But for me real 'traditional' France started that summer at Sète, a place that could well be described as France's Venice. A town of some 43,000 population, it is the end of the Canal du Rhone à Sète and the start (or end!) of the older Canal du Midi. It gives good access to the Mediterranean and clearly grew on the trade generated by the two canals. The town centre is crossed with a system of commercial, locked basins and in the past was a hive of intense shipping activity, particularly in the 17th and 18th Centuries whose architecture still dominates the town. During the 19th Century the railways began to displace traffic from the older canals. The commercial sea traffic has largely gone but has left behind a network of waterways which are a huge feature of old Sète.

Every week in the summer you can see water jousting between rival oar-driven boats with their stern-mounted jousting platforms which carry the crouching combatants. We moored with limited marina facilities in the town centre, avoiding the big modern marina at the sea entrance. Perhaps that was a mistake; it was truly the noisiest place we stayed in with the night orchestrated by buzz bikes, rail freight trains and fast passing fishing craft. Still, it is a lively town which we enjoyed, well worth a couple of days.

The town had good marine services for over-heating engines but, unfortunately, when needed they seemed to be all on holiday. We moved on.

Westwards from Sète you enter the delightful Etang du Thau. It is said to be the second largest lake in France being 23 km long and 8 km wide. This compares with the Solent which is a curved shape of roughly 32.4 x 5 km. The mean depth is 4.5 m but the navigable channel can be 10 m deep. The Etang is open to the sea at Marseillan Plage but only for small boats that can take the restricted bridge heights. The Etang de Thau is not huge, but it is big enough to get a real feeling of space as you cross. To the north is the low-lying mainland running back to gentle hills in the distance. To the south are the modest sand dunes separating it from the open Mediterranean. Only in the direction of Sète does the land rise with the town climbing the landmark hill, Mont St Clair.

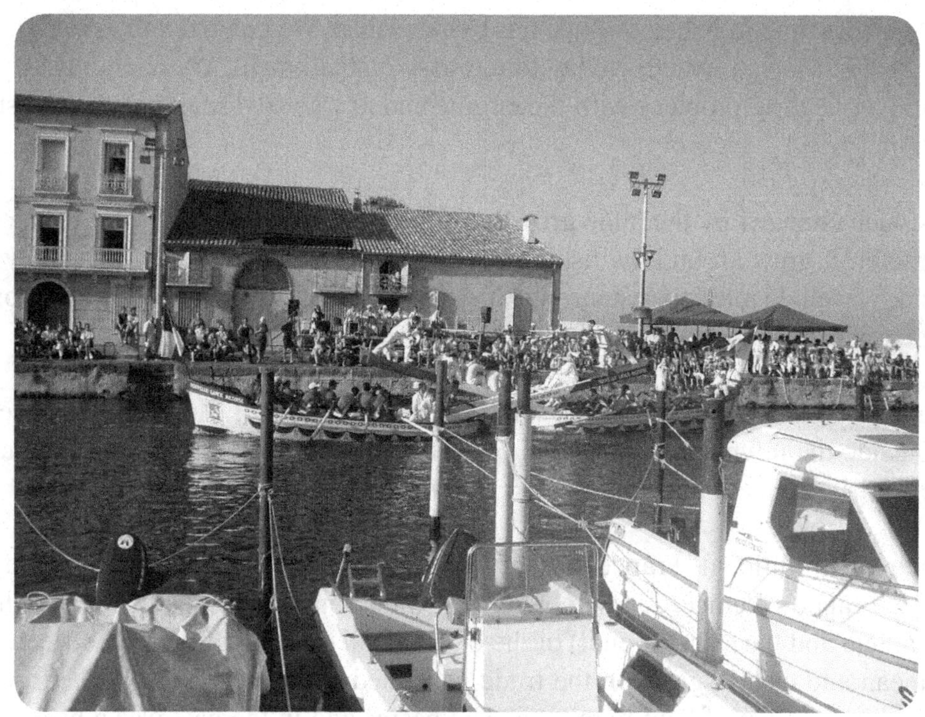

Water jousting

The Etang can be exposed to high on-shore winds. It seemed so peaceful a place that the idea that it could at times be closed to traffic because of bad weather seemed strange. Part of the reason, I am sure, is that the deep channel is fringed on its north sides by miles of oyster and mussel farms. These show themselves as forests of poles each supporting metal beds of mussels. If you were driven into the shellfish farms by a powerful cross wind you could do a great deal of damage to yourself and, perhaps, to the mussels. Here water purity is a matter of priority, controversy and dispute and the shell fish industry can on occasions be suspended while 'Grade A' water standards are restored. Some 13,000 tonnes of oysters and 3,000 tones of mussels are taken out each year.

However the Etang du Thau can meet the need not met by the canals – swimming! The water is fresh, gentle, clean and just there over the edge of the deck !! Time passes and with it some clarity of memory. But it is possible that Jacky said something like:
"This place is absolutely the greatest. Why don't we stop, hang around here, swim, soak up the sun and the rosè. We could really be here for *quite a long time*".
We were around the Etang for some four weeks; but I think Jacky was thinking of four years... Of course we had no fixed plan but the non-existent targets needed to be hit and the *Yellow Brick Road* still led us westwards.

Along the northern shores of the Etang du Thau are the old villages and access to the traditional communities of Balaruc, Bouzigues, Meze and Marseillan (where Noilly Prat is made). All can be good stay-over places although for the winter Balaruc is possibly the least expensive (and least aesthetic). In Bouzigues we watched the small town's population enter the Etang in a variety of small boats to celebrate its bounteousness with the patron saint, garlands, bedecked priest and 'umpah' band. In Marseillan eat at 'Le Marmettiere' (i.e. 'the cooking pot') for the very best of grub. These small places are all well worth visiting and spending some time just enjoying the small French port atmosphere. Mèze was our favourite, but in all we met nice people, drank nice wine, ate mussels, tielles (squid pies) and red peppers; and relaxed in the Mediterranean sun.

Drama comes in many forms. In Marseillan a heavy chartered power boat lay along side us crewed by a middle aged, British foursome. Frantic and lengthy adjacent cockpit conversations were overheard (as you do) as they tried to find a last minute way of returning home for one couple to reach a sick relative. Jacky stepped in with critical information
"There is a plane from Narbonne in about three hours and if you go NOW you could catch it".
My crude French sorted a taxi (with a little help from the nearby bar) and the harassed couple were on their way.

The remaining couple and ourselves repaired to that adjacent beach-bar in some mood of triumph (although I wasn't quite sure why) and the drink seemed all to be on our new friends John and Chris. He is the owner of a London restaurant which we are invited to visit; but these things, I guess, are of the passing moment. (I think they would be very surprised to see us in London.) They left for Agde early the next day and we remained to sort out an annoyingly intermittent, engine over-heating.

The last yard to attend to the motor had removed the thermostat and not replaced it which certainly contributed to some confusion although the actual problem was simple when eventually diagnosed. A casting plug in the outlet manifold had perforated leading to an occasional loss of cooling water pressure (and dramatic overheating). It took a long while to be diagnosed but, when the problem was understood, was then simple to resolve. The plug is a bottle-top size and shaped steel cap which is simply hammered into the casting hole. Problem at last solved by a mechanic from Sète. Time now to move from the Etang du Thau into the Midi at Agde

Chapter 7

The Skipper in the Cooler

Before moving on there is one small matter that needs to be cleared up. The atmosphere on board has always been one of perfect agreement between Skipper and Mate. On most things anyway. Actually who is the Skipper and who the Mate does remain a small issue, but all generally speaking works well.

Until, that is, we came to the question of the 'cooler'.

Keeping stuff cool and fresh going down the canals was a problem. I sought to solve this by the purchase of a low powered 12 v camping box which was not designed for this job and was therefore rubbish (for our purpose). Because the temperature of the cabin could be very high and the cool box motor could drop the box temperature by only a limited amount compared with the cabin ambient, it tended to warm-up food bought very cold from the shop and we did better simply with bags of ice. Jacky expressed her view:
"I cannot continue another single day with these ridiculous arrangements. To survive we have to keep food cool and if you can't sort it out I will buy a 'fridge".

It would have been helpful if she had come off the fence and been more specific.
I had two problems: firstly how to power the 'fridge and secondly where to put it. Actually, running the 'fridge when on a motor boat progressing from one fully serviced 'halte' to another was not difficult. Where to put it was a whole different issue. The best solution would have been to do a conversion of our (well used) food 'bin'; but midway through our journey seemed the wrong moment for that. There had to be a quicker answer.

The day came in Sète when we had the use of a hire car. Jacky set a careful trap involving a trip to Belaruc (Why? It's not very pretty!), where there is, I swear, Europe's largest supermarket. Here I found myself in the white goods section ('les refrigerateurs' it said) looking at a two-foot-cube white box like the one we used to have in our student kitchen. I noted that there was no ice tray but then, a 'larder' fridge doesn't have one. Now the Skipper is, as we know, Master-Under-God and I said
"Non; absolutement, non!". Then, (mistake this, smacks of appeasement), I said "We must go back to the boat to measure up a space to see if it will fit."
This piece of undeniable logic gave away the principle and got me nowhere and I found myself at the check-out weakly waving a piece of plastic.

It was a minor set back that the biggest supermarket in the world closed its goods collection desk for lunch. In the thumping heat we sat silently in the car eating something indescribable while the car's A/C slowly flooded the nearby tarmac.

Eventually we returned to Sète and our small pontoon. The object in its packing was much bigger than two-foot-cube and could hardly be carried through the security gate and past over-hanging bow anchors. When aboard it took up most of the cockpit even with the boom scandalised. Even stripped down it had to be eased down the companion way before a final resting place could be found. But where the hell to put it?

Jacky said:
"Bolt it on to the cabin table".
I mean. Come on! Joking? It would have taken up most of the cabin volume and probably have collapsed the (rather fragile) table. She said:
"Stick it on the quarter berth".
Also a problem. Under there lie all my tools. Behind there is the purpose designed chart shelf. On top of the charts are stored the waterproofs and safety gear. NO WAY !
"It could" I said doubtfully "go *under* the table. And then, helpfully
"The table drop flap then won't quite go down, but it nearly will. That flap will have to be raised to open the cooler door and you will have to lay flat on the cabin sole (i.e. floor) to reach the cool contents. One side of the table will be almost unusable; but the other side and one end will be OK. We won't have a main cabin double bed through dropping the table; but then there are generally only two of us. It could be made to work."
(You see a partnership on board relies on everyone being flexible). Thinking it all through, as a chap has to, I observed:
"The canals are pretty flat with little pitch or roll. When we leave the canals we would probably ditch the 'fridge (give it to a boy scout) because it will hardly be practical at sea".
Actually we didn't; I devised a means to lash it back to the bulkhead and down to the sole. Compromise by everyone is always important on a small boat.

We ran a cable to the ship-to-shore mains link. We connected up; a little light went on; a small whirring noise sounded good so we left it alone and at peace. The next morning we found the bacon frozen not just satisfyingly cold but positively frozen into a solid block. That's when we noticed the word 'congelateur' which, after some research, we discovered meant that we hadn't bought a 'fridge but were the proud possessors of a freezer …

Disaster? Dump it now before we get into more trouble? Actually it must be one of the best things we bought for the boat that trip. We froze stuff in it and transferred from the freezer to the cool box. We could always keep things cool OR frozen. We always had ice and frequently surprised our bigger hosts by providing the ice for the G and T. ("You've got ice? Where did you get that from?"). . Eventually it found its way on to the quarter berth which enabled us to use the table properly and open the white box while standing up which I thought was a great improvement. It certainly got in the way but, curiously, we learnt to live with it. Well there were only two of us. It goes to show (I suppose) that the Master Under God is not always wrong; but can be.

"Another glass of rosé please, my good man, and make it cold."

Chapter 8

Wizard Paul's Watery Dream and we meet the Tin Man in Carcassonne

The Canal de Midi will always be associated with Pierre-Paul Riquet. He was born and grew up in Beziers, becoming a wealthy business man in the world of 'tax-farming' (whatever that is; it smacks of banker's tricks). We have already seen that the canal link had long been a matter of speculation and serious study. Paul Riquet believed he could solve the practical problems which could be tackled with very creative engineering (including the involvement of Sabastian Vauban), as well as with a great deal of money. 'Come the hour, cometh the man' and the opportunity lay with the great wealth and ambition of Louis XIV.

Paul petitioned the King, received considerable support (including financial) but put in perhaps half the cost himself. This was in 1665 when he was aged 63. (SAGA would have been proud of him). The first task was to build the watershed feeder reservoir for which he damned the Laulot River at Naurouse. At the time the dam was only the second such major dam in Europe. The canal progressed from there, requiring a 173 m. tunnel at Malpas, the first canal tunnel to be built. In all, the canal was 240 km, it had 91 locks and it included 328 major structures (aqueducts, bridges etc). Paul Riquet died in 1680; the canal was opened in 1681. The Riquet family benefited from an income from the canal for many years but it took a hundred years to clear their debts.

Agde is the last (going westwards) of the post-war holiday towns which the canal closely by-passes. From Agde the uphill canals unfold. My sister Maggie and family live in Beziers which is a town worth time to explore. It is a city of some 70,000 population with a major historic core. Brother-in-law Norman's working life has been at executive level with a series of multi-national companies. Maggie has been heavily into hospital management as well as family and Norman management. Politics, music and literature have always been their driving interests (and family, of course). Their lives have been split between Bogotá, Pakistan, Belgium, France and sometimes the UK. Now retired, their place of choice is France with which they clearly feel a great affinity. Matthew is a nurse working in Beziers. Piers and wife Emer (with young Sam) write music and sing in a group working across SW France. Alexandra designs, makes and markets jewellery and lives in nearby Lunel with husband Francois and small Maxim. Ben is an arboraculturalist in Essex. They are a lovely family that keeps us entertained (but never give us an easy time) and are very useful when we are travelling in southern France. (Except for Ben, that is.)

Unlike many major towns we visited, Beziers has made a significant effort to accommodate travelling boats with a well set out nautical halt. What a pity it's not maintained since access to electricity, fresh water and toilets are always very welcome.

You do have to climb up from the canal since the cathedral on top of the hill must be the destination. The town has ancient foundations. It was occupied by moors in the 8th Century. It was a stronghold of Catharism in the 13th Century and was sacked by Papal Crusade. (More of that later). You can then reward yourself with a meal at the modest side street restaurant 'Cep d'Or', close to the cathedral, where we ate with Maggie, Norman and Matthew. And explored the local Languedoc wines. And why not.

We always had a lively discussion with Norman and Maggs

The canal at Beziers now really starts to make its impact on the landscape. It is carried over the River Orb on a (later constructed) many-arched aqueduct before leading on to the nearby eight-lock 'stairway' at Fonserannes. This dramatic flight (and very early, in the history of canal building) rises some 21m. The chambers are an ovoid shape, giving more room for stationary boats waiting passage and seems to be unique to the Canal du Midi. In 1983 an inclined plane was added for boats too large for the locks but this seems currently out of use. Matthew cycled out of Beziers to give us a hand through the flight and see us on our way. It was all an enjoyable experience and made us feel we were really now into the Midi itself.

30 Flight at Fonterannes

The next stretch of the Canal would give us the iconic destination of Carcassonne. But before we got there we had an appointment with old friends, David and Anne who have a house *and swimming pool* in Sellelas d'Aude, pretty much on our route. David is a long standing Leicester college friend who latterly has practiced as an architect in France in between singing in various regional choirs with Anne. They had a lovely house just off the Canal du Jonction. To reach them we turn left from the Midi into the Canal de Jonction which leads to the Canal de la Robine and on down to Narbonne. After visiting David and Anne we then had an appointment in Narbonne with friend-from-home Sylvia who was to join us for a few days to discover Carcassonne by boat. And it all worked well; including a hugely welcome soak in D and A's swimming pool (this was July and hot!). Our very hospitable hosts kindly also gave us a couple of days of their time and a tour of the Cathar Country, of which more later.

The diversion down to Narbonne was itself interesting and Narbonne well worth a visit. For a period it was under Moorish control as part of the Emirate of Cordoba. It prospered as a Mediterranean port until silting and shifting of the River Aud took away the port role from the 14th Century onwards. The abandoned river bed is now beautifully landscaped to form a green and pleasant strip close to the town centre. Only in the 16th Century did Narbonne become established as part of France.

We enjoyed the canal Nautical Halt in Narbonne which is particularly attractive with boats generously moored along a clean and well treed quayside. The city has much of historic interest. The Cathedral of Saint-Just is a huge and ambitious structure which however was started and never completed. The C13th ambition was to rebuild the earlier Romanesque church but they only managed the apse and part of the choir built to a vast and abandoned scale. There remains a bit of the earlier church which still, after 700 years, awaits progressive demolition. It is understood that at the time the rebuilding of the cathedral it required the demolition of the remaining Roman walls. The 'Consuls' of the City Council resisted this piece of vandalism and, surprisingly, the church did not have the clout to overrule them.

It is not alone in its abandoned state. In a nearby market town there is an exact parallel at a smaller scale: a very big local church was under ambitious reconstruction but managed only the choir. It is true that the area's economic fortunes suffered through the loss of the sea port and the impact of the Black Death; it is also true that the area went through deep political troubles. Whether these matters are related can be debated.

Sylvia was successfully met. We have known Sylvia for a long time and sailed together before in the Solent and in the Netherlands, so she was no stranger to *Wise One.* In case we should need it she brings with her skills as an office manager and as a masseur – both could be useful for us old folk. We retraced our steps back up the Canal de la Robine; said "hallo" again to Dave and Anne (and to their swimming pool; thank you D and A !); and moved back to the Canal du Midi.

We enjoyed the village of Homp and the three lock flight at Trebes before hitting the green 'halt' of Carcassonne. This is a place of two cities; part 18/19th commercial heart; part 12th Century fortress. Old Carcassonne is a 12th century fortified citadel which played a significant role in the Cathar heresy period of the 13th century. It was besieged and eventually fell to the Papal and Royalist forces. Many of those seeking shelter were simply burnt alive in their hundreds as heretics.

The substantial and 'imaginative' restorations of Carcassonne carried out in the 19th century by M. Viollet-le-Duc are lampooned as being 'Disney-like'. His creative and romantic interpretation of history went well beyond that which would now be acceptable. Nevertheless the old town with its many-towered walls and the citadel are still very well worth a visit. The citadel, though heavily restored and 'improved', at its zenith it certainly was a huge and fortified city which must have looked fairly substantially as it does now. It is, of course, a great tourist destination and some would find that too big a disadvantage. But we enjoyed it for its huge walls broken by towers frowning over the distant countryside. The deeply fortified main gate embraced us sternly as it had done countless thousands over the centuries. Inside, the narrow cobbled streets and substantial masonry houses, shops and warehouses spoke of its power and prestige. It now swarms with travelling visitors - but then it probably always did.

Sylvia and Don, Carcassonne.

If nothing else a visit to the C14th church of St Nazaire within the old city makes a trip worthwhile. The feature there is the unique apsidal East End where transept and apse fall into one transverse space. The east wall so created holds 16 stained lancet windows stopped at the north and south ends by large, stained rose windows. The pierced east wall is supported internally by a free standing 'avenue' of slender columns, off-set from the wall itself. It is a stunning experience of original gothic creativity. Unless perhaps influenced by M. Violet-le-Duc? The next time I am in that part of the world, I must make an early morning pilgrimage to see the rising sun shafting through those wonderful windows.

But we couldn't leave Carcassonne without witnessing real (horse) jousting. After all, we had seen water jousting in Sète and Mèze so we had to see the earlier dry land version. It was good fun with colourful equinine gymnastics, threatening lances and much galloping and some armour - yes! We have tin men! Good fun but not much blood.

Before leaving Carcasonne we ate in the old town and sampled their famous cassoulet. Now we had left the coast behind the menus included good, rural, peasant food and cassoulet must be the French version of a Lancashire Hot Pot. In Paris it is turned into High Cuisine. We were happy to eat it in its 'locale' of origin.

We said farewell to Sylvia at Carcassonne rail station and moved on.

Chapter 9

All about a heresy and bloody Villains

The Cathar Heresy has been mentioned more than once and you can't get away from it in SW France. So here's a bit about it. (But if you know it already you can skip this bit). Across southern Europe the Cathar Heresy was generating panic in the Papal corridors of power. It was a threat greater than the Moorish expansion both in Spain and in the near east because it was internal to the Catholic Church, the self styled 'Ark of Salvation' or, as Bosch depicted, 'The Ship of fools'.

This was the time of the Crusades which were mostly (but not all) directed towards recapturing Jerusalem. For some 200 years Western Europe embarked on a series of Papal-directed, bloody attempts to dominate the Near East; wresting it away from growing Moorish and Muslim control. The Crusades have become shrouded in a child-like nineteenth century romantic sentimentality. In fact they were driven by Papal bribery and blackmail, by Princes' greed for land and heavenly forgiveness at a monumental cost to lives and national wealth. They were characterised by political and military incompetence and, in general, humiliating failure. In the end Saladin invited Christianity to look elsewhere for land glory and wealth. It has been said that: *"There was so much courage and so little honour, so much devotion and so little understanding. High ideals were besmirched by cruelty and greed, enterprise and endurance by a blind and narrow self righteousness...". (History of the Crusades, Sir Stephan Rinciman).* George W Bush could not have known what he was proposing when he advanced a 'Crusade' in response to 9/11; (or could he?).

A few Crusades were also directed against Christian 'variants', notably in northern Europe. The Cathar Heresy fell into this camp and was a rebellion against the excesses and corruption of the Roman Catholic Church. It could only be met by a full bodied and (typically) very bloody Papal-directed crusade. So that's what the Pope did.

We are talking about the spread of the heresy in the 12/13th Century, particularly in what we would now call south-west France, but also northern Italy. Pope Innocent 3rd called on the King of France to take action. An agreement in the City of Albi established the Albigensian Crusade under the leadership of Simon de Monfort. The 'Oc' area SW of France was not under direct control from Paris and indeed saw itself as an independent 'Occitan'. Simon de Montford's force was essentially made up of French noblemen who saw the opportunity both to consolidate the authority of the French King and, perhaps more important, to extend their own personal land holdings. (As well as getting a few important heavenly credit points).

A massive army marched on Oc in 1213. They must have expected a rapid victory but none was achieved and fighting went on across the region until 1229 when Oc at last became established as a part of the Kingdom of France (Treaty of Paris).

The sheer scale of the military action demonstrates that the heresy did not just lie with a few inconvenient 'nutters' but encompassed the whole of society, from top to bottom. The campaign had been desperately ruthless, perhaps the most famous atrocity occurring in the city of Beziers. There 20,000 citizens were slaughtered on the instruction of the Bishop Commander. When the troops asked how they should differentiate the dissidents from the honest Catholics, they were famously instructed to kill everyone since ''the Lord will know his own''. I understand that Cathar followers were instructed to wear a yellow cross on their clothing in case the Lord was uncertain about 'his own'. (An interesting precedent of ethnic branding) Even after 1229 the heresy had still not been wiped out and the infamous Inquisition was born to search out every last threat to the Roman Church. The mountain-top citadel of Montsegur survived until 1243 when the final remaining 200 surrendered and were burnt to death on a massive pyre.

The area remained one of independent and liberal thinking and in the 16th Century it became a centre for Huguenot and Calvinism.

What's this got to do with the cruising yachtsman? Well apart from knowing a little about the area you are going through, the history certainly had an impact on the villages and towns. Old villages and churches were often located defensively on small hilltops. Sometimes those inconvenient but defensive positions have been abandoned over the centuries but the remains can still be seen. The local churches themselves were often built like small castles with little, high windows. They were used as defendable places of refuge against casual roving bands of armed men.

There is even a possible architectural spin-off into the construction of great churches. This is the only area of Europe where I have seen a number of huge gothic ecclesiastical project started but unfinished. A vast and hugely ambitious local church got only as far as the choir before being abandoned. The cathedral in Narbonne had a very similar experience when normally one expects the great establishment of the RC Church to find the means somehow to complete an important building project, even without the support of the local Consuls. In Toulouse the cathedral, St Etienne, is a fascinating melting pot of architectural styles over the centuries. The C13th rebuild of the earlier Romanesque was 75% complete so it has a grand and very usable nave although the gothic west end was never built. The Romanesque nave, which is off-set and at an angle to the new, was never demolished and remains as an odd 'extension' to the later gothic nave.

For long periods the regional economy was on a roller coaster through civic unrest and the fall of Narbonne as a trading/coastal wealth generator when its access to the sea became totally silted; and through the Black Death (1348-50ish)which decimated the population. These curiously incomplete building ambitions of a number of bishops seem unique and seem to speak of regional poverty but also the political marginalisation of the region: perhaps punished by Rome for failing to control the Cathar heresy?

Chapter 10

But back to the Canals

Lets talk a bit more about the 'caneaux des deux Mers' themselves. Typically the canals are double lined with mature trees which provide shelter from the sun and stabilise the embankments with their matted roots. The much photographed image of the Midi is of a curving watery avenue of 200-year-old plane trees. But there are places where Scots Pines dominate. Others where a mixed deciduous woodland including oak, chestnut and beech crowd the canal banks. Or sometimes a lone walnut tree. The Canal du Midi generally follows the contours as it climbs higher, i.e. it bridges many a crossing stream. Long views of vine-striped hillside lead to the Black Mountains to the south and the distant Pyrenees rising blue in the far distance. Here the major wild life are the feral hire power cruisers-of-minimal-control but generally good humour. They exist in much greater numbers on the Southern Canals than the Central Canals. Their skippers appear to have only brief introduction to power boat control and are exempt from CEVNI Certification which governed us. Wilful bad manners occurred occasionally but mostly we shared the waters with mutual goodwill.

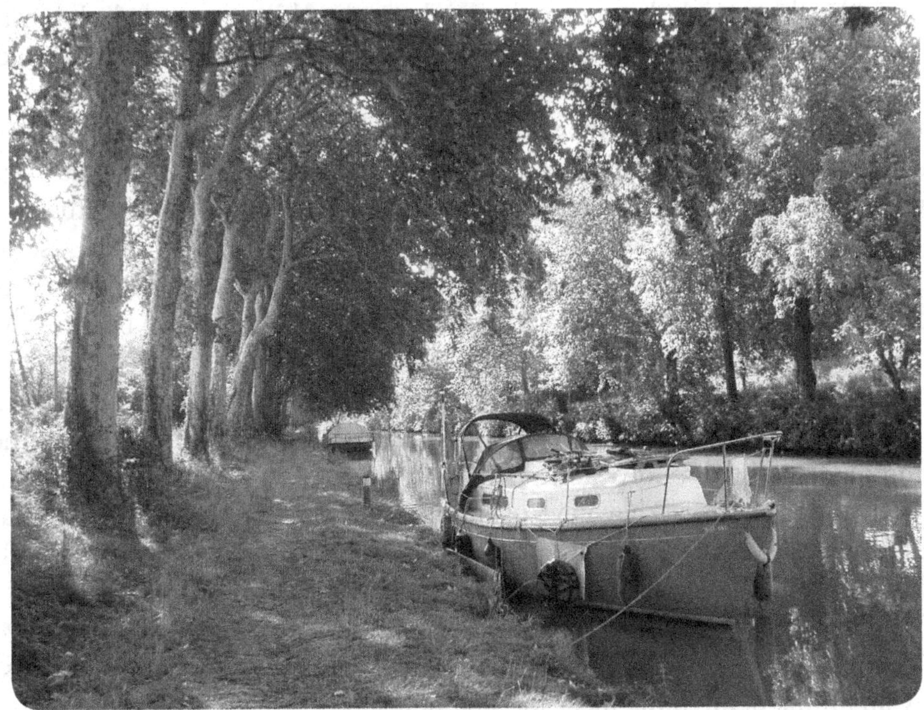

Canal du Midi

"But", people ask "how do you spend your evenings? I mean, what on earth do you say to each other?" Not quite sure how to answer that one. We took along a great deal of music, initially on disc for the boat's music centre which has repeaters in the cockpit. The cockpit speakers can be switched to the VHF Radio so we can follow any incoming VHF messages from there. But (used with consideration) can also give us leisure-time music. Later in the trip an ipod tended to replace the discs. We also took films to be run through the laptop. You might think that this would tend to replace the TV hours at home. In fact we very rarely watched films. The long, balmy French evenings invited you into the cockpit with book and music; not ensconced below with a film. And, of course, there was often company and the business of the day past and the day to come to be chewed over and analysed. Ever bored, frustrated, ill or cross? Well, no; not really. I suppose we must have been sometime, but not noticeably or memorably. There was just too much to see and do and plan for. If you ran out of all those options, there was (as a friend once said to us) always something to mend.

With our slow westward progress the Mediterranean climate gradually becomes more Atlantic as Languedoc gave way to the more gently rolling landscape of the Garonne. Instead of crossing contours, we now ran beside the River Garonne as the canal and the land gently falls to the sea. Hire cruisers become less numerous. As the miles and the summer rolled by, vine gave way to soft fruits of apricots, peach, plum and cherry alongside fields of ripening sweet corn. Sunflower fields changed from blinding yellow to an autumnal and pre-harvest brown. Soft fruits gave way to later season apples and pears. On the long hot days the cicadas played their endless tune. At times the nights were too hot to stay below and I would sleep in the cockpit. If you were lucky there might be an evening nightingale while coypu and glow worms accompany our westward wanderings as the *Yellow Brick Road* took us where it would.

From Carcassonne we moved on to the very attractive little town of Bram and then to the historic Castelnaudry, the true home (they claim, correctly I am sure) of the Great Cassoulet. It was a memorable stop amongst many pleasant interludes. The small town is situated on a hill overlooking the canal which circles its foot. At this point a large basin (or small reservoir) was created as both a water supply for the canal and as a barge/freight assembly point. Now it appears simply as a watery and tree-lined setting for the town and a leisure boat resting spot.

For us this was a short stay interlude; for some live-aboards it was a more-or-less permanent mooring. We made friends with livaboards (and retired) Barbara and Mike on their steel barge 'Lemmin' Times' from Lowestoft. With their ready wit and warm hospitality they entertained us in equal measure. They gave us much useful canal information and a number of glasses of red wine. Their life seemed to be pleasantly spent within a few dozen kilometres of Castelnaudry. In fact Jacky's comment was:

"This looks a pretty nice place. An interesting town, usable shops, local restaurants, people to chat to. Can't think of anything nicer for a bit of a stay."
And stay we did for several days.

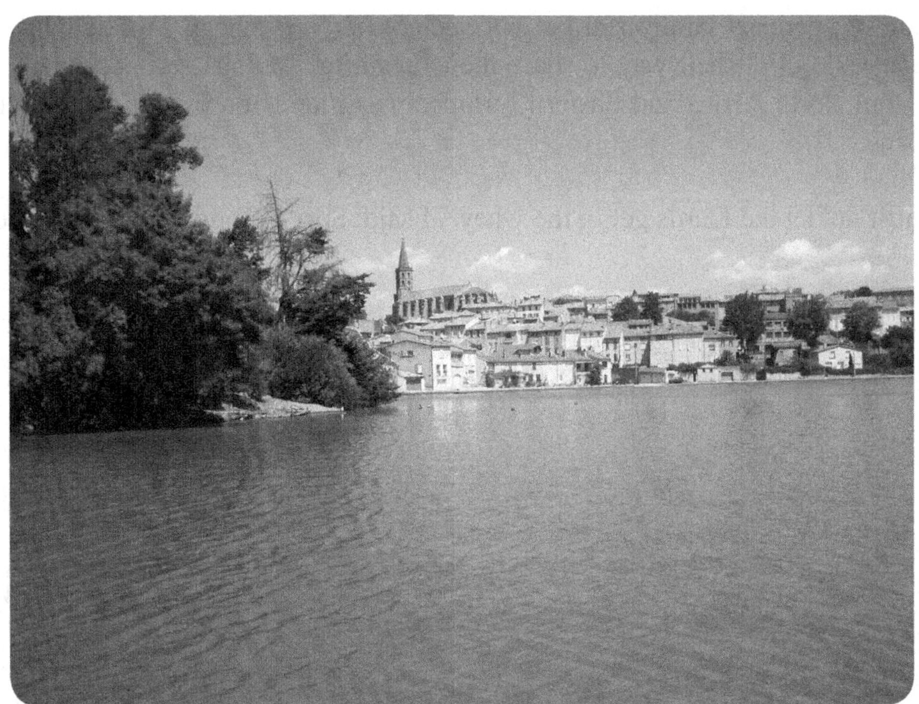

The basin at Castelnaudry

So people come in all shapes and sizes. We invited on board a passing 52-year-old, be-whiskered, cycling German yachtsman to have a glass and entertain. He did, at length covering the history of Europe over the last 100 years and the respective Anglo-German roles played. Drama dominated his life as he came right up-to-date by informing us that his partner of 31 years was to leave him for ever the very next day. We were quite uncertain as to how much this mattered, but he himself had to stay in Castelnaudry. He was to be the witness at the marriage of the Spanish hobo-who-lived-in-the-bushes (and in plastic bags) just close to our mooring. The lucky lady was to be an elderly Italian resident of a local old folks' home. The Hobo claimed to have an extensive Spanish spread but she said that she knew it wasn't true. We left the next day for Toulouse and never found out if the partner did leave or the marriage was consummated. Or where. Somehow its better that way.

Toulouse was, of course, one of the major cities of our travels. It is the fourth largest city in France at a population of 1.1.m people. It is the centre of French space industry and houses the Head Quarters of Airbus. It is a regional capital and has a long history. As seems typically French, the extensive, historic core has been well preserved and enriched with fine buildings, including the already-mentioned magnificent Romanesque St Sernin and the Cathedral St Etienne.

It also has a half-decent marina as the Canal goes through its centre. Clive and Rose, living on the small Dutch Barge in Toulouse, gave us an over-wintering option that they were releasing in Moissac while they changed plans and went the other way to the Danube. As we wandered the historic central streets looking for that absolutely 'right' restaurant (not too expensive;

not too touristy; perhaps family run but not *necessarily* very cheap…) a delightful French couple went well out of their way to share their favourite. Toulouse is a cosmopolitan city. All races from North Africa and Eastern Europe appear here and this must have an impact on the cuisine.

"But we must not let the Kurds get in the whey", I said. Sorry. Good place, Toulouse.

Chapter 11

Lateral to Biscay

From Toulouse we entered the Canal Lateral de la Garonne; the replacement for the partially navigable River Garonne. The Canal du Midi is a canal whose purpose is to climb over the headwater that looks to the Mediterranean into the headwater that looks to the Atlantic. The job of the Canal Lateral is to run with the River Garonne down to the coast. The Midi runs with and climbs the contours and therefore has many bridges and small viaducts of watercourses that cross its path. The Lateral runs across the contours falling generally with the valley of the Garonne. It doesn't sound very different, but the character of the 'Caneaux des deux Mers' does change as we found ourselves gently falling to the Atlantic and Biscay coastline. We were now to enjoy the attractive settlements of Montech, Castlesarrasin and (the best) Moissac.

Moissac is a small town on the banks of the canal. The 'nautical halt' is treed and grassy with clean and well managed support services. There is room to over-winter and the Harbour Master would have found space for us. The very nearby little town centre and market was all you could want from a southern French country town.

"Hey! We could happily stay here for a while. It's got everything." I agreed with her.

Now we always visited the local church and the bar, (thirst after righteousness) in that order; so please forgive me for a few words about churches and things since the churches and cathedrals are the record in stone of the communities. But they are different in SW France to the UK. You think you know what you are looking at until you realise that it all has to be modified by the obvious adjacent influence of Italy and the not-so-obvious influence of Moorish Spain. In the UK (as you know) we call the early, rounded arch on massive rubble-filled stone columns 'Norman' simply because in 1066 the Normans brought with them the building technology. The French learnt it from the structural evidence of the plentiful Roman remains; think notably of the three level, multi-arched aqueduct, Pont du Gard near Nimes. In France therefore it is called 'Romanesque' and it dates a building to the C11-12th.

In Moissac, however, we find a church described as pre-Romanesque but with small round headed arches and a distinctly un-Roman/Gothic modelling of the porch way. In Britain, 'pre-Norman' would be 'Saxon' when the rounded arch had yet to be understood. Technically, therefore, this is far in advance of the English Saxon construction. In Moissac the technical influence came from further south. The Iberian Peninsular was, of course, under Moorish control from the 8th to (finally) the 15th Centuries when the Christian forces eventually drove them from southern Spain. ('The Moors' last sigh?'). Their control at one stage even went as far north as Narbonne, Beziers and Bordeaux. In fact the Moorish advance into central France was only stopped in battle at Tours, after which they retired to consolidate their hold over the Iberian peninsular. The wonderful architectural (as well as scientific) heritage in Spain can still be enjoyed in places like Cordoba, Toledo, Segovia and Granada and it would be surprising if that influence had not spread into the Occatin. In Moissac we seemed to find an early Moorish influence both over the advanced building technology and in the decorative details, notably in the west end doorway. Perhaps this is also some reflection of the independent tradition of this (larger) Languedoc area.

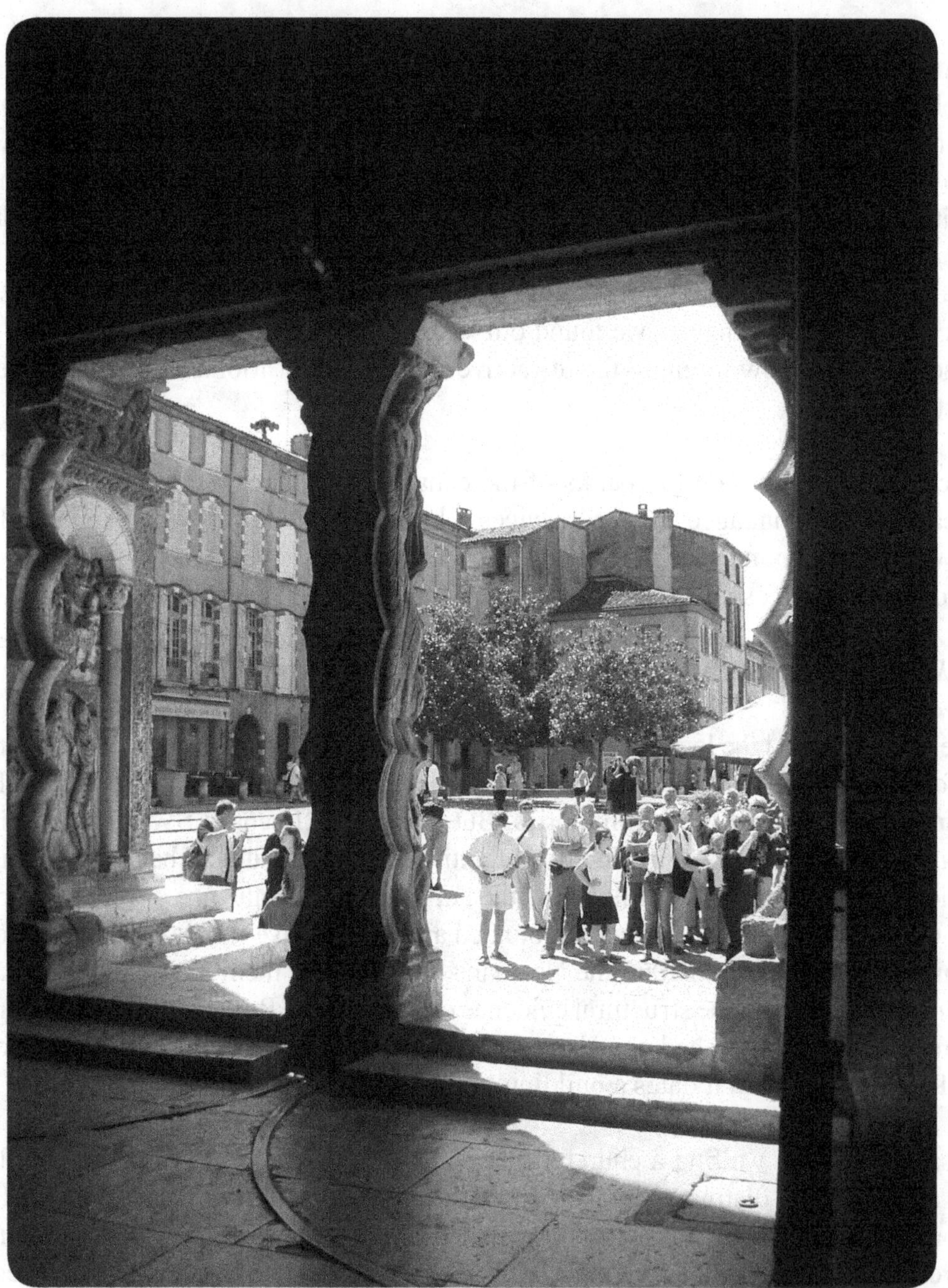

The church in Moissac

The parish church in Moissac was also distinguished by its beautiful gothic cloisters graced by elegant columns with sensitively decorated capitols. After having enjoyed this medieval church, you may then eat at l'Auberge du Cloister in the elegant town square. The cloisters reminded me of our visit to the Cloisters Museum in New York a few years ago. The story is that during the First World War some American service men with a wider cultural interest than the next battalion advance, noticed scattered medieval remains across some French fields. They returned after the war and researched the masonry bits-and-bobs. In short they identified crumbling remains of an abandoned medieval church and cloisters scattered across farmland and, no doubt, incorporated into the structure of field walls and barns. This led to a wider search of France's crumbling history, a selective purchase of the finds and a heavy export to the USA. Judicial reconstruction created a setting of several interlinked ecclesiastical courtyards and the display of related medieval memorabilia.

The whole ethics of the enterprise might be debated although there is precedence on the grounds of preserving that which is not being preserved. If you are in New York the museum is well worth a visit. If you are in Moissac go and see an original in place. In both you will see intricately carved stone capitals in both their finished state but also partially carved and unfinished. The interest to me of the latter was to see how craftsmen drilled many a hole into the stone to weaken the bits that needed cutting away and their technique is well displayed where the work is unfinished.

* * *

From Moissac we continued to Buzet and the junction with the Canal Baise. This waterway was a bit shallow for *Wise One* so it was time to get the folding cycles out and explore the Baise on wheels. The Baise had a very usable canal path and our folding bikes came into their own. Either side the banks rose high and wooded, the canal a silent black ribbon curving round the contour. We cycled for some distance just enjoying this small side arm of the main canal.

Our next stop on the Midi was at the little town of Meilham-sur-Gironne. It is set on a high bluff from which we enjoyed the long and distant views of the river as it curled around many a shallow patch or little island that seemed to be floating in mid-stream. River banks and islands were overgrown with a tangle of beech, oak and chestnut. As Paul Robson says. "only God can make a tree" Far in the distance a couple of anglers waded in shallows.

Notices around the town made it clear that a village feast was to be held on the big, tree-shaded square that very evening; all welcome. In due course it slowly assembled. Trestle tables come out. Open sided vans took up position to serve all manner of goodies for hungry (and thirsty) villagers, and we were adopted by a trestle table full of hospitable locals. Clearly Munchkins at feast. A good evening was had by all and we eventually staggered down the steep path to the canal bank and our own village home.

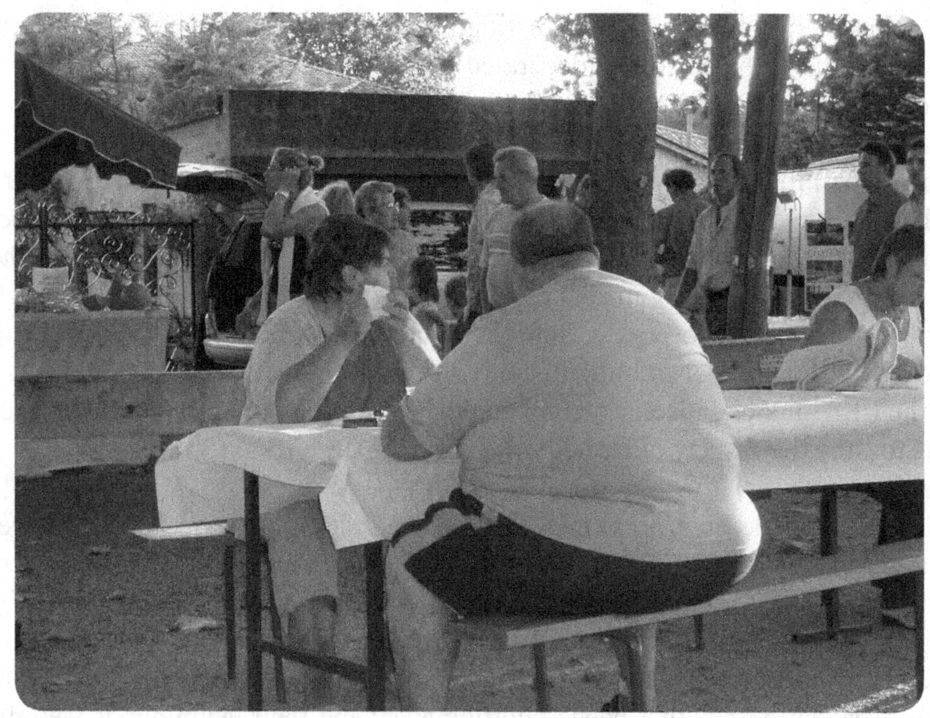

Munchkins at feast

We stopped briefly at Agen, an attractive old city which equally deserved more of our time. We did note the forthcoming Pruneau Fest-Noz and were introduced to a new and delicate prune experience. Although the butt of jokes in Britain, here in SW France prunes are a toothsome delicacy. We bought a selection to put on the cabin table and be eaten like sweets.

We were now close to the end of our canal journey. Castets-en-Dorth is a small town at the point where the final canal lock drops you, tired and tested, into the fully navigable but very tidal River Garonne. The contrast to our two years in the sheltered canals and rivers was quite scary as we were swept at great speed down the 67 km to Bordeaux. Once again we really missed our sail-rig, feeling that another source of power would have given us a bit more control.

Just upstream of Bordeaux lies the small marina at Begles, scoured through by the roaring spring tides (''double your mooring lines, guys''). There is another yacht 'halte' downstream of the City centre and within a locked basin. We elected to stop at Begles – for one thing had we gone past Begles we would not have been able to get back, at any rate not on that tide. So Begles served us well enough but could not be described as a comfortable stop. At night we could hear the roaring of the flood tide through the marina making Jacky question my mooring techniques. My concern was for baulks of timber being carried down stream and dragged through the moorings. We survived. The next day we took a bus and tram connection to the centre of Bordeaux.

Bordeaux is, of course, a serious city of some 805,000 population. It has a huge and proud history and particularly grew during the 18th and 19th Centuries. Its architecture reflects the depth of its cultural and educational foundations. This is the centre of a great wine growing region and tasting the product must be obligatory. Interesting to note that the city was plundered by those Moors from the south in 732 and emphasises again the impact of the Iberian Moors on southern Europe.

Interesting also to note that Bordeaux did not become an established part of France until 1653. It took France a long while to define its southern borders and for several centuries Paris eyed its south-west frontiers as a sort of no-mans land over which it certainly had ambitions. As part of the process of subjugation some seven hundred small towns were built between 1222 and 1372; known as Bastides, most were fortified on construction or at a later date. Special trading and tax arrangements were made for these towns both to attract citizens and loyalty to the French crown. Many survive with their medieval core and walls substantially intact and are now an attractive record of this medieval French period. At that time the same Simon de Montford used the same 'colonising' technique for just the same reasons in the English borderlands with north Wales

* * *

Now we are well into our second summer (2006) in France, we must talk about FOOD ! This important subject has come up several times; but let's see if we can pull together one or two thoughts.

Our travelling has given us both a discipline as well as a freedom. In the BF period (i.e. Before Freezer) we had a problem of keeping things cool, even with a picnic 'cool' box. PF (Post Freezer) we ran the cool box in tandem with the freezer. The latter could store frozen food (of course) but also provide a supply of solid water bottles and freezer plates for the cool box in which we kept fresh food. Rosè or white wine were decanted from three litre boxes into 25cc bottles and placed into the freezer to be drunk or transferred to the cool box before solid. (A certain amount of management skills needed here).

The French miracle of the boulangerie was hunted daily on foot or cycle to supply the inevitable pain-au-chocolat, croissant and baguettes of many types. (Not to mention tarte au pomme, tarte tatin etc). Baguettes must, as we all know, be eaten within the day if not the hour. And then thrown away (what an inspiration of marketing). What can be better 'on the hoof' than fresh baguette, rillettes, local cheese, red wine and spicy local olives? But all this is just the human rights of anyone anywhere in France.

What impressed us as travellers was the extent that food could be regional and seasonal. This was particularly noticeable as we moved from Port Camargue on the Med up to a modest 190 m. altitude and down to the Biscay coast; and moved at the same time from May to mid-September. The landscape changed from the Etangs and salt marshes (Marais) up to the lower Pyrenees and foothills of the Black Mountains down the lush Garonne valley to Bordeaux and the Atlantic seaboard. In July and August we were eating cassoulet in Carcassonne and

Castelenaudry and duck in the Perigord. Some things we avoided. Andouilles are chittereling sausages and were not our favourite.

In September we spoilt ourselves with fresh and ripening melons, pears, small strawberries, peaches and grapes. In Marmand there were big, fat tomatoes and in Agen there were prunes fit for a 'Fest-Noz' with music and dancing. (And there was one of those too). In Bordeaux there were local wines aplenty for us to wash down Bordeaux specialities; including the tasty little canneles cakes.

Closing the coast brought the fresh seafood back into play. Of course it all travels and moules might be ordered and served anywhere. Just north of the Canal de Bourgogne summit tunnel we attended a village Auberge moules 'fest'. The whole village was there and it was a major event. But that was the point, it was not routine. Hey! We are not experts but down on the Biscay we became aware of the differing sizes of (it seemed to us) southern moules and Normandy moules. Some might say the smaller ones are sweeter but the bigger ones are meatier; take your choice! The smaller ones are at greater risk from over-cooking and we have been known to send back a plate of wizened moules that were 'end of the batch' and not cooked just for us.

Fresh fish straight off the boat can only be the privilege of coast dwellers. Spider crab, chucked away in Britain, can be much appreciated in France and make for a whole evening in the cockpit cracking and delving. There clearly is a reason why they don't appear in restaurants. A little further north we encountered superb oysters in St Denis (Ile d'Oloron) and generally crustaceans improved as we went north. Although any coastal town will produce an 'assiette de mer', the 'fruits de mer' seem better in cooler waters. As we closed Brittany, Breton specials became evident such as Breton Far (made with prunes), Kouign Amamm, salted butter and globe artichokes.

Assiette de Mer plus Alex

So what can you do with two gas rings and a small oven? Well, a favourite on board is the 'pot de feu'; a sort of mixed meat, sausage, beans, veg, stew cooked slowly and eaten with chunks of fresh bread over several days. Humm!

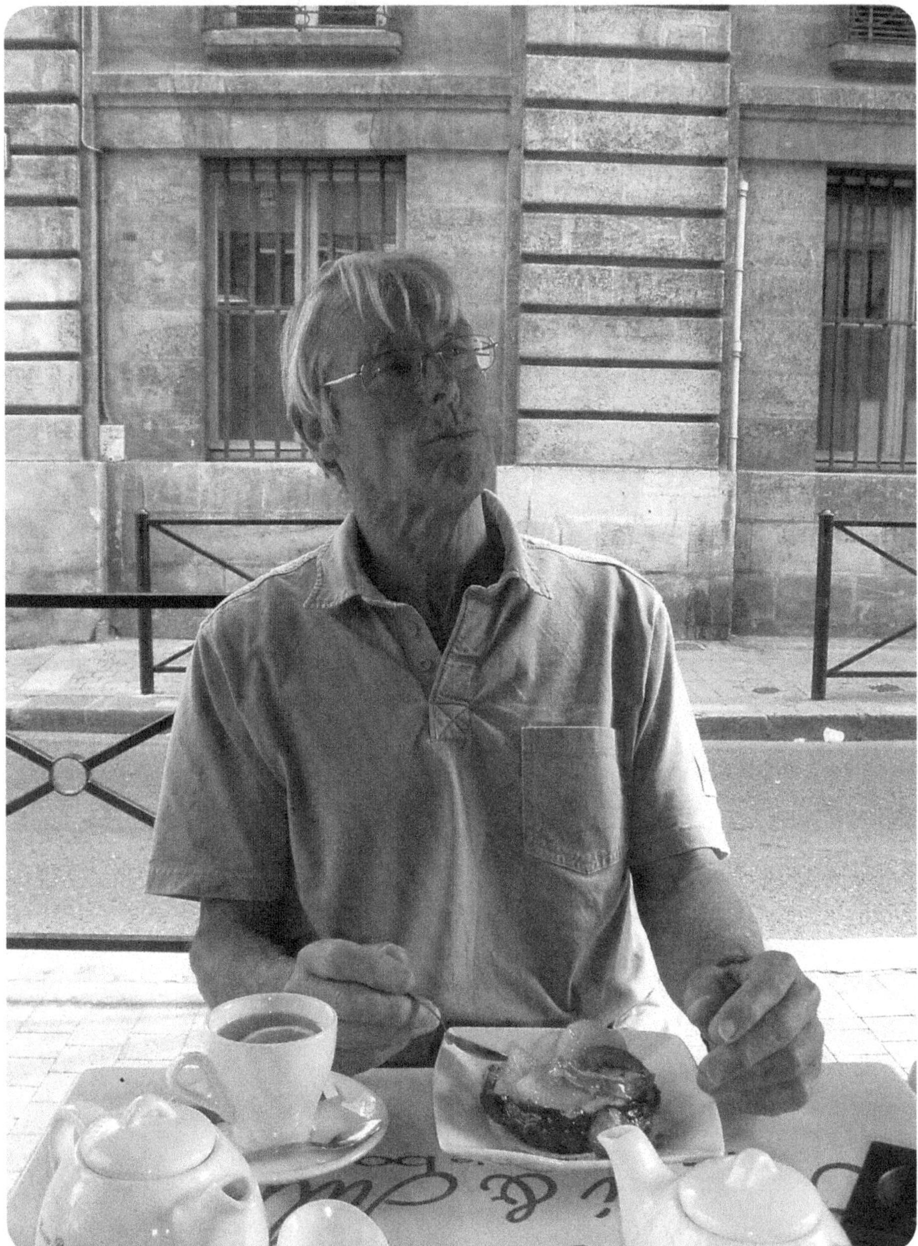

A pastrie of delight plus Don.

Wines are another subject. We bought what was available but usually tried to go regional if not local. We fell in with a number of favourites notably Bourgogne Alligote and Madiram. Curiously we drank far more cool rosé in the cockpit lunch times and evenings than we ever would at home. In the UK rosé is for wimps who can't make up their minds. In France a good, cool rosé is refreshing and light on the head with sufficient flavour to keep the buds alive.

Chapter 12

Exposed on the Estuary and the 'Yellow Brick Road' gets rocky

From Bordeaux the Garonne was joined by the Dordogne. We had left the inland waterway system to carry the ebb tide down the widening Gironde Estuary. The settled weather (of which I have said very little) broke, it rained and blew and visibility closed in. Navigation was not difficult but it was quite important to identify the right channel as small tree-clad islands appeared.

One fascinating feature of these tidal waters was the frequent appearance of small wooden structures on the bank. Typically, tall posts had been driven into the ground at around bottom of the tide level supporting a wooden shelter accessed by a wooden bridge to the bank. The purpose was given away by the long bendy masts sticking out over the water and supporting large horizontal nets. These were dropped into the water by a simple system of pulleys so that the net lay on the estuary bed. On lifting the net anything above it was secured and was that night's dinner. These fishing huts can be hired for a day and you can hope to catch carrelet (plaice), anguille (eel) and bichet (prawn).

The estuary was quite choppy and our progress with the tide very fast. You will recall that *Wise One* is a yacht with no mast and just its auxiliary engine; in the circumstances we felt quite vulnerable! Fortunately we did not experience the 'Mascaret Wave', a two metre high tidal bore that is said to sweeps the estuary at 20 mph at high water in August and September.

* * *

I guess that centuries of seafarers have felt the same about these waters. Certainly in WW2 twelve British Commandos must have entered the Gironde from the sea with some trepidation. The 'Cockleshell Heroes' was the name given to the twelve British Marine Commandos, crew of the six canoes which raided Bordeaux Harbour in 1942. At the time, Bordeaux was an important base for the supply of German forces in SW France. It was also a German submarine base with direct access to the Atlantic. German surface ships accessing Bordeaux from the Channel could be attacked; but ships supplying Bordeaux from the South were more difficult to reach. The harbour could be bombed but only with serious risk to the civilian population and with inevitable loss to the RAF of aircraft and men. This project was called Operation Frankton and the objective was to sink ships and damage Bordeaux Harbour.

The commandos had special training but they were only told their target when they were on the RN submarine Tuna to be dropped off at the mouth of the Gironde Estuary. The plan was to paddle the five miles to the estuary entrance; then seventy miles to Bordeaux; lay limpet mines on shipping and escape via neutral Spain. One canoe was damaged as it was being launched from Tuna and those two marines remained on board. A second canoe (Conger) was swamped in heavy seas at the entrance to the Gironde. The two crew were towed closer to the shore to enable them to swim but sadly they did not make it. Canoes Coalfish and Cuttlefish were caught by the Germans who shot the commandos. The Germans were now thoroughly alert and increased their patrols.

The operation leader, Major 'Blondie' Hasler in Catfish, with crew member Marine Bill Sparks continued with Marine William Mills and Corporal Albert Laver in Crayfish. They travelled by night and hid by day until they reached Bordeaux. They were spotted by a sentry at the harbour entrance but, perhaps thinking they were just drift-wood, the alarm was not raised. Limpet mines were placed and delayed action fuses gave them eight minutes to get clear. One ship was sunk and four were damaged. The harbour itself was severely damaged and its use disrupted for months.

The Marines escaped on the tide to link up with the French Resistance in Ruffec from where they moved 125 km northwards. Laver and Mills were caught and shot; Sparks and Halser reached Spain, Gibraltar and, eventually, England. At home their deaths had already been assumed and they were at first treated with some suspicion. In due course, however, their exploits were celebrated in film ('Cockleshell Heroes') and 'Blondie' Hasler went on to become in peacetime a very well known pioneering small boat yachtsman.

* * *

So the Gironde is full of memories and serious ghosts of the past; recent and ancient. Our next destination was the attractive small town of Pauillac (set in rich and famous vineyards) lying on the south bank some 45 km from Bordeaux. The old fishing harbour, now entirely occupied by a well managed marina, projects into the estuarine waters with high masonry walls to give great shelter. To make the entry on the ebb you approach along the low water shore line up stream (keeping an eye on your 'echo'!) and slide into an up-stream gap in the harbour wall. Had we allowed ourselves to lie somewhat off the shore before cutting in, we would probably have been swept past the entry and would have had a fight to return against the ebb. The entry cannot really be mistaken; it is marked by a giant 8 m high simulated wine bottle with 'Pauillac' inscribed.

We enjoyed the small town. There were posters displayed for their local annual marathon which appeared to be run around a number of the local and very distinguished vineyards. There did seem an opportunity here for some rather inebriated athletes so how this was supposed to work we were not certain. Had we stayed longer I am sure we would have done more research. Eating was, as is often the case, an exploration of local delicacies, notably estuary-caught carrelet and anguille.

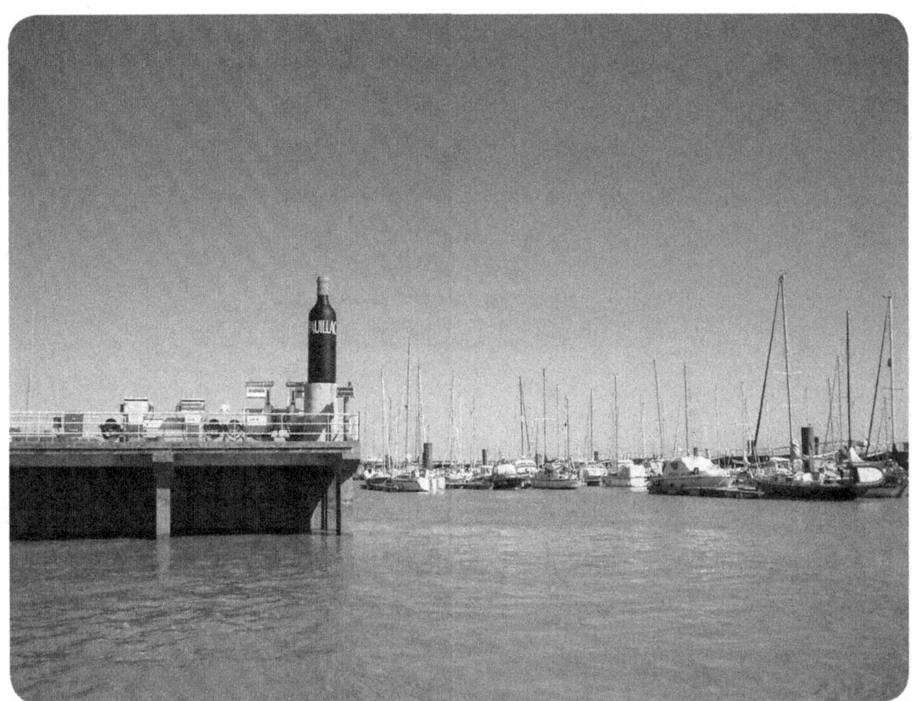

Pauillac

Autumn was now setting in and Pauillac was one of the places we had considered for a winter stop-over. Unfortunately they have no local yacht support for wintering purposes, no resident mechanical services or chandlery (that I could see); no quayside lifting available (although no doubt all these things can arrive by road). So wintering would need to be at our next (and last) choice; on to Port Royan. We left, of course, on the ebb which swept us quickly seawards. Port Royan is on the north bank and so we worked our way across the current to ensure we were well placed to enter the port. Here the estuary at places is 11km wide and dominated by shallows, small islands and swirling currents.

Heavy ocean-going vessels were encountered; including those delivering airframe parts to the Airbus quayside terminal just west of Pauillac. The waters at Royan are officially categorised as 'sea', continue beyond Royan and you are into the open Biscay so Royan was very important to us. Entering Port Royan was a very auspicious moment. After two summers of travel our whole summers will now change radically. Some 2400 km of canal and river were behind us along with 408 locks. Our days as a motor boat were over and *Wise One* will be reinvented as a yacht. Sad? No, not at all; more excited by the next and coastal phase of our adventure.

That night we were lulled to sleep by the sighing of the restless sea on the rocks.

Royan is a town largely flattened by the British in 1944/5. (The Germans didn't seem to flatten much. They didn't need to). The modern marina gives comprehensive security to yachts passing through or over-wintering. A separate port basin holds the major fishing fleet which fishes widely into the Biscay and beyond. The (post war) waterfront has a wide range of seafood restaurants and the market is second to none.

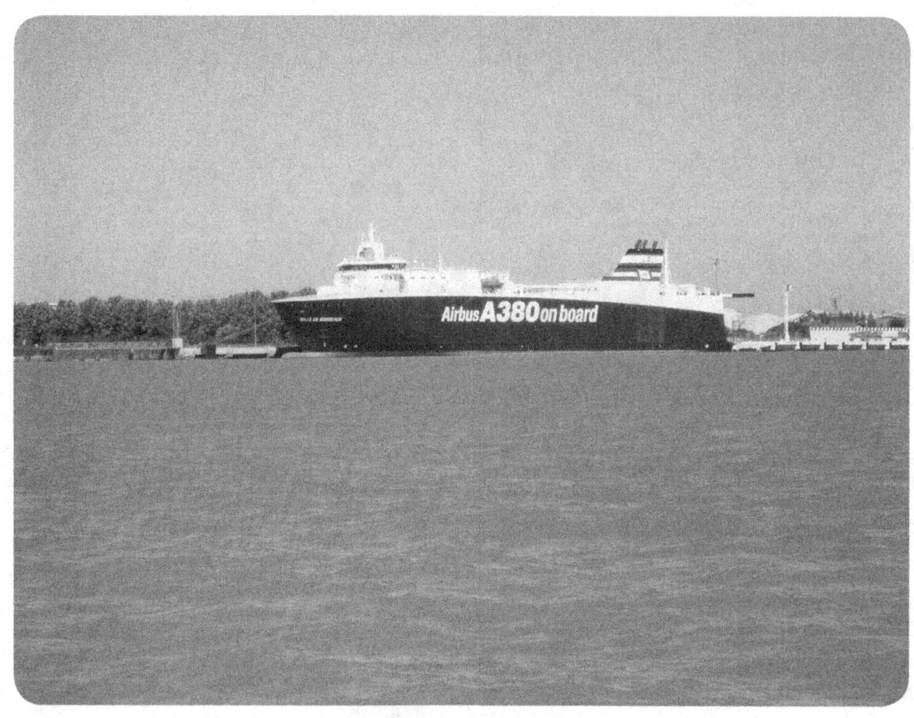

A380 on board

* * *

The new cathedral deserves a visit. It dates from the 1970's and is a worthy and sculptural concept in in-situ concrete and glass. The space, forms and modelling of light through stained glass are well worth a visit. Sadly the quality of the concrete is a disaster. Poor detailing and construction means that thousands of rusting steel bars are blowing off the surface of the concrete, inside and out. This is generating a daunting and now ongoing renovation problem.

The marina has an adjacent beach and we swam with pleasure in the (just about acceptable) waters of the Atlantic. The beach was popular and it was there we saw the slim, blond haired girl with very long brown legs, bare feet and a distinctive red dress. As she strode the beach she called above the sound of surf and sea bird: "Beignet; ChouChou; Glaces". I had to try a beignet.

The month was again September and with it, I found to my surprise, comes a wedding anniversary. It seems it comes every year. Jacky reminded me that last year we dined royally on freshly caught mackerel donated by French pontoon neighbours which were really very nice. Apparently something more was expected this year for our 41st.

Of course Jacky had already some thoughts.
"I've got an idea for something a little different" she said. Very cautiously:
"Tell me". (I'm always up for something new. Naturally).
"There's a Novatel nearby which advertises weekend deals".

"Sounds good". Relieved, shouldn't be too damaging.
"No, hang on. There's more to it".
"Go on". Suspiciously.
"The weekend package comes with thelasotherapy ."
"What on earth is that ?".
"Not quite sure but it involves water based 'good-for-you' activity sometimes with rubber sheeting, water movement and dolphin music. And you feel great afterwards".
"OK let's give it a whirl".

So we did and the ambience was fine and the food OK and the wine quaffable. The water massage, dolphin music, seaweed overcoats and optional mud came with much hands-on therapy – not something I'm normally into with strangers but well hey! this was anniversary time!. I wasn't quite prepared for the tiled cubicle with a drain in the middle, which reminded me of a heavy interrogation room where the off-spill from questioning can be discretely hosed away. Alone with just my Speedos (or, as Jacky calls them, my budgies smugglers) I faced a fierce woman with a fireman's a hose like the ones used for throwing French rioting students over the barricades. If nudity does not exist immediately, it soon does after a bit of selective power hosing. Afterwards it just might also involve large, soft, warm white towels, a good evening meal and *a night in a large, comfortable double bed....*
"Are you sure", Jacky said "about continuing with this round France thing in an old plastic boat that's a bit like living in a rather small bathroom ?" I thought that was rather unfair. But she could also have been referring to our sleeping quarters which take up a triangular fore cabin in which two pairs of feet compete for resting space at the sharp end and going to the loo requires a headspring over the pillow end to get out.
"I don't know why you are raising this matter now" I said.

The marina pontoons were still mostly French with the Red Ensign only occasionally seen. That was to change as we progressed around the coast but at present we enjoyed the short holiday friendships with our local neighbours. There was Jean Pascal, Michelle and Marie-Francoise, the French live-aboards, who end-of-season fare-welled us with a freshly caught 'Thon' and helped us clear our stock of red.

So there we were in Royan. We have got here at a steady four knots, which is very pre-industrial, leisurely and self-indulgent. Who on earth can have the time for this? Haven't we got anything more important to do ? Pretty good point really. We haven't seen India or China yet but not, I think, at four knots.

The mast will now be transported from Port Camargue and the boat re-rigged. The elderly and dysfunctional Autohelm 4000 will be replaced with an amazingly smart new model (that's how we will all go). A Clipper NavTex 'Weatherman' will be installed and other matters carried out involving paint, varnish and money.

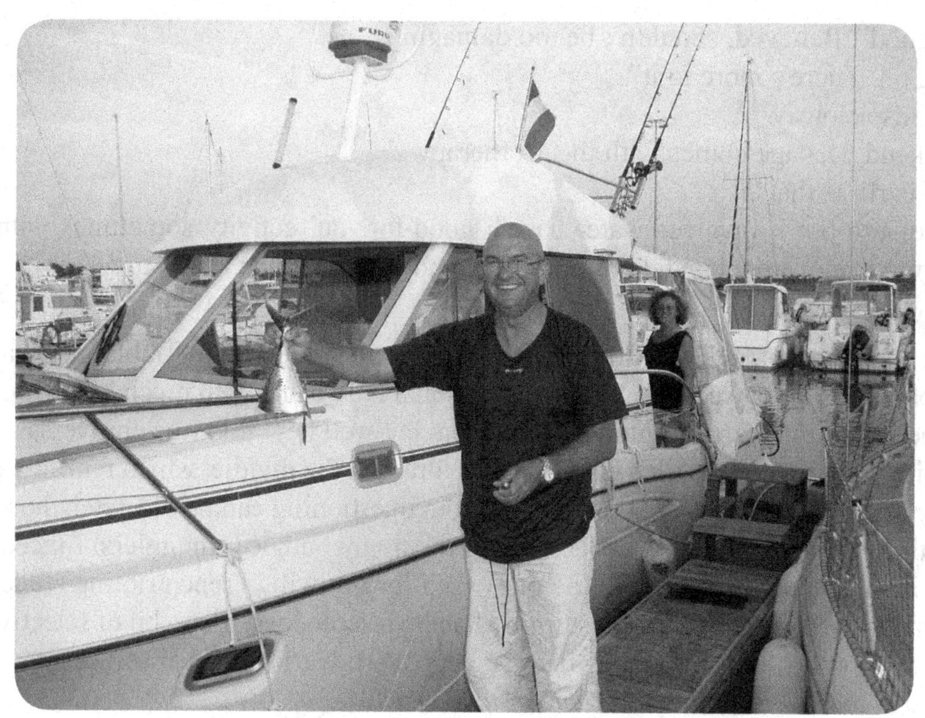

Just a Thon at Sunset (in Royan)

Next
And so we came to the end of the summer 2006. We've talked just a little about food but perhaps we should leave that to the expertise of Rick. Did we mention ripe figs, succulent prunes with goat's cheese ? 'Ile Flotant' or eel pie ?; or of John and Jan and the story of the frog with a straw up its bum, (all was revealed years later at the London Boat Show); or the crowd from Dundee or why all French mechanics are called Didier? I could, though, for a pint. Or perhaps you could go yourselves and see. In May '07 we will take off for La Rochelle and, I imagine, beyond. Who knows ?

In the meantime, a glass of your rosé please, my good man.

Readers' Notes

Part 3
Summer 2007. Gironde to Vilaine

In which we soak up La Rochelle, eat blue in Rochfort, shake hands with Wizard Vauban and rest in La Roche Bernard.

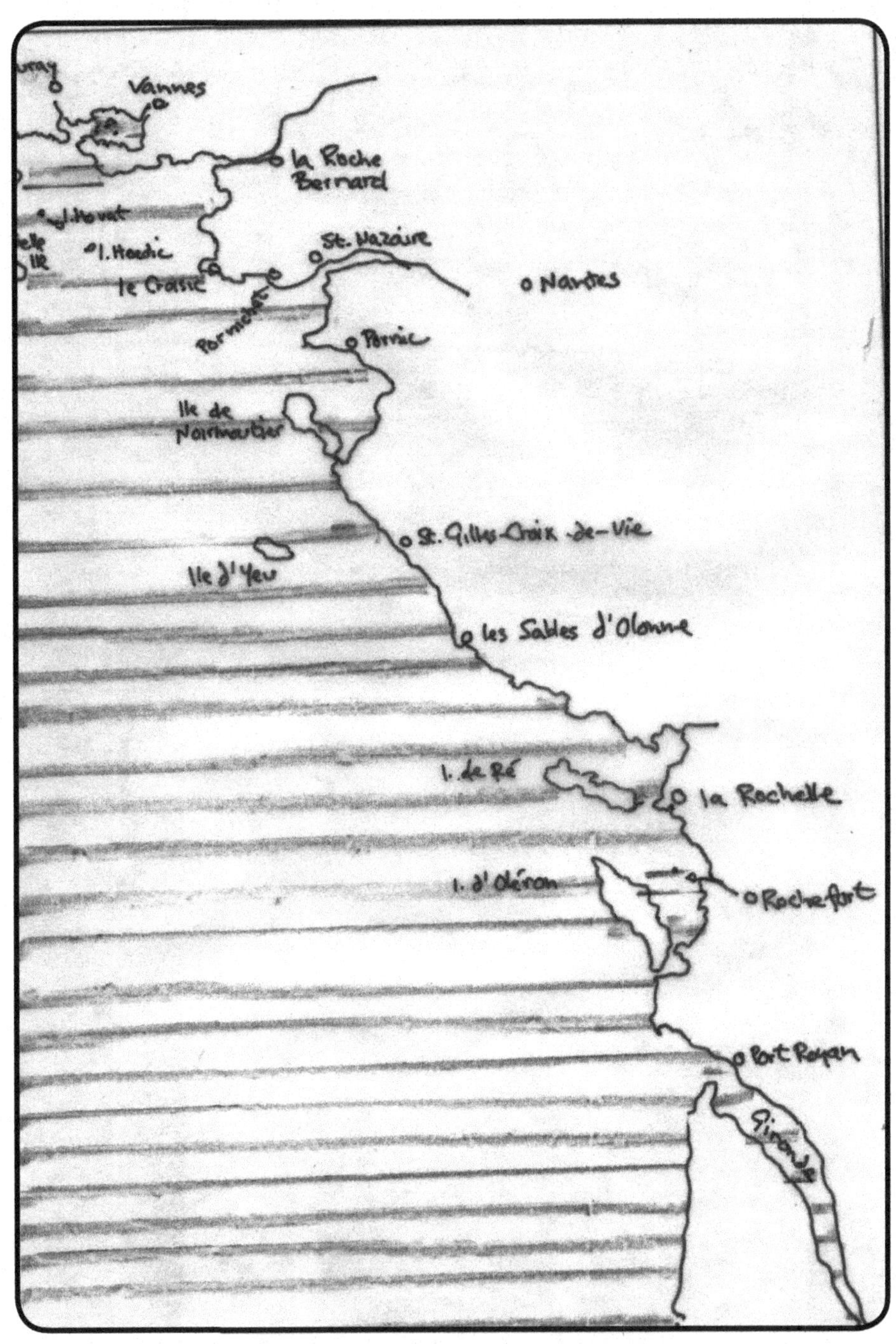

Map 3: The Gironde to the Vilaine

Chapter 13

Biscay Beyond Port Royan

Back to Port Royan and Year Three of the French Circumnavigation attempt. The spars and rigging had been hauled from the start point, Honfleur, to Camargue. The reason was simply so that at the end of Year 1 we had boat and gear in one place. The gear could be checked and repackaged for another winter's storage. Now the spars and rigging had been road hauled from Port Camargue to Royan. The yard had craned our Snapdragon 890, *Wise One,* on to the 'hard' to be re-rigged, anti-fouled and re-launched as a yacht. As the good Lord intended.

There was a great deal to do to make her our home again and fit for off-shore cruising. We had thought seriously about the state of our gear and were now well loaded with a new hard-canister life raft, overhauled life jackets; new Navtex Weatherman, new Autohelm, new steering compass, new battery monitoring system, well overhauled set of sails, new charts and pilots etc, etc. Moving from canal to open water means re-equipping the boat with a great deal that had been taken home. We were happy to find *Wise One* bobbing to her pontoon just waiting for it all to be bolted, screwed, wired, and generally put in working order.

The *Yellow Brick Road* for the summer of '07 took us out of canal mode to sail gently out of the Gironde Estuary and northwards along the coast, exploring as many inlets and little ports as time and tide permitted. We had no destination in mind, thinking only that somewhere on the south Brittany coast a good winter stop would emerge. (Let the *Yellow Brick Road* take care of us.) There was work to be done by us and by the yard before we could leave Royan so we had time to inspect and instruct the boatyard before heading by car for the first of our destination: not La Rochelle but southern Spain.

A villa had been booked from 10th May in southern Spain, thanks to Alex from whom it was birthday and Christmas presents. We drove down from Royan. Alex, Anna, partner Daz (vocalist in a heavy rock group working in Manchester area), seven year old Amelia, Jacky's sister Peta, partner Dennis and little Josh all variously arrived by air. Peta and Dennis live near Dorking and work in the insurance world. Both have done the London Marathon (Dennis serially). Peta took in Kilimanjaro but missed an Everest Base Camp when Josh came along. (That omission was to be corrected in 2010 but on the very day of departure the flight was cancelled due to volcanic ash in the atmosphere …. It is said that some language was used.) This objective was finally achieved in 2011; well done Peta! We made a lively group and a good week was in store.

Jacky and I had long planned an extended Spanish/Moorish historic cities tour down and back + the bit in the middle. Going down we enjoyed Segovia (with snow topped hills), Valencia and Granada (with the absolutely stunning Alhambra and Albaicin). On the return we enjoyed

Cordoba and Toledo. The villa lay in the hills of El Bosque not far from the hill town of Ronda and the chill weather warmed up just in time. The family assembled.

For us there were two objectives: spend quality time with the family and see something of the mind-blowing architecture of Moorish Spain. The villa lay at the end of a 2 km gravel track, 10 km from the nearest small town of El Bosque and looked down over a beautiful valley and distant lake. In the mornings, white mist drifted below up the valley. During the day we looked down on great birds of prey hunting the grassy slopes. Our mixed age group meant much pool-swimming and 'al fresco' eating at the villa as well as beach visits. We also visited the historic Seville and the famous horse fair at Jerez. The latter was more an informal parade of traditional Spanish costume than a serious market in horse flesh. But it was all a colourful and fun addition to the week.

The Moors occupied the Iberian peninsular from 8th to (ultimately) the 15th Centuries. They brought with them a sophisticated urban living and architecture as well as learning which was generally in advance of Western Europe; in particular in science and maths. As we have already noted, the Moors at times controlled not just Spain, but also towns like Narbonne, Beziers and Bordeaux. (None of these at the time were part of Royalist France.)

Although over the centuries Christian forces slowly pushed the Moors southwards and eventually out of Spain, there must have been considerable mutual respect between the opposing cultures. The great Mosque in Cordoba was in effect a broadly based university, library of international importance and centre of learning. As Christian forces slowly ejected the Moors, you might imagine that there would follow a systematic destruction of all that the Moors stood for. A great deal of Moorish building was indeed lost over the ages, but their greatest architectural heritage was generally not just kept, but cherished.

The Great Mosque at Cordoba was, however, seriously altered by the new rulers. It originally took the form of a huge covered space with the roof supported by a forest of elegant columns and arches. It is so big that a (Christian) cathedral was inserted into the middle of it; retaining the vast and covered columned space. The King of Spain is quoted as saying to his Archbishop: "You have destroyed something unique and beautiful and repaced it with the mundane". Don't suppose the Bish was pleased.

Our return north to Basque country at the end of the week enabled us to meet up with old college friends Eric and Liz from Vancouver Island, Canada. Eric and Liz are again friends from our Edinburgh days. Liz has worked for much of her life for the Canadian Government on 'First Nation' issues. Eric, architect and town planner, has worked in Canada in both professions. Both have families and enjoy sailing and skiing. Together we visited Bilbao to spend time at the Guggenheim galleries; arguably one of the most important bits of modern architecture for many years.

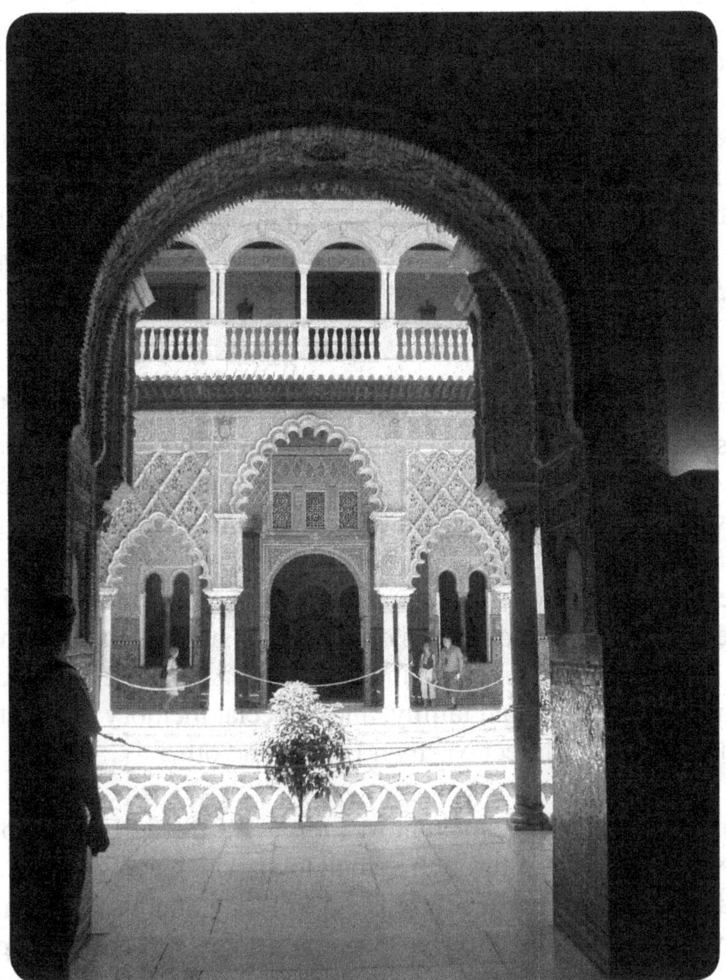

Moorish Architecture

And so back again to Port Royan. We expected to find *Wise One* fully fitted with new gear and ready to go. After a long drive from Bilbao we arrived late, tired, and in the rain to find that all the jobs were started, nothing finished and the boat in chaos….. Despite mutterings of hotels we eventually got sorted (several days).

At the same time we visited Saintes, Cognac (ate at the café d'Or in the central square), St Emilion, toured the Marais by car and watched a series of 'lows' go through doing what 'lows' do best (i.e. rain and wind). The drive across to St Emilion was through attractive, rolling, green vineyard countryside. St Emilion itself is well worth a visit simply as an unspoilt example of an early, southern French country town with ancient foundations and building generally dating from the C15-C18. Its tightly packed little streets and heavy Roman tiled roofs have remained unchanged for centuries. Partially fortified, it is possible to walk a section of the walls and look down on the rich pattern of sculptured, mature, locking clay roofs. Of course the wine features and there are many opportunities to stock up. The underground cathedral (cut out of the hillside rock) is said to be an absolute 'must'. Sadly it was closed when we were there.

Following the booze theme, we had then to visit the town of Cognac on the river Charante. In a region full of medieval-to-eighteenth century town treasures, this is an historic town worth a stop and a walk. 'Vieux Cognac' is the medieval quarter which runs from the town centre down to the river. There are many old and interesting buildings and, of course, cognac is distilled here. A reception area in the distillery has a unique display, including some Picasso material since he did some promotional and label drawings. Not far from Cognac lies Saintes, also on the River Charante. Saintes is a big, elegant, C18/C19 town with an extraordinarily complete Roman amphitheatre.

From the towns and inland countryside it was back to the coast and the 'Marais'. The name 'Marais' reoccurs along the coastline and indicates salt marshes, that had probably been used for salt panning. And in some cases salt production still continues. This is reflected in the flat open landscape with salt fields mixing with more traditional marsh-land habitat.

Back on-board severe weather warnings found us doubling our lines, jumping in the car and heading off to see family and friends (again) in Beziers. That was the best thing you could do with a force 7/8, gusting up and precipitating like a fireman's hose in a thelasotherapy cell. Nice memories though of friends and family; and a special memory of the stunning bridge at Millau designed by British Architect Norman Foster (and others!)..

What can you say about the bridge? It removes an awful traffic black spot as the old road wound its way down a steep valley, through a small town with narrow streets and a little bridge and circled its way out again. The structure is 2.5 km long and higher than the Eiffel Tower at 343 m. over the valley bottom. Most suspension bridges have two support pylons. This has seven. It cost 310 million euros and was built in 39 months. I don't suppose the planning inquiry took very long either. Behind the raw figures lies a structure of outstanding beauty. Crossing it by car (on a clear day) is an experience; but it also needs to be seen from up the valley on the old road. From there you can see the pylons reaching to heaven as they march across the deep valley. High above your head but slung between the pylons the black spider's thread of a road links hill to hill.

So when the weather was bad, or family called, or gear needed to be shifted, it was good to have a car. It does give another series of options to the casual coastal sailor. There are of course times when we had to travel back to enable the car to catch-up with coastal progress. This could mean complex arrangements involving buses, taxis, (folding) bikes and trains. It seems to us that most bus networks were based on the 'Departement' and stop at the boundary. At one time we even had to take a bus to the local boundary, take a taxi to the next village to catch the next 'Departement' bus onwards. But as long as you regard this as part of the fun, it's not a problem.

Chapter 14

La Rochelle Beckons

Back in Royan once more we waited patiently for a weather slot which is the benefit of having no time pressures. We now had the chance to test boat, gear and crew. Our first leg was northwards and out of the Gironde Estuary, past the length of the Ile d'Oleron leaving it to starboard to reach St Denis at its northern tip. It would have been good to have been able to go between the Island and the mainland, leaving the island to port. The water would have been more sheltered and we would also have had a series of alternative destinations on the way. Our French pontoon live-aboard friends showered us with local wisdom "Don't ever attempt the Couteau d'Oleron. Noooh!" (i.e. the inside route). At any rate not without heavy and reliable twin engines. Most of these scary warnings can be overcome by careful study of the tidal currents and depths. But we had been given the serious local warning from the local fishermen and so we stayed outside. Pity, the inside route looked far more interesting and the outside meant a 40 mile open water northwards without any escape or alternative on the way. Fresh stuff on the nose for 40 miles didn't seem necessary, so we waited.

There were fond farewells as at last we got our slant and left for St Denis. The entry into St Denis marina is tidal with a fixed sill, but the tidal window was fairly wide and the day went according to plan. The general landscape here tends to be low lying and un-dramatic with no off-lying dangers and so we tracked fairly close inshore, registering each little village, church and water tower as we passed. It was just wonderful to be a yacht again and an off-shore north-easterly gave us a good sail and a gentle and considerate sea. It was invigorating to feel again the power of those two well balanced sails drawing us westward, kissed by the early summer sun. The day slipped by until forty miles on, we were dropped neatly through the tidal window into our first new port of '07. It was satisfying to be on our way again and good to explore a new haven

St Denis marina is modern and efficient; a good stay-over or jumping off point for further destinations. The old market town of St Denis is a pleasant ¼ mile walk to a small historic centre with a good market, super fish monger and the usual cafes. David and Stella on *Boheme* shared red wine and 'winterising' destination information about the Vilaine River. Sounded good; we must research. It was good to be here.

The next leg was to take us to our major focal point of the summer – La Rochelle. We had seen the Rochelle bay (i.e. Rade de Basque) as holding a lot of interest for us with Rochelle being a feeder-port to a number of destination. La Rochelle itself is accessible at all states of the tide, hence (presumably) its historic importance. All the feeder destinations are tide-bound so a tide-free common departure point is always helpful.

La Rochelle has two marinas. In the city centre are many yacht mooring spaces but mostly taken by locals or on a long term basis. Visitors are encouraged to the huge marina facilities out-of-town. New pontoon work in the city centre meant that it was in any case closed to us. Despite the ambitious size of the marina, the genuinely available visitor berths are quite restricted and help from le Capitaine non-existent. It was a game of bluff and counter bluff as boats of all sizes manoeuvred to spot and capture the next available vacancy. (The lack of help from the Marina staff is a matter of wide-spread gossip over cockpit drinks). Not to worry. The city centre is a very pleasant half hour walk along the river front; or a fun 20 minute water-bus ride.

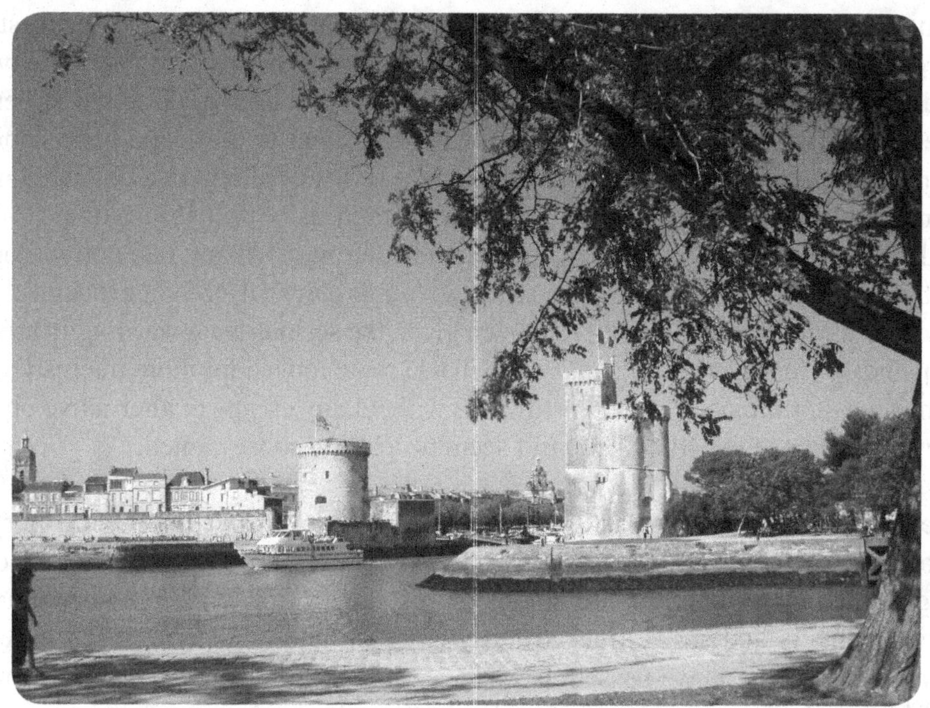

La Rochelle

La Rochelle has ancient foundations based on sea trade. It was declared a Free Port in the 12th Century which encouraged enterprise and growth. The city was greatly fortified in the C13th. During the 15th century it was a strongly protestant city and held in collusion with the Brits against Royalist/Catholic Paris. Despite that it was the biggest 'French' port on the Atlantic coast and trade with Spain, the Netherlands and England featuring strongly.

Until the middle of the 16th Century it was a centre for Huguenots and port defences were significantly developed with the British to keep Royalist Paris out. The old docks were then well defended and the entrance towers and adjacent walls still stand. However Louis X1V could not allow that to continue and the city was attacked and eventually occupied by Royalists in 1628. The king's great siege engineer, Sabastian Vauban (see Appendix 2) was then involved in making La Rochelle part of the 17thCentury Atlantic Wall against (particularly) the marauding Brits. The city centre is elegantly stone built, mostly in the 16/17/18th centuries on an older street pattern and all this makes the city irresistibly attractive.

In the C20th la Rochelle, Ile d'Oleron and Isle de Re were defended by a garrison of 20,000 German occupying troops against the Allied invasion. (Their own Atlantic Wall). They were by-passed by the invading Allies and only surrendered on the capitulation of the Nazi powers on May 7th 1945. The whole coastline has always been a turbulent front line between competing interests.

As always the pontoons are sociable areas. We now found ourselves well surrounded by the Red Ensign and the cockpit of 'White Lady' provided a good setting for gossip-share with Audrey and Norman. We had time to kill (the weather again) and a day was also profitably invested in the walk-through modern aquarium. Well worth a visit.

From Rochelle there are a number of local destination, perhaps the most significant being Rochefort which lies some 28 km to the south/east across the Rade de Basque. It is very tidal and approached by a canalised River Charante through a lock. In the C17th Louis X1V needed to rebuild his navy and establish an Atlantic coast naval port for building, repair and provisioning. Rochefort was built from scratch on a site well sheltered from the Atlantic by the Ile d'Oleron and well defendable from the marauding Brits. Defences were built by the infinitely energetic Vauban both around Rochefort and on the approaches to the River Charante. Dry docks of huge size were stone built in the 17th Century along with their support buildings. The rope works, to take one example, are more than 370 metres long and built more like a C17 royal palace than an industrial shed.

The shipyard was only closed early in the C 20th but the historic buildings were nearly lost through neglect and vandalism (e.g. retreating occupation forces in 1944). A move totally to demolish in 1946 was defeated and restoration has been in process ever since. The marina space lies in an old port basin which is part of the historic town. In one of the historic dry docks is a project to build a replica C18th, 14 gun warship, the frigate 'Hermione'. The original was built here in six months (!) in 1778, played a part in the American War of Independence and later was wrecked on the French coast. The full size replica has been under construction since 1997 and leaves you in no doubt about the ship building skills of the 17th and 18th centuries. The hull is now fully planked and completion planned 'within a year or two'. Perhaps whilst it is a major tourist attraction, finishing is not the first priority. So go there; by car if you must; by boat if you can. The fortified little Ile d'Aix, off the entrance to the River Charante is worth a high-ish tide visit but don't stop too long if you can't take the ground. Port Buyardville on the Ile d'Oleron is also tidal and needs careful calculations to get in.

But our next destination was back north/west to Rochelle and then St Martin on the Ile de Ré. We were joined by old college friends Brenda and Doug for this short trip, (after they had taken us back to Royan to collect the car). Brenda and Doug date back to our old Leicester collage days when he and I studied architecture. His life has since been spent in architectural practice in Leicester and dress-designer Brenda has brought up a family and latterly managed and owned her own shop. We have more or less kept in contact over the years and it was good to have them aboard. One advantage of the long architectural course is that there is plenty of time to build a useful student rugby side. Doug was a robust fly half in the Will Carling mould. (Well he would have been if he had been born a bit later.) We can still reminisce over pints about the disgraceful behaviour of youngsters in the 1960's.... I'm surprised that Brenda puts up with him.

The Ile de Ré is pretty flat (good cycling country); it is 30 km long and 5 km wide. It is joined to the mainland by a dramatic curving, 2.9 km bridge, built in 1987, with good clearance (for us, anyway) through the central arches and doing wonders for real estate values. The island has a winter population of 16,000 and summer population of 160,000....

Bridge to the Ile de Ré

The principle port, St Martin, is one of a delightful series of former little fishing and commercial ports along the north Biscay coast that make this such a compelling cruising area. Some have a marina grafted on. Others, like St Martin, just accommodate yachts (elderly or modern) as best they can. Typically the towns retain a medieval street pattern with modest stone houses from the 17th and 18th centuries – an endearing combination. The downside is that the visitor economy takes over the shops. The up-side is that there is the typically French respect and value for the historic townscape and a rich plethora of restaurants and cafes.

The pilotage to St Martin was straight forward though again the timing has to be right to enter into the locked basin. This is an old sea port and the long sea basin prescribes an arc through the centre of the small town. There are now few fishing vessels and so the wharfage is devoted to leisure craft. This very pretty town is a major destination for yachts and cars. The latter are banned from much of the centre; the former can lie five deep on the visitors' pontoons.

St Martin also shows the once-French preoccupation with keeping the Brits out of French coastal fringes. St Martin was further fortified by Vauban (that man again) in 1681. We climbed the church tower and were fascinated to see the town and coast spread before us and the full extent of complex geometric defence works emerge. We then walked Vauban's huge star-shaped earth mounds and troop-traps. We absorbed a couple of hours imagining the attacking and defending manoeuvres with the huge earthworks absorbing the incoming cannon fire before enjoying the more peaceful preoccupation of the local cuisine.

We sailed back to La Rochelle where *Wise One* was closed down for a few weeks. The return to Le Havre and the ferry was used also to explore the very attractive Vilaine River. It didn't take us long to find the small Foleux yard at Beganne, track down the owner and make wintering arrangements. We then had serious appointments at home with two weddings and a grand-birth. Congratulations to all, especially Anna, Daz and small Elliot (who is doing well).

Chapter 15

Westwards to the Vilaine.

Going home was an enjoyable interruption to our planned progress. In fact we missed a chunk of peak season congestion and the frustrating delay of the arrival of the summer Azore's High. Many sailing Brits prefer to cruise April-June and September-October; we returned for six weeks from mid-August. Persistent northerlies 5-6 had given way to clear skies and 3-4 north-easterlies. Bliss! We left the bay of Rochelle (i.e. Rade de Basque) to launch ourselves onwards and upwards. The first stop was a return to St Martin where we were joined again for a couple of days by old friends Pete and Kate who had seen us across the Channel two-and-a-half years earlier. This time they came by camper van, the 60 mph touring alternative to the 4 knot *Wise One.* We have thought about it at times.

We were helped into our berth by Jackie and Simon Smith + Alan off a new Southerly 45 'Augusta'. As they took our lines they announced that they also have a Snap 890 (of course called *Dancing Bear 3*) which they purchased as a bare hull and completed themselves. We lay to the quayside five deep.

Leaving Port St. Martin for deep water and Les Sable d'Olonne in the morning took some unknitting. But it led to a great sail up coast in a force 4 on the quarter. Les Sable is a small modern town (population some 15,000) with a large enclosed dock system substantially turned over to yachts. Extensive facilities enable it to host long distance blue water events (eg the four-year Vendee Globe round the world yacht race). Got a great beach which gets very crowded. Time to move on. The next call, St Giles, is another town that grew up around a very busy fishing and general purpose dock. Its deep water entry is marked by an C18th breakwater which seems to run for ever out to sea. We were hosted comfortably in this old town before moving on again; this time off-shore.

The summer theme seemed to be 'islands'. With the wind off-shore and force 4 on the quarter, with full head sail and main drawing well, it was just a joy to be sailing. *Wise One* surged over the slight sea, dipping to the gentle swell and chucking the occasional cup-full of spray over the foredeck. We rarely used the auto-helm on these modest trips, preferring to feel the life of the working yacht through helm and fingertip. That's, after all, what we were there for. A great sail.

The Ile d'Yeu is a strangely understated place; little seems to have changed since the 1930's. It must always have been a poor fishing community with agriculture at a subsistence level. Fishing remains important and the mainland ferry brings a daily quota of visitors (in the season). Initially we found it hard to know what they came for. Shops, cafes and restaurants hardly seem to recognise the visitor trade; perhaps the season is simply too short. Hotels were hard to find and specific 'attractions' non-existent.

But we became tuned into an island geared down for cycling, walking, beaching and relaxing. A two-wheel visit to le Vieux Chateau de L'Ile d'Yeu was a small highlight. It is built on the cliffs and its ruins spell of isolation, contemplation and great sea views. New development across the island is low key and clearly must be in a C17/18th cottage-architectural idiom. One imagines that it must be dominated by retirement and holiday dwellings and be very quiet in the winter. In fact, however, we became very fond of the island perhaps because of, rather than despite, its gentle approach to the C21st. We found perhaps the only respectable cuisine on the island – les Bafouttes – where we ate in some disgraceful sophistication.

Ile d'Yeu - le Vieux Chateau

So you've got to do the islands and 20 miles up coast from Ile d'Yeu lies Ile de Noirmoutier. The major town, Noirmoutier Sur Ile, is accessed from the sea by a shallow ditch or gut drying at low tide, used by local small craft and some older vessels. However it is Port l'Herbaudiere that contains the ferry terminal, the remnants of the fishing fleet, the deep water marina and the little bistro which hosted our 42nd wedding anniversary dinner. Don't scoff, marina haters; it's worth the marina to have deep water access not to mention electricity and water. It's an attractive waterfront and they have done their best to soften, by landscaping, a previously working waterfront with new paving and planting. There are good supporting marine services and the coastal sailor quickly feels at home. A half hour cycling puts you across the island to Noimoutier town which was well worth the effort with its medieval streets and large open market. It is dominated by a huge fortified 15th Century bastion and chateau, the walls of which you can walk. There is a bridge and low-water causeway, the Passage du Gois, linking the island to the mainland.

From the marina we long-walked the foreshore to the far headland. Now although a chunk of the island is low lying flat salt pans, on the North West side the shore was now fringed with granite reefs. Here we left behind the flat Morais and stared at the beginnings of rock-bound Celtic Brittany; geologically if not politically.

Our next stop was the extremely pretty inlet, harbour and small town of Pornic. It lay NNE by some 15 miles and a NNW wind + a favourable tide took us happily across the Baie de Bourgneuf. The delightful town estuary, however, dries to a modest trickle at low tide so we were very contented with our bolt-on, all-tides marina. The walk into the very pleasant old town centre was a delight along the river frontage and past the C13th castle and on to the town quay overlooking the old commercial basin. Commercial vessels have long since gone and the space is now taken by small, local fishing craft and leisure boats. The pleasure of walking and cycling the area made it quite hard, eventually, to leave.

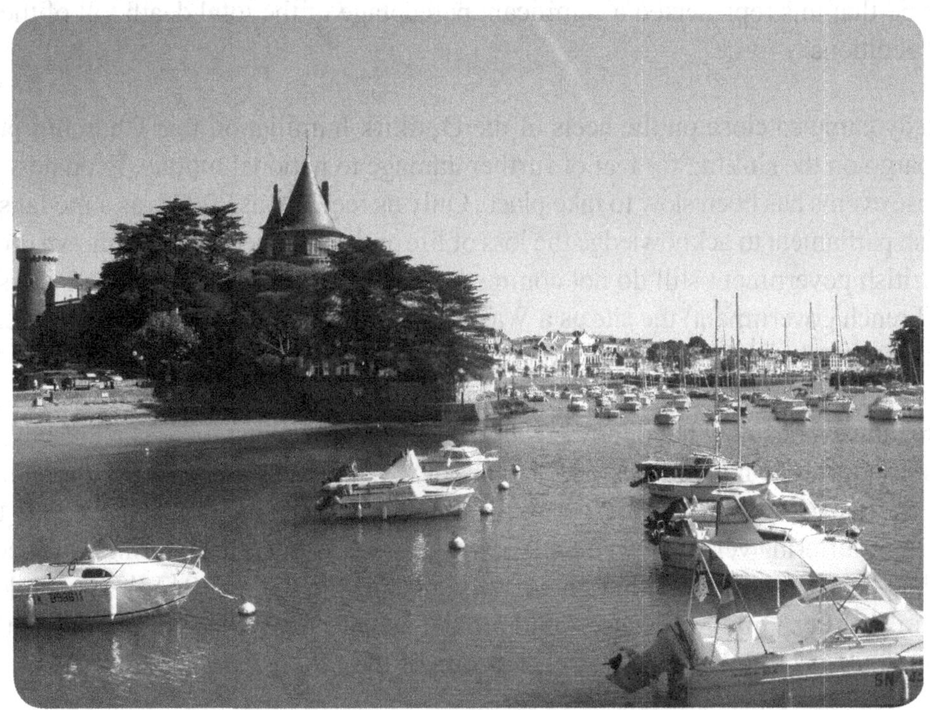

Pornic

After Pornic the coastline makes a great indent into the Loire Estuary.

A few miles off the estuary entrance a modest red buoy marks the spot of horrendous scenes in June of 1940. It was early days of the Second World War and two weeks after the humiliating evacuation of the British Expeditionary force from the beaches of Dunkirk. After Dunkirk, there were still left in France many troops and civilians needing to get home. The south western ports of France must have seen huge numbers of British, confused, exhausted and desperate. St Nazaire was a major centre of an evacuation attempt entitled Operation Ariel. Ships were sent to St Nazaire but the journey both there and back was at risk from submarines and from the air and hazardous in the extreme. That part of western France had yet to fall to the German forces, but they had command of the air and bombing of the docks was a frequent occurrence.

A Clyde-built, ex-Cunard liner, the troop ship RMS Lancastria, was part of the evacuation attempt. She would normally have taken some 2,200 passengers and crew but on this occasion she was simply filled with as many people as could be crammed aboard. How many she took is put at about 6,000. The estuary down stream from St Nazaire is wide and shallow except for the narrow and deeply dredged big ship channel to the busy and industrial port. The Lancastria was lying some nine miles down stream of St Nazaire, waiting for an escorted return to Britain. She was hit by three bombs and sank within 20 minutes. Rescue craft were quickly on the scene but so were German aircraft strafing survivors and, presumably, rescue craft. The ship's oil tanks were ruptured and 1,400 tons of burning fuel was released into the sea. It is estimated that some 4,000 lives were lost, making this by far the greatest maritime disaster in British history. In fact it is said that this represented a significant percentage of the total death toll of the ill-fated British expeditionary force.

This tragedy came so close on the heels of the Dunkirk humiliation that Churchill put a total news embargo on the sinking for fear of further damage to national morale. Even now recognition of these events has been slow to take place. Only as recently as 2008 was a medal struck by the Scottish parliament to acknowledge the loss of life and associated heroism shown on that day. But the British government still do not commemorate the disaster by medal or by designating (with the French government) the site as a War Grave. So if you see a small red marker buoy at the entrance to the Loire Estuary, doff you cap briefly in respect for those lives lost.

St Nazaire, however, is now not of any great interest to small boats; there is a locked basin that takes leisure craft, but not in any comfort. The few small vessels there are probably locals. However, again back to WW2, it was certainly of interest to a lot of people in 1942. At that time the allies were suffering very heavy Atlantic losses through U-boats and German surface raiders. *Bismark* had been sunk but the giant *Tirpitz* was still operational. In 1942 she was holed up (so to speak) in Norway. Only St Nazaire could provide an alternative base for *Tirpitz* in the shape of the huge Joubert Dock built for the construction of the *SS Normandy* in the 1930's.

St Nazaire lies in the Loire Estuary, some 10 km from the mouth. The dock itself is a basin 1,148 ft x 164 ft with lock gates of 35 ft thick caissons. These are 167 ft x 54 ft and moved on great rollers. Winch and pump houses were located close by and adjacent were docks and pens for smaller warships and U-Boats. The complex was protected by some 100 heavy guns, searchlights, minesweepers and coastal defence craft manned by some 5,000 German forces' personnel.

During the night of March 28th 1942, the redundant American destroyer *HMS Campbeltown*, a number of accompanying MTBs, 611 British commandos and RN marines launched Operation Chariot with the intention of putting the great dock out of action. After dark they entered the Loire estuary and penetrated the river defences. At first the German guns were puzzled but soon realised that they had a serious raid on their hands. Firing onto the raiders became intense and the fuel-packed MTBs (and their crew) suffered very badly. However the *Campbeltown* reached and rammed the lock gates. The Commandos swarmed ashore and, in an intense fire-fight, attacked the shore installations. The destroyer, packed with delayed action explosives, was occupied by German troops searching for anything significant while the Captain was taken into custody. He was being politely reassured that there was little fundamental damage done and the dock would soon be in working order again when the explosives blew. The dock was out of action for the rest of the war.

As the Allied offensive on mainland Europe took shape, the German army faced up to the reality of retreat. In Western France they established a series of strong points into which they could withdraw and then defend against the advancing Allies. Some enemy enclaves were bypassed by the advancing Allies as of not sufficient importance to capture. For example La Rochelle and the outer islands.

St Nazaire (and Lorient and others) were seen as being too important to leave in German hands. After a leaflet-drop to warn residents, St Nazaire was devastated from the air. Despite incendiary bomb attacks, the U-boat pens refused to surrender and remained in German hands until after D-Day. There is a museum in the town established adjacent and within one of the several surviving U-Boat pens where there is a submarine on display but, disappointingly, not a U-Boat. However a French Naval sub built in the '50s is still well worth a visit along with the general exhibition.

* * *

North of Pornic are two marinas that serve the area of la Baule: Pornichet and la Turballe. There is little to say about either except that they may be convenient breaks going coastwise and provide good main rail connections. At Pornichet we met with 'Intrepid Bear', a voluminous cat, and hospitable owners Jo and Mario. No doubt we will return their hospitality another year.

From Pornichet a satisfying and relaxing 12 mile sail took us between the off-lying and disturbed shoals of Le Plateau du Four and the mainland to the delightful fishing port of Croisic. It lies deeply indented into a low lying and sand banked inlet. A long training wall leads you past marshy fringes, past the deep water pool for fin keels and on into the town. A number of old fishing and commercial basins along the waterfront service the locals while one basin is fitted out for a mixture of local and (limited) visiting leisure traffic. At low water we dried out in shelter and comfort. And ate at the modest restaurant 'le Stream' for a proper French Sunday lunch.

From Croisic we had only a short hop around the headland to our last coastal stop of Port Piriac. The approach is tidal and the marina is ducked behind a sill which rises (or falls) at half-ish tide (says the Pilot). Three weeks of an Atlantic high had given us stable conditions of gentle winds and clear skies

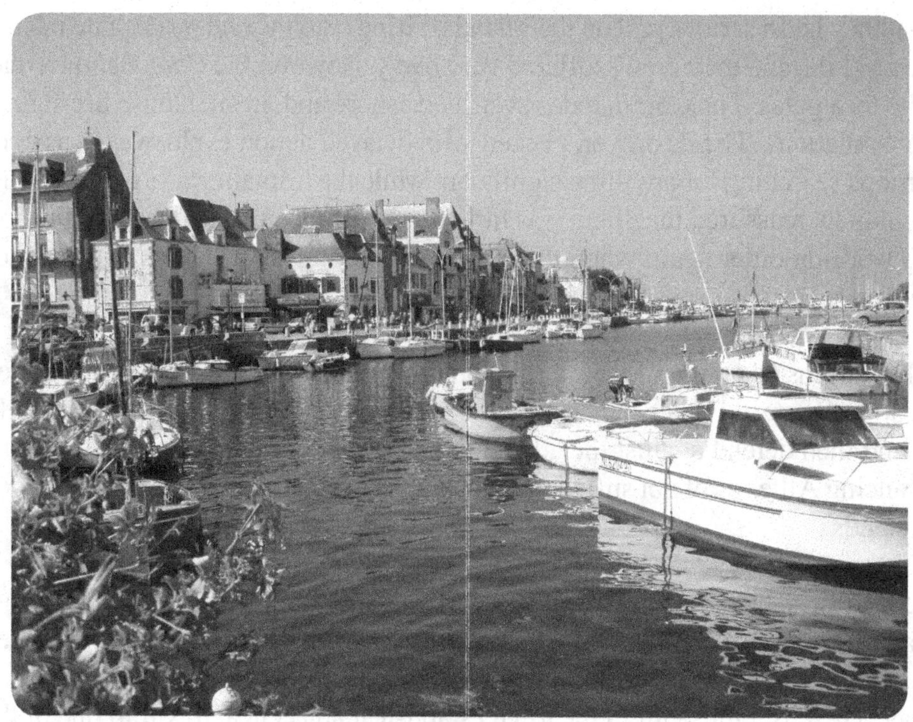

Croisic

We now sensed a change as the evening temperatures dropped and the days got shorter. The French had long since gone home leaving their coastline to the Brits (Louis X1V and Vauban wouldn't have stood for that).

Piriac was another delightful place in which to finish our coastal travel. The days were still warm enough to enjoy the beach walk though the evening meal tended to be more indoors. That was no hardship in the bistro 'Chez Grande-Mere'. Sally and Tony on their own-built, 40'(ish) James Warram cat Tika Roa showed us another way of doing things. Clearly the deck awning provided the principle covered space and cross-legged on Persian carpets seemed to be 'de rigueur'. They run the cat in tandem with a camper van which takes over when the weather cools down and a fast trip south is needed. But I guess we will see them again in southern Brittany sometime.

Piriac was one of many small towns that were deeply devoted to the 'France in bloom' competition. The natural side street presence of wild hollyhocks was accompanied by dazzling displays by town and private gardens of intensely colourful planting on every corner. We also greatly appreciated the French use of wild flowers to enhance roadside borders and roundabouts.

We now took this chance to use the local bus service + a taxi + two trains to return to La Rochelle for our car and deliver it to Roche Bernard. At the same time we also thoroughly enjoyed looking in on the walled medieval town Bastide de Guerande on the way. We have already talked about the Bastides. Over the centuries some have developed into reasonably sized towns of wider local significance. Some have grown little beyond their original walled limits. Those provide us with lovely pictures of modest, rural, southern French living of earlier years. They are therefore always worth searching out as possible small gems.

And so to the Vilaine Estuary. The Vilaine is no great distance across the bay from Piriac, but we had to time the (potentially) strong tides and shallows of the Vilaine estuary and time our arrival at the Vilaine barrage at Arzal. The barrage creates a fresh water reservoir of the damned-up Vilaine. The result is that when the lock is negotiated, beyond it is twenty-five miles of sheltered, non-tidal, deep water estuary. At first it is high sided and deeply wooded. Up stream towards Redon it expands into open countryside; clearly many smaller boats never leave the river. (But more of the Vilaine later).

Our destination in the Vilaine, la Roche Bernard, is an old port; the town lies on a steep bluff with moorings streaming up the river and tucked into the short inlet (le Vieux Port). Just up-stream are the sky-high Roche Bernard and Quiberon Bridges. This is a special place so tell no one. Unfortunately, it's too late. It's not hard to see why the Brits are here. It's 200 miles south of the Solent; a lot cheaper (or was before the recent devaluation of sterling); better sailing and easy to get here by car or 'plane. Initially we were reluctant to enter into an area where the red ensign is such a common sight; so far this simply had not been so. It has to be said, however, that as we settled into la Roche Bernard, we made many friends from 'home' which added another dimension to our trip. But, again, more about Roche Bernard later.

La Roche Bernard

A few short miles up-stream lay our winter haul-out at Foleux. First we continued beyond to Redon. The town is a working place of 10,500 population. If you can't find what you want in little Roche Bernard then Redon probably has it. However, although it has attractive central streets and a canal/river frontage, it is not a visitor destination. When we stayed there in 2006 we struggled to find anywhere interesting to eat (though no doubt the locals know better). The yacht canal basin is flanked by the through road to Rennes. Yachtsmen do spend the winter there and no doubt it is more economic than alternatives. But it wasn't one for us so, dropping back down stream, we spent our last 'free' night at a river-side rural 'halt' of Rieux, green, gentle and deep in early morning mist. Autumn was on us and it was time to go. We slipped down to Foleux where we met Mirage 28 owner Christian le Dreau, skipper of 'Veri-Titeuf' who was interested in the existence of the Snapdragon and Mirage Association. We put them in touch.

But we had hard work to do and, sadly an appointment with a crane. It was goodbye to Project France, Year 3 and 'au revoir' to all that.

In the meantime " Deux rosé, s'il vous plait Monsieur !"

Foleux - end of season

Readers' Notes

Part 4
Summer 2008 The Golf du Morbihan and the Vilaine

In which we brave the Vilaine and the Golfe du Morbihan and the Bai de Quiberon without any damage to anyone. And thank you George Millar.

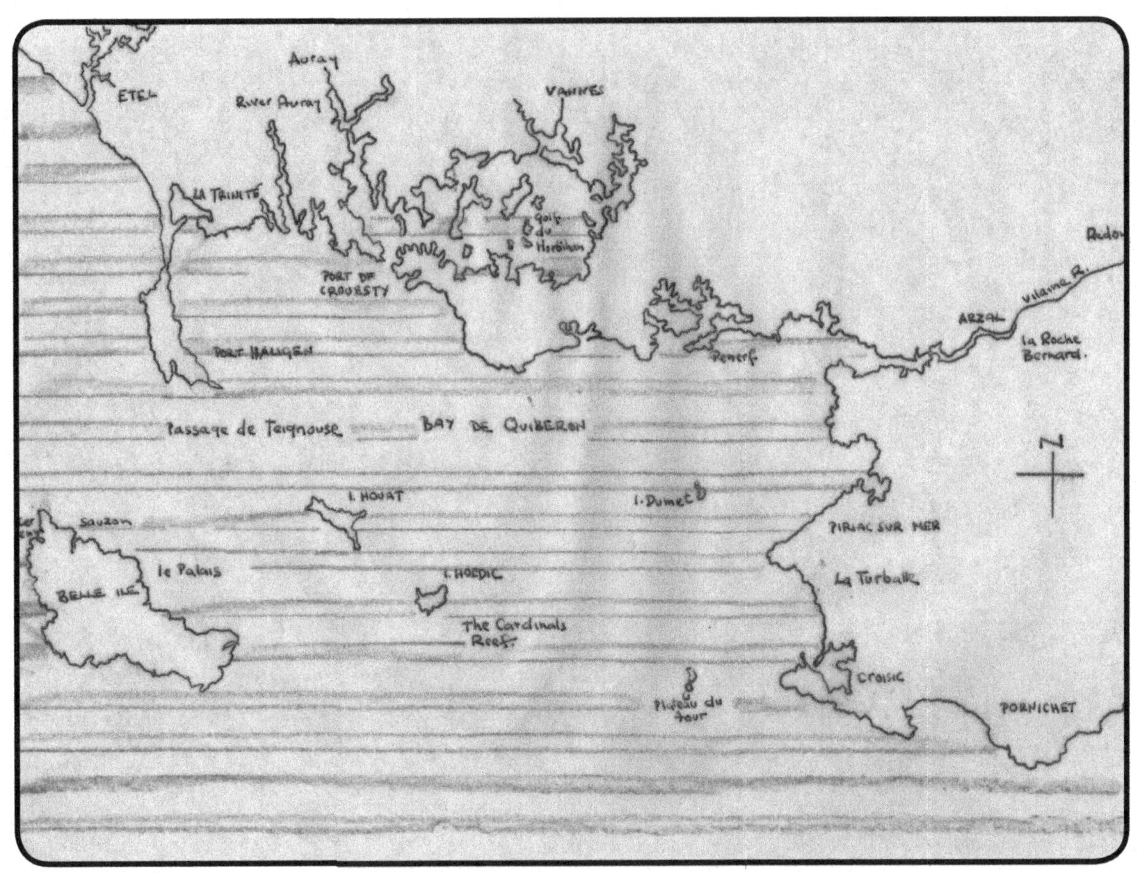

Map 4: Golf du Morbihan and the Vilaine River

Chapter 16

The 'Little Sea' calls

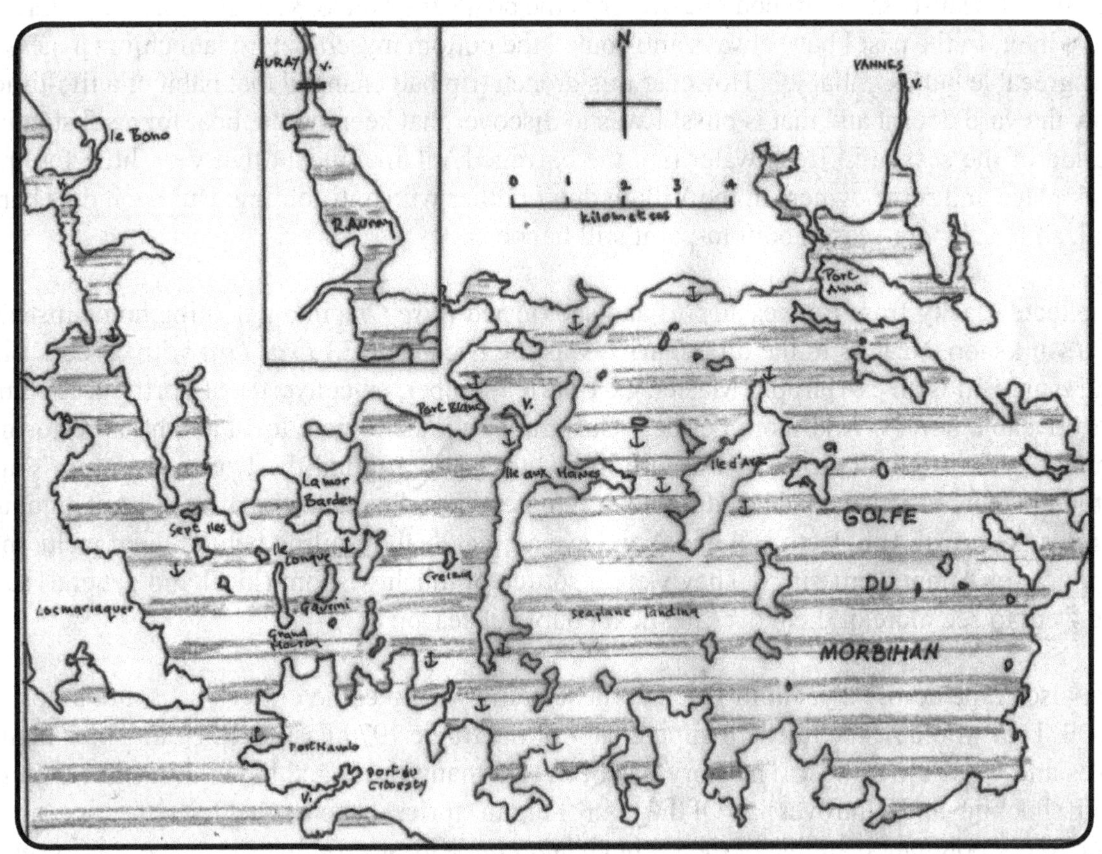

Map 5: The Golf du Morbihan

This is the fourth year of our French project. Now, rather like life, we find ourselves at present happy to avoid the longer passages and fresher winds. Jacky and I have been sailing together for 43 years so we can be forgiven for being into a little consolidation. In fact the damp and blustery summer of 2008 became largely a story of two sheltered waters: the Vilaine and the Morbihan.

After a May yacht charter with friends in Croatia we were a bit late starting back on the *Yellow Brick Road.* I drove with a mountain of gear and spent a week re-assembling the vessel in Foleux. M. Jean-Francois Renou, the owner of the boat yard, had looked after *Wise One* during the winter. In the past I have always anti-fouled the bottom myself before launching; a messy, disagreeable but essential job. However this French trip had changed that habit of a life-time; now the yard does it and that is bliss! I was to discover that keeping the boat for a substantial period of the season in fresh water (i.e. the barraged Vilaine) meant that very little fouling took place and some owners in the Villain don't bother with anti-fouling. But habit dies hard and, so far, my pre-season bottom-paint still happens.

I collected Jacky from Rennes airport and she turned *Wise One* into a floating home instead of a workshop. Near us in the little marina was the Nicholson 33 *Frai Tira* with owners Bill and Ann. Bill is an ex-Harbour Master, ex-Charter skipper, ex-converter of Portuguese ruins into liveable homes. And more besides. Currently he is help-mate to Mac who is restoring an elderly sailing hull (at present ashore in Foleux) into a round-the-world adventure ship, although there is no launch date admitted or remotely in sight. With a lot of Irish good humour Ann puts up with Bill. Both Bill and Ann have a great deal of sailing behind them including a couple of Atlantic crossings. They were a source of much wisdom (local and general) and we were to see more of them over the next couple of seasons.

We also came across a yacht in Foleux whose name was to come onto every sailor's lips in 2009. That would be the thirtieth anniversary of the tragic 1979 Fastnet Race in which many lives and vessels were lost. The story has been told many times and the circumstances were both shocking and controversial. Of the many human stories that emerged from the race, none were more poignant than that of the yacht *Grimalkin.* With several lives lost, she was eventually abandoned in the Irish Sea but later recovered and towed into a southern Irish port. Here she lay, dis-masted, damaged and neglected for a while (the principle actors in the drama had other things on their mind). She was eventually restored and changed hands. We now met her young owners who were coastal cruising having placed her in the Foleux yard for one winter. She still had her old name; it is after all bad luck (it's well known) to change a ship's name.

Eventually we un-glued ourselves from Foleux and dropped back the short distance downstream to La Roche Bernard. A further five miles took us down to Azal and the locked barrage. With the small frisson that we must all have, we were looking again at the estuary and the open sea. Below the barrage the estuary can reduce to a shallow channel – and so do your sums ! The tidal currents can be quite strong and unexpectedly reinforced by a surge from the barrage. We will return to the Vilaine a bit later.

Entry into Crouesty

Our destination was the Golfe du Morbihan (in Gallic: 'the Little Sea'). The Crouesty/Arzal track has now become so well used by us that I swear you can see our twin keel furrows permanently inscribed on the surface of the sea. Here you enter the Baie de Quiberon; not a totally enclosed Bay but well surrounded by the curling mainland coast, associated islands and extended turbulent reefs. The Bay is some 30 miles in length and 14.5 miles wide compared with, say, the Solent which is roughly a curved shape 20 x 3.25 miles. In close weather you see little except the passage of the main coastline lying to starboard as you forge westwards. On a clear day however, a great deal can unfold as you move up the coast. Initially, on leaving the Vilaine estuary, the mainland stretches away to the south and Piriac-sur-Mer emerges on its own small headland.

A small island lies off the coast leading some to comment on how close Hoedic looks. Not quite true, this is the smaller island of Dumet that lies just off Piriac. As you move further westwards, land appears across your south-western horizon and little by little you can identify the islands of Hoedic and Houat with the much larger Belle Isle rising mistily behind them. Further on still and beyond the main headland of Pte de Grand Mont, (leading to Crouesty and Navalo) emerges a strip of land across the horizon, apparently joining up with Belle Isle. It doesn't, of course. This is the Presqu'ile de Quiberon. An island it jolly nearly is, almost (but not quite) split from the mainland, but separated from Belle Ile by the turbulent Passage de la Teignouse. Hoedic and Houat are part of the sweep of shallows and reefs that extend the Presqu'Ile de Quiberon half way round the Bay. These were the islands we wanted to explore.

The morning lock gave us a good ebb tide shove down the estuary and, after a twenty-five mile 'hop', we made a mid afternoon entry into Port Crouesty. Crouesty, just outside the Morbihan entrance, is a big modern marina strategically placed as a launch pad for the Morbihan, la Trinite or the Quiberon. Its advantage is that it is sheltered and accessible at all tides; it has all support services and conveniences and you can freshen up your freezer. The quay-side Monday market was one of the best we had seen. But at 22 euros per night (for a 29-footer) it was relatively expensive.

* * *

So, a few words about the Golfe. It is an enclosed sea of about 19 km long and 9.6 km wide. This compares with Poole harbour which is roughly 7.5 by 3 km and with the Etang du Thau which is about 23 by 8 km. The Golf has open sea access only via the fiercely tidal Navalo channel. Most of the 60 islands are private and many quite small; but a number can be walked and several have small communities linked by ferry or low water causeway to the mainland. It is fed by three small rivers: the Riviere Vincin at Vannes, Riviere d'Auray at Auray and the Riviere du Bono at the small town of Bono. The substantial city of Vannes is serviced by a mile-and–a-half canalised river. As a result, the change of direction of the tidal currant does not coincide with the time of high and low water at Navalo.

The flood tide naturally runs from the Navalo Channel like a tree, branching up to Auray and Vannes. In places it runs at 5 knots and just inside the Navalo Channel it can achieve 9 knots…. (we are told). However there are many, many places just outside the main flow which are quite secluded and calm, untouched by the passing rip stream. The useful reverse eddies are the secret and privileged knowledge of the locals. Only thirteen miles from Port Navalo, Vanne highwater is two hours later and so it seems that the tide is always on the move somewhere trying to catch up with itself.

At low water there is quite a lot of foreshore with shell fish farms revealed and I initially did wonder how much deep water there would be to sail in. Do not worry; there is plenty for everybody at all states although no doubt our deeper brethren need to keep half an eye on their echo sounder. The islands are generally quite low but well wooded. All this makes for a gently modulated landscape; but the wind does tend to puff, back and veer around and between the islands. This may seem a bit daunting and no doubt some are put off. Don't be. Sailing here does need more than the usual patience but in the end it is all extremely rewarding.

There are many, many places to drop a hook or (more likely) pick up a mooring. There are visitors' buoys and generally we were not approached for fees. There are private buoys, and we always had to be ready to hand over to their rightful owner at any time. There is no other modern formal marina once Crouesty has been left behind. Our first stop, however, was to be the city of Vannes (population 34,000). As new-comers this gave us a run the length of the Golfe from which we immediately got a really good idea of its scale, variety and moods.

The Morbihan

So from Crouesty we slipped down the Navalo Channel, past Port Navalo. A sharp turn to starboard around La Grand Mouton left the River Auray to port to be explored later. We rounded Ile de Longue and Ile Gavrinis and powered with the flood tide northwards past little Creizig, up the Port Blanc Channel and past the north end of Ile Aux Moins. This island would become a favourite destination but on that day we were pushing on while the flood lasted. Ile d'Arz was left to starboard as we threaded our way through the Port Anna narrows. A well marked channel that slims down dramatically at low water with mud flats encroaching on either side led us to the Rivier de Vincin and the big road swing bridge.

The opening of the swing road bridge was time-linked to a locked basin which has to be negotiated (get the times from a local harbour master). Yachts gather in some mood of competition before opening time since it is fairly apparent that once through the bridge there is unlikely to be any overtaking. The gathering tension, however, was dispersed when a Vannes Harbour Master's launch arrived to allocate places for all before we were even allowed through the bridge. (On a later occasion there was no Harbour launch, but a loud hailer from bridge control gave each passing vessel a berth number.)

The yacht pool (previously a busy commercial basin) is very organised and pleasant and right in the heart of the medieval town. The old town is well worth a visit just in its own right. We went to a concert of baroque music in the cathedral where a mixed choir of 150 and a quality orchestra with soloists to match filled the vast place with the sound and fury of Vivaldi and friends. There are many places to eat but you can do a lot worse than the restaurant over the top of the harbour master's office. (There's even an internet link you can use.)

From Vannes we dropped down with the ebb to look for the open moorings which tuck into the south side of the Ile d'Atz at Cale de Pen Raz. Anchoring would have been easy but we were seduced by available and very professional looking (visitor?) mooring buoys. If we had stayed to our anchor we could have enjoyed a walk ashore to explore the little island and its small village. But that waits us next time we visit. A comfortable, scenic and fine weather evening and night was spent with great pleasure. Around us lay wooded islands of all sizes with masts tucked into every little cove. The shore fringe is estuarine and so there is rock and weed aplenty – but also white beaches inviting a dinghy-driven swimming party. Shallow acres are taken by oyster farms whose metal racks emerge as the tide falls. Private yachts, dinghies and public ferries criss-cross the water lanes and gaff-dun-sailed wooden veterans of the water work their passage between the islands. There is always something to watch. And it all falls quiet at night when the only sound is the occasional call of a sea bird or of a hunting owl over the woods. The faint slap of wind driven wavelets on the hull is a lullaby before sleep. The boat lies quiet to the mooring and during the night will silently swing to the changing tide.

And so we sailed on (with the tide, of course) to the only serviced pontoons of which we were aware in the Morbihan itself. These lay at the north end of the Ile aux Moines at the Pointe de Rechauds which we had passed on the way to Vannes. There are two short pontoons with water and electricity, detached from the shore and serviced by free water taxis during the hours of daylight. The pontoons can be well used. We welcomed a youngster-filled Glenans sail training yacht beside us; another fell alongside them but we protested when a third tried to fall outside those two to the great amusement of other French neighbours. The young sailors all piled ashore across our deck, but were no trouble.

The Glenan Sailing School may be well known to people who sail the western coastlines of France. But their origins may now not be so well known. The Iles de Glenan are a small archipelago which lies off the south west Brittany coast, not so far from Benodet. The school and the tradition were established in 1947 by previous French Resistance workers for French youngsters. The tradition was a very Spartan one with simple open boats being used to slip around the coast as well as act as tented accommodation at night. All 'services' were basic but the seamanship taught was absolutely thorough and very French. ("Engines? What's wrong with a good sculling oar?"). For the last 40 years we have been meeting these simple, basic craft with their informal young crew (and skippers) around the coastline – invariably good humoured, courteous and knowledgeable. The Glenan Way has been celebrated in sailing instruction manuals over the years. Now, however, this delightful group had a boat with a cabin roof on! But otherwise they weren't much changed.

Ile aux Moins is the largest in the Morbihan and well populated. The small town of Locmiquel was a local delight and a pleasant fifteen minute up-hill walk. A general store, fresh fruit and veg stalls, the inevitable boulangerie and bars all served to keep food lockers and morale topped up. From here we walked across the island with its ancient stone cottage corners, colour crammed old gardens and endlessly fascinating water fringe. We even stumbled across an impromptu Brittany country dance group on a remote headland. Our chosen mooring also has the ferry link with the mainland and is a calling off place for the trans-Morbihan vidette.

Busy, for sure, but we didn't mind that. (It all falls quiet at night). We topped up our freezer, water tanks and walking legs as we hiked the island.

That evening we ate very well at the unprepossessing-looking 'Chez Charlemagne' on the waterfront. It is an old sailors' bar; and still looks that way but also produces very satisfactory grub. We paid pontoon fees of 22 euros per night which rivalled big brother Crouesty. But then, we enjoyed it more.

From the Pointe de Rechauds we had a short but enjoyable sail to Lamor-Baden. We last visited this place some 40 years ago, camping close by and sailing our mirror dinghy from the sandy fringe. As we picked up a visitors' buoy we felt quite nostalgic. The anchorage is well sheltered by the mainland close to the north, the Ile Gavrinis to the south and Ile de Berder to the East. The inevitable trip ashore explored the immediate port area but also led us via the low-water causeway to the (private but welcoming) tree-clad Ile de Berder. A scramble, a beach, a refreshing swim all led to a good appetite aboard (smoked duck and new potatoes) and a sun-filled evening cockpit.

From Lamor-Barden it is only a short sail (on the flood) round the headland, between Ile Renaud and Grand Vezid and then threaded between Sept Iles and le Grand Huernic before heading north up the Riviere d'Auray. The wind was fickle but the tide was a help and with patience we slowly worked our passage. Navigation is all eyeball stuff and fun and satisfying. Off to starboard lies the little Riviere du Bono where we lay between fore-and-aft buoys and dinghied ashore. It is an attractive little town lying on higher land falling down a steep little hill to the old tidal harbour. An extensive art exhibition/market on the quay delayed our walk ashore. Once in the small centre a pavement café (and a totally mad/effete waiter) served us family Sunday lunch before we walked a distance along the river's edge. On the cards were a pre-prandial swim (there's no stopping Jacky), a quiet night and a departure the next day for Auray.

The final approach to Auray involves a 14 m clearance bridge which we could pass with yards to spare. But I stopped short, picking up for-and-aft visitors' moorings from which we again dinghied ashore with no trouble and over no great distance. There are those who swear by sailing right in to the old stone harbour basin to share its historic atmosphere. I confess I was as glad we had stayed out of the complications and congestion and was happy to visit by dinghy.

Both Bono and Auray are well worth the effort with Auray being much the bigger town. It has a larger historic harbour overlooked by a beautiful C16/17th frontage; and an impressive medieval bridge and superb old streets running up to a C19th town centre. The Morbihan attracts restored and historic sailing fishing and trading vessels which gravitate to the older harbours like Auray when not gracing the open waters. Eat on the waterfront and you might even meet the delightful French couple who gave us so much advice and offered hospitality. But avoid Jacky's boiled tick salad.... (thought to be baby calamari ?).

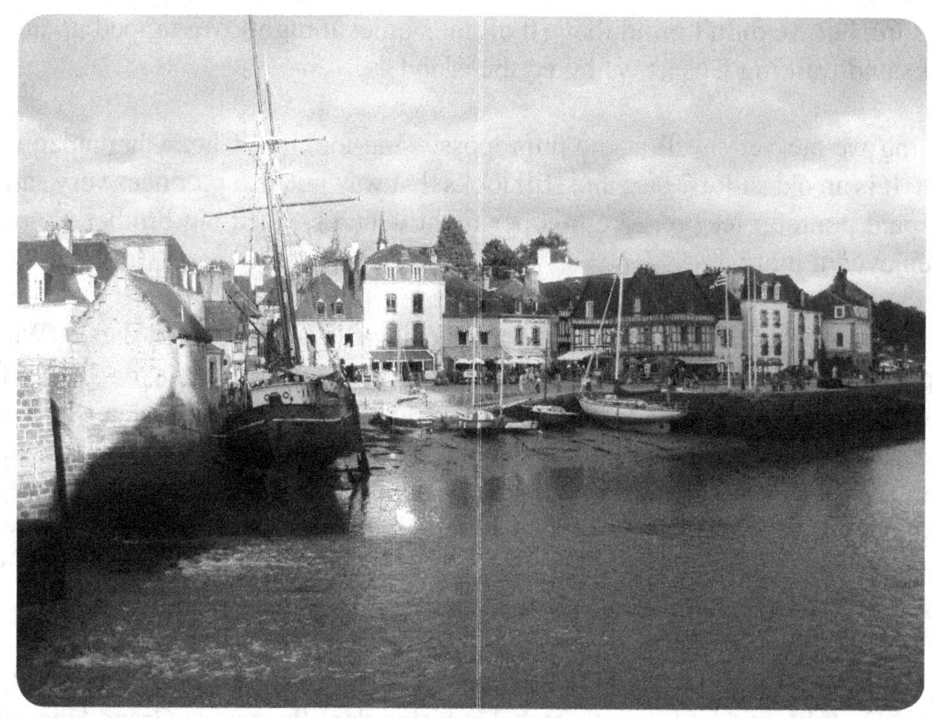

Port Auray

We will most certainly return to the Morbihan to revisit these places and enjoy other corners of this delightful little sea. It was time now to drop back on the ebb to Crouesty, top up the freezer, fuel, water and food. Time to go coastal again so the next day saw us in a sleigh ride of an ebb tide sail to Crouesty through a heavy swell off Port Navalo. We had a family appointment back in the Vilaine, but not before we had looked in on la Trinité.
La Trinité is a famous and distinguished sailing centre with an attractive river approach (Riviere de Crac'h). The marina pontoons lie behind a timber palisade breakwater. With winds in the south this gives insufficient protection, and we had 40 knots over the deck from the SE ! Gusts funnelling up the river shook and bounced the marina craft, especially at high water. After a blustery and noisy night (why don't French tie back their halliards ?) the wind moderated, we left and headed back east again toward the Vilaine.

You are not obliged to go straight back to the barrage. It is possible to put into Penerf which is about half way to the barrage. It is a little estuary with some moorings and anchoring ground. There is a small fisherman's chapel but not much else to attract. Then there is the Billiers estuary just at the entrance to the Vilaine. It is very pretty and hosts a small fleet of local vessels lying to fixed moorings carefully placed in the channel. When all dries out you then see the steep mud and sandy banks that fringe the river. If you want to go there it would pay to have a careful look at low water by car.

On the move

A much more attractive proposition is to accept a pleasant sun-drenched sail to our old friend, the delightful Piriac. We always enjoy this town and port and the beach walk with a late season scatter of sand worshippers. Here we saw again a slim, fair haired girl in a distinctive red dress calling "Beignet; ChouChou; Glaces". She seemed to have difficulty with her trolley in soft sand.
"I think I'll just give her a hand".
"Don't think it's necessary" said Jacky.

The rising (and falling) sill does not get in the way of the departure to the Vilaine which needs to be taken with the benefit of some flood both to give you a helpful push and stop you ploughing a furrow in the bottom. So that's what we did.

Piriac to the Vilaine barrage was another gentle sail and even produced a few mackerel on the line. ….

Encore du vin rosé, M'sieur, s'il vous plait ?

Chapter 17

Vilaine and La Roche Bernard

The River Vilaine is some 225 km long; no mean river. At its exit into the open estuary the barrage at Arzal retains the freshwater reservoir (see also chapter 16) some 25 miles long as far as Redon. At Redon the navigable river accesses the Nantes-to-Brest Canal and the trans-Brittany canal which exits near St Malo. It also accesses the canal system that reaches as far as Le Mans. Sadly the Nantes-Brest canal, although under restoration, apparently in 2008 was not navigable throughout and the St Malo link only coped with maximum of 1.2 m. draft. (We are 1.4m.). Charter 'peniche' are available on the inland waterway system and may occasionally be seen down-stream as far as Azal.

The barrage was conceived in 1936. Work was not started until the 1960's and completed in 1970. The barrage has a lock which normally handles leisure traffic although there appears to be one sand dredger based in Redon which frequently works the nearby coastline. The Vilaine management are, naturally, very keen on water purity. Holding tanks are encouraged and may 'soon' become a requirement both here and for other French sheltered waters. Pumping out facilities exist at La Roche Bernard. Anti-fouling practices and waste oil disposal are the subject of Authority guidelines. There is a very useful booklet handed out which gives advice as well as schedules times of the barrage lock and the swinging bridge at Cran.

The barrage is crossed by a road which opens with a lifting bridge. This device crosses over the lock itself and so only when the bridge is up can the whole lock be used for fixed mast vessels. When you are going up don't despair if the lock seems full on approach, if the bridge is not raised then there is another 30% of space still to go. The lock seems capable of taking up to 30 boats at a time, depending on size and the fierce directions of Dominique, the eclusier. ("If that's how you handle your boat, why don't you play football?"). There are waiting facilities on both sides of the lock.

Port d'Arzal has two marinas, one on each side of the river. Most of the support services appear to be on the Arzal town side (i.e. north) including restaurants and (amongst other services) a large USHIP chandlery. We secured alongside for an hour and the restaurant overlooking the lock produces excellent pizzas. August nightly fees are 15 euros. It is notable that fees are less within the Vilaine presumably reflecting the perceived inconvenience of the barrage. There are secure wintering options both ashore and afloat.

The five miles to La Roche Bernard (LRB) is between high and wooded banks. Roche Bernard is set on a rocky bluff with the 'Old Port' tucked into a short arm on the southern side. The newer marina space is along the south bank of the main river.

The lock at Arzal

* * *

Westerly winds can funnel along this stretch making the western end of the marina pontoons surprisingly exposed. These are the visitors' berths. There was one occasion when we wanted more shelter and the Harbour Master very readily offered us temporary use of a more sheltered, vacant permanent berth. The only thing that woke us early the next morning was a repeated hard knocking on the hull toward the stern. It seemed that the normal occupier of the berth would be up early feeding the only goose on the river. The goose's powerful beak on the transom would protest if breakfast were late.

In the middle of these river moorings there is a water activity centre which, one imagines, is at its busiest in the school holidays. Of course we enjoyed watching the French doing what they really do best: i.e. getting very small youngsters onto the water no matter how small, apparently no matter the weather. These are ideal conditions being fairly sheltered and non-tidal. Even so the commitment of both the young adult instructors and their very young clients was impressive. No wonder the French 'do sailing' pretty well.

By contrast the old port can be very sheltered – but also swelteringly hot on a summer's day (what's one of those?). Long before the barrage, LRB was a busy, but tidal, trading and fishing port around which grew a very attractive town. It is still the destination of many visitors, by boat and otherwise. Close to the town is the fast N165 / E60 highway with the sky-high Morbihan Bridge (clearance 50m) crossing the ravine. Also with the same clearance is the newer Roche Bernard Bridge and the stone buttress remains of an earlier bridge.

The Old Port, La Roche Bernard.

I spoke to the Harbour Master M. Sygogneau. He told me that the marina has some 500 berths mostly on pontoons and a full range of support services. Contrary to gossip, there was no quota on British boats in the marina and no attempt to limit their number. In 2008 there were about 20% British permanent berth holders although the numbers might rise in the summer with casual visitors who are never turned away. (Well nearly never). The marina, like many others in France, is a municipal funded venture that has to be commercial to cover its costs (there are no revenue subsidies) but whose tariff rates are controlled. In 2008 a maximum of 2% tariff up-grade per annum was allowed. A trading 'surplus' is expected which is reinvested into the facilities.

During the peak season permanent berth holders are offered a free lift out to release space for casual visitors. In 2008 there was a 4-5 year waiting list to get a permanent berth but the Authority requires the Management to make a significant number of berths available each year on a six months contract. Applications for such berths must be made each year in July and the allocation is made in the December. There is a federation of coastal ports between Rochelle and Benodet which allows a free (but limited) inter-use of berths between permanent holders using the invaluable issued 'Morbihan Passport'.

We found LRB to be a friendly, very attractive town with a long and busy history. We were greatly welcomed by French people – yachtsmen and trade folk alike. (And why not ? We had money to spend !). The harbour management was helpful as was English-speaking (well anyway, a bit) M. Gerard Quidort of the local boat yard.

A very excellent street market takes over the centre on a Thursday and we could find there almost anything of use. Of course the quality of fresh fruit and veg reminded us how much French food is fresh, local and in-season. Hot food is also prepared and the Vietnamese stall sold (not very local) delicious solutions to our cockpit lunch where we were happy to carry that eastern aroma with us.

Madame Jacqueline of café 'Le Relais' (up the main street, left hand side) was always ready with WIFI and her own Daily Telegraph to go with the excellent coffee. The marina itself has WIFI as do several establishments in town; notably the old waterfront theatre 'Sarah B' (Sarah Bernhart used to live near-by) and the computer shop off the main street on the left hand side going up. Restaurants there are aplenty. Up the main street on the right hand side there is the 'Belle Epoque', a simple town café for good and unpretentious grub. In the central square there is the 'Café du Vieux Quartier' for good French food. A plaque nearby tells explicitly where Mme. Guillotine was located; and why. A little more special (but not bank breaking) is the excellent floating restaurant on the waterfront and the 'Panoramique', a roadside restaurant just on the north side of the Roche Bernard Bridge and looking across and down the river.

The Old Port is dominated by a huge rock (hence the name) which towers over the old port entrance. Steep paths climb up behind the Harbour Office to the high bluff overlooking the river and the new moorings. At the most prominent spot a cannon has been mounted which controls the main river approach. No doubt early morning yachties slipping away without paying can be dealt with. The climbing footpaths continue towards the town centre where we found a small local museum. We enjoyed an hour browsing through the recent and distant past of the town and its port.

The cannon emplacement was a pretty good spot for us to see the 14th July evening fireworks. They naturally don't start until dark which is quite late in France in July. But we sat with a gathering little crowd of picnicking neighbours patiently waiting the hour and sharing the bottle. It's always a good place to see the river, the great Morbihan Bridge in one direction and the winding, tree-frowned silver strip making its way to the sea in the other. Evening shadows drained the landscape of colour as the sky fell dark. Suddenly from the base of the far buttress of the great bridge huge rockets split the sky and another French memory to the great Revolution was under way. The French do love the 14th of July even though there was no one in that stormed Bastille. But that needn't stop you having a good time.

Before our guests arrived there was just time for a further trip by car. On entry into La Roche Bernard there is a sign which announces 'La Petite Citie de Characteur'. This indicates that it is part of a designated group of perhaps eight small towns of particular historic quality within the 'Departement'. Also included are the very lovely towns of Rochefort-en-Terre and Gacilly. The latter has an impressive international outdoor photographic exhibition which we had to see.

So indeed Rochfort-en-Terre proved to be delightful and unspoilt by modern development with an historic central square dominated by C17th and C18th buildings, beautifully maintained and enhanced by a riot of colourful planting. (The French really make the very best use of geraniums!)

Cannon emplacement, Roche Bernard

There are good eateries and interesting local shops and galleries and, of course, many visitors. The visitor impact has its own downside as shops and galleries seek to meet a popular taste. Still, it is a town well worth a visit.

We did some pleasant walks from the town which is dominated by a fine chateau on the highest point. The grounds of the chateau are open (and free) and well worth a visit if only for the sweeping long views over the nearby countryside. The C18th Chateau itself replaces a C15th castle of which there are few remains. It is understood that the chateau was in desperately poor condition at the end of the C19th when it was discovered by a wealthy American family who fell in love with the area, bought the chateau and lived there for most of the C20th . A major restoration job was done and the family established an annual, international artists' summer school. It is understood that it is now in university hands and the Summer School tradition certainly continued until fairly recently. There are two small exhibitions of memorabilia and art work open to the public and the buildings themselves are open at times (timetable available from the Tourist Bureau).

Gacilly is also well worth a visit. From its (unremarkable) town centre runs an artisan quarter down the hill to the river and the local Yves Rocher family firm. Yves Rocher are now global manufacturers of natural beauty products. It was founded here and sought to use local herbs and flowers in the production of a 'natural' product. There was at least one influential mayor of Gacilly from the family and as a result the historic townscape and community importance of the artisan quarter was recognised. The family already had property ownership in the old quarter and they persuaded (and no doubt helped) the purchase of most or all of the 'quarter' so that it fell into Town/Trust ownership. It was then restored and held for 'artisan' occupation and to be managed for the community benefit. It is now a beautiful group of small streets and alleys of the C16, C17 and C18 running down the hill and with great views over the countryside.

Arising from this background, the area became host to a number of small artistic workshops and from that arose the concept (and execution) of an outdoor photographic exhibition which has now become of international importance. The exhibition occupies a number of the galleries and open spaces with fairly traditional and themed presentations. What is absolutely exceptional, however, is the tradition that has emerged of using many of the open spaces, structures and facades for photographic prints some on a large scale. My memory and impression is that some could perhaps be of 10m x 8m (big for these modest streets) making a huge impact on the street and river scene.

We walked to the Yves Rocher factory which is at the bottom of this town hill fronting the river and set in fields cultivated for the ingredients of the beauty products. We were able to explore a 'jardin botanique' adjoining the factory, laid out to display the plants and flowers of interest. We also got involved with an interactive display within the factory of the research and development of perfumes and creams over the years and, indeed, currently widely marketed.

Go and see for your selves, you won't regret it !

* * *

Anyway, La Roche Bernard was a good place for non-sailing guests, Jacky's sister Peta, partner Dennis and 4-year-old Josh (we met them all in southern Spain) were to join us. After a couple of days we all took off for Foleux, five miles up stream. Foleux is divided between the south bank boatyard and the north bank or Foleux Beganne yard and marina. Both yards will winter vessels although I understand that the south bank will not take bilge keelers (us). This winter will therefore be our second year ashore in Foleux Beganne. The marina is small, perhaps 100 modest boats, mostly locals. The yard takes perhaps 150 boats ashore and (English speaking) M. Jean-Francois Renou provides basic yard services, getting specialists in for work he can't do himself. A very pleasant restaurant with a basic menu is run by the affable M. and Mme. Pascal. Some touring boats prefer the rural quiet of Foleux to the more bustling and touristy LRB. Baguettes and croissant, however, can only be found three miles away in the village of Beganne – unless specially ordered from the Harbour Master's office the day before. We stayed awhile with our guests enjoying beautifully settled weather and a few impromptu water sports involving the inflatable dinghy, lifejackets and swimming before moving further up-stream.

Our next destination was the even-more-rural stop at the village of Rieux, perhaps 6 km short of Redon. On the way there is the swinging bridge at Cran which opens according to a timetable available from any local harbourmaster. Don't be late; the man doesn't wait ! At Cran there is a restaurant of some fame for its value-for-money approach. We went one evening to 'sus' it out and found it disappointing in cuisine and almost empty. Perhaps it's a lunch time event.

From Cran, Rieux is perhaps 3 km and here there are two pontoons of possibly ten berths each. At a busy time boats will double up. Water and electricity are available for those who can reach. The small village is 10 minutes walk away and this year a very pleasant pontoon-side café/bar has been created from earlier derelict buildings. The facilities are pleasantly shared with an adjacent camping site and the whole provides a very pleasing rural interlude. Really good when it's nasty the other side of the barrage. We swam and did watery things and picnicked on the generous grassy areas.

Redon is a commercial town with an ex-commercial basin in its centre now laid out for yachts. We did not find it comfortable or very welcoming so on this occasion it was not for us. However we did visit (by car) the 'routier' cafe by the canal connection which will give you an unrivalled lunch. Dear reader, you probably know all about the French 'routier' tradition, but let me explain to those who don't.

The format is aimed to appeal to commercial drivers, or indeed anyone else who fancies joining in. They might be found anywhere and we found several village sites, but they may often be in an industrial location where there is parking for heavy vehicles. The general style is that you pay a set price on entering which includes table wine and, on Saturdays, may be slightly increased to include an aperitif presumably to cater for the social as opposed to the commercial clients. The first course is a cold collation buffet and those we have seen are generous in both volume and quality. There seems no check on those returning again to the buffet and in truth that could be your complete meal. However there is then a choice of three or four simple main courses; some basic dessert choice (help yourself from the cold cabinet) with coffee perhaps as an extra. Accompanying the meal would be an automatic one litre of red which, in our experience, can be freely swapped for white or rosé on request. The wine is basic but drinkable. Commercial drivers seem to respect this and alcohol consumption by them seemed very moderate.

Typically the price might be 12E per head (or 15E on Saturday evenings). From Roche Bernard there were three within reasonable reach (if you had a car) and the favourite could be found off the E60 to Vannes; take the left hand turn (D139) at the big roundabout heading toward Arzal; almost immediately the 'Routier' might be seen in the adjoining industrial estate on your right hand side. Warning: if you go there once you may want to go again.

* * *

So with our guests we made our way back to Foleux and their hire car. The summer was coming to an end, the days getting shorter but before we could get away, Jacky reminded me

"There is one more event to recognise".
"Really ? What's that ?"
Our forty-third wedding anniversary. And no mackerel or beheaded thon, thanks."

"And no fierce women with fireman's hoses either. Got any ideas?"
"Well yes." said Jacky, predictably. "I hear that there's a rather nice place at Penlan in Billiers called 'Hotel la Vilainfrelais'." (Where does she get this information from?).
"Sounds good to me. We could at least go and have a look".
We had our car so we motored westwards along the north bank of the Vilaine estuary.

Billiers is a short distance inland on a drying inlet, clearly an old, very local fishing port. At the sea entrance to the inlet is a site of a previous priory near which has been built the Vilainfrelais Hotel. Use appears to have been made of architectural remnants to re-create an 'historic' atmosphere. Whatever its origins there has been created a number of apartments and support accommodation, set in beautiful gardens and on the edge of a rocky promontory overlooking the estuary and open sea. I guess we could have sat on our balcony for another week just soaking up the late summer sun and the view and watching small vessels negotiating the Vilaine entrance.

There were, however, alternatives so Jacky enjoyed a massage experience and I walked to see the inlet with a view to future use. (It has a small stream running through which has carved out its own steep sided channel, only visible at low water. It's really only for the brave or very knowledgeable). And we ate well (surprise, surprise) and drank to another 43 years. The wine waiter insisted on choosing our wines for each course. When we commented that we did not recognise the vineyard, he just said enigmatically "Well you wouldn't, would you". It was, of course, delicious.

Do go and see for yourselves.

* * *

So back to *Wise One* in Foleux. We haven't talked about the many friends we made. Perhaps the Vilaine is designed for this with French and many Brits spending a chunk of the summer in and around the estuary. They do tend to be 'of an age' when they have the leisure time and can place their boat away from home. Mid-sized Moodies and Westerlies are a common sight. Owners are grey haired, wrinkly, brown, fit and relaxed. The evening cockpit sees red wine consumed and many a tall tale spun. (Suspend disbelief and just enjoy it). Friends are made quickly and generously shared, along with information about sailing/weather/place/family. It is sometimes difficult to keep up with people who are typically known by three names: his, hers, the boat's.

"Isn't that James and Ann from '*Blue* Water'?".
"No, no. It's James and Mary from '*Seven Seas*'."
" I thought Mary was with Bill on '*Yogi Bear*'".
"Can't be; anyway '*Yogi Bear*' was a 40' cat. and Bill's got a Westerly."
"So who was on *'Draught Dodger'?"*.
" I dunno. But he couldn't have been British".

Thanks of course therefore to Chris and Sue, Roger and Verity, Bill and Ann and many others generous with their wine and advice.

Certainly more of that next year. But now the evenings were beginning to draw in and temperatures drift gently downwards. We were reminded that Brittany has a real winter and boats need to be well protected from hard frost, particularly those wintering ashore. We were told that the previous winter had seen the (freshwater) Vilaine ice over so be sure that your own vessel is well prepared !

But, with all preparations made it was time to go; we once again had an appointment with a crane. Leaving the boat for a period is always a bit fraught with a great deal to do. As we eventually motored off for the ferry, there was a little tense silence in the car. Some miles down the road and justifying my own labours, I said:
"Well at least I turned off the gas, last thing". Jacky said:
"And so did I "....

In the meantime "Deux rosé, (encore) s'il vous plait Monsieur !

Readers' Notes

Part 5
Summer 2009 The Quiberon Islands
The Circumnavigation (alors)!

In which we find the Celts, explore the Baie de Quiberon, have a brush with the Natives

and *<u>complete the circumnavigation !!</u>*

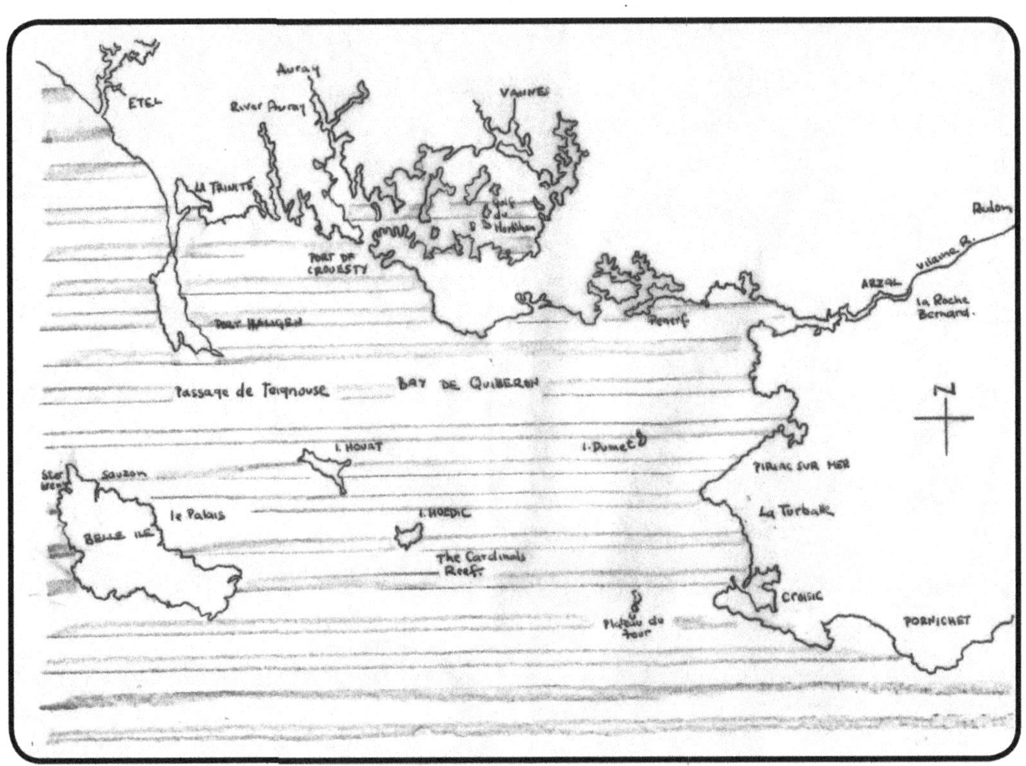

Map 6: Baie de Quiberon

Chapter 18

A bit about the sea-faring Celts and others (or 'The last of the Amoricans' ?).......... And some thoughts on early sea travel.

Woody Allen said that "eternity goes by awfully slowly. Especially towards the end." So it must be relevant to say just a few words about Celtic Brittany since the Celts, after all, are still around. We found a huge awareness of the Celtic tradition across Brittany, perhaps particularly in coastal areas. Wherever older boats were gathered together, there would be contingents from the Six Nations, i.e. Scotland, Wales, Cornwall, Ireland, Basque and Brittany. They would fly a complex burgee which was a combination of all six emblems. So what about the Celts ?

Until the expansion of the German tribes and the Roman Empire, most of Europe was dominated by the Celtic cultural traditions. But slowly the Celts were pushed to the edges of Europe and Brittany itself is now seen as one of the six Celtic 'nations'. If there could be a capital town of the Celtic Veneti it would probably be Vannes at the head of the Morbihan Sea. So the Veneti were the Celtic sea-faring people who lived in Brittany before the Roman invasion and the Romans called the peninsular 'Amorica'. In reading up Celtic history I find references to both the Veneti and the Amoricans and the difference between seems to be that the 'Amoricans' are simply the Celts who lived in Roman occupied Brittany.

Anyway, I have found one reference to Veneti retreating to Britain from Roman occupation in 56 BC and occupying Maiden Castle. This was not a theory supported by the Dorset CC Archaeological Unit. It does seem clear, however, that there were Iron Age ports at Hengisbury Head, in Poole Harbour and in Portland. There is archaeological opinion that " it is not inconceivable that the settlement at Ower was established by Amorican refugees".

A lot seems unsaid here. Refugees don't settle easily into an established rural community. Perhaps they landed in force and took (and held) enough land to support themselves. Certainly to leave behind an archaeological record they must have been there in numbers and in family units. Clearly we can assume that cross-channel Celtic trade was well established before the arrival of the Romans or Phoenicians who travelled into Cornwall for tin (or tin ore?). And that people from Brittany used that knowledge to retreat from Roman occupation in Gaul.

Where is this bit of historical diversion leading us ? Well, it's clear that before the Roman invasion of Britain, the short seaways were not regarded as barriers, but rather as routes of (fairly) safe passage. There were competent Celtic craft which certainly gave the invading Roman navy a very hard time in Southern Brittany in 56 BC. We know from modern small boat travels that very simple craft can safely cover long ocean distances. But, to go back a bit, in 600 BC the Greek historian Herodotus tells us that the Phoenicians circumnavigated Africa. (A replica Phoenician vessel, the Phoenicia, is currently recreating that voyage). Another Greek historian, Diodorus, reported in 100 BC that the Carthaginians knew of a large land far out in the Atlantic. Coins made in Carthage in the period 350-320 BC are said to show a map of Europe with a land mass across the Atlantic. And there are other claims all generally discounted in favour of Columbus, Da Gama, Magellan and Cabot. Clearly the Phoenicians, the Romans, the Arabs, the Indians and (later) Scandinavians and Venetians all had very competent sea going vessels. The C15th Venetian boats, for example, could be up to 150 feet in length and carry 50 tons of freight.

Let us just take this a little further. It seems now generally accepted that the Chinese were trading across the Indian Ocean in vessels up to 200 feet in length in the first century AD. and by the C15th it is claimed that their trading vessels were up to 400 ft in length. There has recently been a 60 foot Ming dynasty replica junk, the Princess Tai Ping, (built with C15th techniques and materials) that happily covered 17,000 miles of Pacific Ocean visiting Japan, Hawai and the west coast of America. Sadly it was cut in half by a freighter within sight of Su Ao, Taiwan, its destination. The organisers, however, claim that they comfortably demonstrated that the Chinese C15th Admiral Zheng-He could well have rounded the two great Capes as well as landing on the American continent well before the acclaimed European global explorers. There is no need to show that rafts made of reed (Ra), balsa wood (Kon Tiki) or sewn leather (Brendan) could survive extended journeys. Far more competent craft have existed from very early times capable of exploring the oceans of the world and the Celts are a competent part of that maritime tradition.

It is perfectly credible that the powerful European tradition extolling the Spanish and Portuguese as the first global navigators is simply wrong. Evidence ? There is a credible if controversial growth of evidence of early global travel by Chinese fleets and it may be that the current research into global DNA patterns will have some serious surprises for us.

It has been said that " to ignore history is to ignore the wolf at the door". (Pity Blair and Bush didn't know that). The past and the present are always with us, after all who really dies? An actuarist will give you your life expectancy; and when you reach that age will give you another one (etc). The professional view clearly is that we are actually immortal - except for the odd busy moment from that tall, gaunt man with the scythe.

But enough of these historic fantasies. Let's get back to the real world.

Chapter 19

Festival of the Sea

Wise One had spent her second winter in Foleux-Beganne. Now it was early May 2009. I had driven out with a car-load of early-season, all-you-need-to-get-you-going stuff. A couple of days of post-launch labour, a drive across to Rennes airport to pick up Jacky and all was GO.

Contact had been made with Bill and Ann again who had requested a consignment of English tea bags. They had sold *Fai Tira* and bought a near-by rural barn with dwelling potential. We visited to admire their present 'home' which was a mobile unit adjacent to the barn. Optimism is always a valuable trait…

Our first move from La Roche Bernard was to have been back to Crouesty as a jumping off point for Belle Ile (or the Morbihan). However we had business in Crouesty involving the car (small matter of a new outboard motor for the inflatable) and took the opportunity to re-visit 'our' old moorings in the port which we hoped would soon be temporary home. We were taken aback (to use a sailing term) to find that all the visitors' berths were taken up by old gaffers. What was going on? 'Our' spot was occupied by a 40' gentleman's yacht from the 1920's: Marconi rig, varnish by the mile, long over-hung counter, creamy white running rigging, mahogany tiller, and polished brass finishes. Outrageous ! Our berth ! And more: the next berth housed a 1930's gaff rigged yacht and beyond that two old working gaffers. I looked around and realised that we were surrounded by classic yachts, power boats and working craft. The Morbihan was about to start their week of traditional boat festivals across the whole 21 km. inland sea. Some 12 centres would each host their allocated fleet of yawls, working gaffers, classic yachts small or large and early power boats.

During the period of the Festival we were told that the harbour of Crouesty would be closed to visitors and therefore presumably the Morbihan would be very busy. So, one imagines, Auray, Bono, Ile aux Moines and Vannes would be 'full' too. This would then have repercussions on the nearby Trinite and Port Haliguen who would take the overflow. In any case Haliguen was just finishing a major pontoon up-grade and so their state to receive visitors was a bit unknown. There was nothing to prevent a yacht from entering the Morbihan and searching for its own mooring or anchorage, but clearly there was a problem. An added complication was an indifferent weather forecast of a depression, associated fronts, and forces variously 5 to 8 and rain squalls. The best plan seemed to stay put in La Roche Bernard and hit the festival by car.

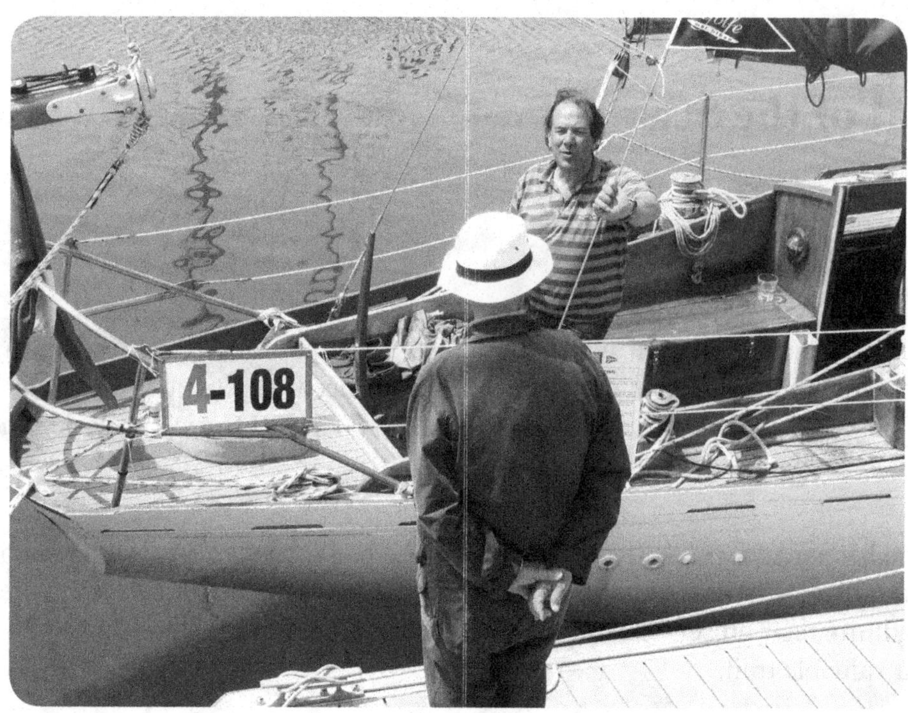

The Festival

The festival is bi-annual. (Brest festival of the Sea is four-yearly and ran last in 2008). This is the Morbihan's fifth event and a 1000 boats are expected to take part (says the blurb). I guess one important difference between Portsmouth and Brest Festivals and the Morbihan event is that the former are based on single port cities and generally you know where to find the vessels. The Morbihan festival is across the 250 sq. km (or so) of the Small Sea and features in some 12 separate locations. We covered over 150 road miles just driving between the centres of Crouesty, Port Navalo, Bono, Auray, Locmariaquer, Port Blanc, Ile-aux-Moines and Vannes, plus several viewing headlands. Going in your own boat is a different experience but you couldn't hope to cover all the centres.

The Festival ran from May 18-24th and the Tourist Office put out detailed events for each day and for each centre. The picture was complicated indeed with craft categorised into seven main groups. These were Yawls, small gaffers, traditional pleasure craft under 8m., classic yachts over 8m., working boats, classic motor boats. And then there were the very large vessels. Each were based on several centres but some gathered during the day and made a tidal descent on one or other of the centres; returning 'home' at night. The Grand Parade was to be an entry into the Morbihan past Port Navalo in four 'managed' flotillas but proceeded by an avalanche of small less-easy-to-marshal little 'uns.

But the events were preceded by near gale force winds and the 18th and 19th were spent with vessels slowly assembling. Port Crouesty was a good place to go to see the assembly since many boats would make a short stop there before organising their tide for a final arrival in their designated port. From the 20th things started swinging; on the 21st and 22nd all sorts of events were held across the Morbihan. The 23rd was the Parade day and the 24th was the slow dispersal day.

The Festival

On Tuesday 19th we went back to Crouesty and enjoyed the assembling Classics. There were many beautiful yachts to admire. The 1922 Italian 45 foot extreme racing machine, pencil thin, Marconi rig, beautifully loved and a thing to admire. Other gentlemens' yachts from the 1930's abounded with TLC. We stopped and chatted with *Aethra* from Marchwood (Southampton Water), busy lunching and looking elegant at the same time. We talked also to *Tom Tit*, an 1890's bespoke yacht sturdily designed with a working boat as its precedent but well restored and gleaming. *Tom Tit* hailed from Keyhaven on the Solent and knew Lymington well.

We then motored to Port Navalo which is a main vidette take off point for Belle Ile and the outer islands. It also hosts the ferry to Locmariaquer and is a (non-pontoon) entry port for the Morbihan. In itself it is an attractive old fishing port with a beautiful cliff-top walk overlooking the main channel and across to Port Locmariaquer on the west bank. This seemed to be the place to be for the Parade. At that very moment the early flood was beginning to run which is the moment of choice to enter the Little Sea heading (perhaps) for Auray, Bono, Vannes or just one of the islands in between.

It was a good moment, therefore, to see the dramatic arrival of a number of classics, small and large. The big, 50m. three masted barques and 45m. schooners were a grand sight but must have been common in the days of deep sea fishing for tuna and sardines. Most extraordinary was the open decked, 40-ish foot, twin masted, ketch-rigged schooner with square-headed lug rig, topsail on the pole masts, an upper mast taking a further square headed top sail above the first tops'l. And, of course, an outrageous bowsprit to carry flying jibs. Was this the place to see the Parade or would it be too congested ?

We drove on to the near-by Point du Mouton at Bilgroix and found a cliff-top grassy sward absolutely designed for boat watching; but with limited parking. Wàs this for us ? Blanket, red wine, filled baguette, camera, field glasses ? Maybe!

The Festival

On Wednesday 20th the programme suggested that entertainment would begin to hot up in most places. We drove to Auray where there is a beautiful old port absolutely designed to show off and enhance working boats. We enjoyed a beer in the sun but – no boats! Perhaps they were all out on the water showing off what they do best. Perhaps the rebuilding of the quay wall had something to do with it. (It'll be good next year). We drove on to Port Blanc.

Now Port Blanc is a very small port near Lamor-Barden and is the ferry port for the ever popular Ile-aux-Moines. This was clearly (from the programme) the primary base for the larger vessels, although probably not lying alongside. We went to see. We had been curious as to why the several large vessels (20 to 50 m.) were all allocated to Port Blanc or Ile-aux-Moines. Space could perhaps have been found alongside for them in Crouesty where crowds could have seen them close to (or even gone on board); or on buoys in Port Navalo. Within the Morbihan itself there is little space really convenient and easily accessible for these larger vessels. However the waters off Ile-aux-Moines and Port Blanc (really the same stretch of open water) was where they could all lie within tourist view and in deep water at all states of the tide.

So we saw the not-too-distant sight of a number including the British three masted barques Kaskelot and the Earl of Pembroke, the popular 32m. langoustie Krog E Barz and the big 50m Dutch three master Oosterschelde. (And others we couldn't identify from the shore). They lay in the beautiful setting of the Little Sea with its many low lying, tree-clad island and busy sails and the background sound of a group singing Celtic songs. The Celtic connection was a constant theme with boats from all the six Celtic 'Nations' and the combined Celtic burgee much in evidence.

On the morning of the 21st we drove to Port Anna where the programme had led us to believe that yawls and working boats would *leave* at 1730; i.e. they must be there all afternoon at least. The very pretty Port Anna is on the Riviere du Vincin approach to Vanne. It is tidal and deep in the wooded estuary. The tide was out, (we should have known that) and the foreshore estuarine mud and shingle well scattered with local small-craft moorings. The quayside tents were up clearly for food and dancing, but where were the historic boats and the people? "Ce soir" they said. We were about eight hours too early; just in time to drive beyond Vanne, out onto the peninsular to Port Locmariaquer and the alternative viewing headland for the Parade.

Locmariaquer is, again, a most attractive old fishing port and small town close to the Navalo Channel but on the west bank. Its tidal foreshore was well covered with local boats resting at peace on the shingle. The broad sweep of the Morbihan lay before us - quite covered in sails of all colours, sizes and ages in every direction. There really was only one option remaining and before very long we were aboard a heavy, fast power boat heading for the action. (If you can't beat 'em etc. etc.).

There followed a delightful trip across the Navalo Channel, past Ile Longue, around the Ile d'Arz and back to Ile-aux-Moines where we landed for an hour. We revisited haunts of last year when we spent an enjoyable couple of days exploring. The festival flotillas were all out as were many, many non-classic yachts just enjoying the old boats and a sunny May day on the Morbihan. Many (too many) photos were taken of tall rigging and spars and old timbers and gleaming varnish and dun-coloured sails and blinding white canvas all on dappled sea stirred by those sweeping currents and backed up by no-go areas of oyster beds and mussel farms and …and ..(well, and *everything*). On returning to Locmariaquer we jumped into the car and headed back to Port Anna.

The evening sky was totally clear and the sun still quite hot. The remote car park in Port Anna left us with a walk across the fields towards the river and along a well wooded cliff track towards the little harbour. The tide was now high and the harbour front was now packed with 25 to 35 foot open yawls, brightly rigged and gleaming with varnish. The heavy poles of gaff-rigged working boats broke the skyline. Sailors in rust-red smocks and rust-red faces mingled with 'beaking' and rubber-necking sight-seers in crowds of hundreds. Black bulwarks, battle flags, burgees, and buntings bedecked the Port from cliff top to sun-reflecting harbour water.

Tented stalls were churning out mass-delivered plates of food and bottles of rude red. Trestles under open-sided canvas were set across the sloping quayside giving some uncertainty as to whether all would not gently slide down the long table and into the (now high) water. But it didn't. And hundreds sat shoulder to shoulder - grannies and children, grandpas and tourists, hoary sailors and deck monkeys with whom we shared a couple of bottles of modest red. Celtic music on the Big Stage could not compete with rising volume of chat, shouted (smiling) ruderies, encouragement or rivalry exchanged and clear boating untruths proclaimed ("bigger, faster, quicker and all in a force 8 and rising"). And not one English voice heard. Generally speaking and all in all, pretty good really.

Feast at Port Anna

The next day was the 23rd and the day of the Parade. We woke aboard *Wise One* in Roche Barnard to the sound of steady rain. It was 'stair rods' as we sorted and loaded water-proofs and wellies. The windscreen wipers worked hard as we drove to the Pointe du Mouton. We parked a walking distance to the viewing field. An ex-Royal Naval Officer once said to me that the two most useless things on a small boat were an Admiral and an umbrella. I won't have that said about the umbrella which was invaluable as we chose a spot just over the cliff edge and a little sheltered from the wet easterly.

Hopeful crowds were slowly gathering as, at 1400 hours, the rain stopped and an avalanche of classic and elderly small craft poured out of Crouesty and Port Navalo (where they had been assembling all morning) and streamed past us led by a vigorously paddled Viking ship. Bizaar but true. For half an hour they sailed/powered/paddled past us – perhaps in excess of 300 in number – keeping us well entertained with a variety of miniature sprits, yawls, little schooners, sail assisted rowing boats, dipping lugs, little cutters, topsail gaffers, bumkins, bowsprits and bobstays. (Everything except a dhow or a junk. Where were the Arabs and Chinese?).

From 1500 hrs the heavy skies lifted, waterproofs were peeled off and the 8m plus vessels came through. They should have been in four categories at quarter hour intervals, but that wasn't very apparent. Since our arrival on the cliff top we had seen the three masted square and schooner rigged 'biggies' out on the horizon waiting to time their entry. For an hour and a half we were now entertained by a steady stream of extreme racing machines from the 1920s; heavy lug-sailed local barges from the 1900's; gentlemen's yachts designed on fishing or pilot boat precedent; fleet mail boats beautifully restored; big tunnymen and sardineries; or just owner's pride and joy lovingly kept with buckets of TLC.

The Festival

Most popular with our crowd (now packing the green behind us) was the 32m. langoustier Krog E Barz, a gaffer with a mighty 'widow maker' bow sprit. She came across to our cliff space, spun round with flying jib backing hard, curtsied and bobbed to cheers and waves before working her way back up-stream. Its all true and captured on camera by a news helicopter missing not one moment, wave or smile.

But what on earth do I do with all the photos ?

The Festival

Chapter 20

Baie de Quiberon and the Islands. Summer 2009.

Our 2009 summer target (apart from receiving family and friends) was to get out to the islands; specifically Belle Ile, Houat and Hoedic (plus any other islands that came our way). The first move was to unglue ourselves from the very comfortable Roche Bernard pontoon space, get down stream to Arzal and through the barrage lock. Once out into the estuary our first destination was Crouesty (again) since it provides the entry point into the Morbihan and gives you a good jumping off point for other Baie de Quiberon destinations. Specifically these are Port Haliguen on the Presqu'Ile, le Palais and Sauzon on Belle Ile, La Trinite and Piriac on the mainland and the small Islands of Houat and Hoedic in-between.

Our days were dogged by westerlies. We waited for some southerly or northerly slant and when promised a bit of southerly we took off. The tide was on the make in the estuary and a small flotilla leaving the barrage punched the early flood and – dammit – a westerly on the nose. Perhaps it would back once outside the estuary but sadly it didn't and the day was condemned to a freshening head breeze knocking up a nice little chop which seemed to stop us dead every few minutes.

* * *

The Bay hosted a major sea battle between the great colonial powers of France and Britain in the C18th, it decided which of the European rivals would control the sea. The Battle of Quiberon Bay took place in November, 1789 during the Seven Year War. The French were threatening to invade Britain but their battle fleet was holed up in Brest for some time by a blockading British fleet. The French intention was that their French Channel Fleet would provide safe passage across the Channel for an invasion armada of transporters which were currently lying in safe havens around the French coastline. The Morbihan hosted a number of such vessels which were also being blockaded by British ships. One of the objectives of the French escape from Brest was to challenge the Quiberon blockade. A second objective was to place the French fleet into the more secure port of Rochefort, further down coast.

During a gale, the British withdrew temporarily and the French broke out. Admiral Sir Edward Hawke with 23 Ships-of-the-Line pursued Marshal de Conflans with 21 ship-of-the-lines after the Marshal's escape from Brest. In an extreme NNW gale the French fleet were chased down the coast as they attempted to reach the naval base of Rochefort.

The local coastal communities would have known nothing of the impending events. They would, however, have seen the huge French battleships (five of which carried over 70 guns) approaching Belle Ile under reduced gale rig and ploughing through a confused and rising sea. From the cliffs of western Belle Ile increasingly excited crowds would have speculated on their escape from Brest. Perhaps this was with a rising tide and plenty of water over the shallow reefs; certainly it became clear that they were to enter the Quiberon Bay.

The main body of the British fleet would have been seen on the horizon. But against the howl of the gale the crowds might just have heard the thunder of the distant cannon as the French stragglers entering the Bay were engaged by a few British leading ships. The smoke of battle would have been whipped away by the NNW gale as the chasing British warships, under full sail, bore down on the eastern end of Belle Ile.

The watching crowds would have expected the English to remain outside the turbulent Bay and the French heavy fleet to anchor in the sheltered lee of Belle Ile or Ile de Houat; or even to enter the Morbihan and real safety. But it became clear that Sir Edward Hawke had also ordered the British fleet into the Bay, in pursuit, through the narrows between the Cardinals reef and the Plateau du Four shoals. The implications would rapidly have been clear to everyone. Far from being safe behind their reefs and islands, the Compte de Conflans had put his vessels into a trap. With the enemy snapping at their heels, anchoring was no longer a safe option. Under shortened sail they were slowly driven down-wind across the Bay with the British commanding the windward position and controlling the battle. Crowds would now have gathered on the cliffs of Hoedic and Crouesty and on the battlement of the Citadel in le Palais. The whole Bay could be seen with forty-odd storm tossed ships-of-the-line in close and deadly combat. Anxious watchers would have seen and heard the smoke and thunder of broadsides as the fleets engaged.

As the ships fought, so damaged square riggers struggled to hold their positions against the gale. The whole engagement would have moved eastwards towards the Vilaine and Piriac lee shores until parts of the French fleet could no longer weather the Piriac and Croisic headlands to safety down-coast. This 'embayment' is the square riggers nightmare. The British vanguard veered off to chase the French remnants that were successfully rounding the headland. Those French that couldn't leave the Bay were faced with either anchoring, beaching on a lee shore (certain wreckage) or attempting the Vilaine estuary. By now it must have been low-ish tide, perhaps ebbing, and the Vilaine would have been a shallow and dangerous place.

With no other options, some seven major French ships dumped all their heavy armour overboard to enable them to cross the shallow Vilaine River bar. Crowds on the cliffs at Billiers and the Point de Halguen would have watched as, in crossing the estuary shallows, four grounded and were wrecked. If the tide were now flooding, flotsam and surviving sailors would have drifted up-stream to be rescued by fishing boats putting out from Peneston, Trehiguir and Billiers. If there was still an ebb, then survivors would have been swept out into the storm wracked Bay.

Other ships were destroyed or taken whilst the remaining ten French vessels worked to escape down coast to the naval port of Rochefort. However they were still not out of trouble. As they rounded Piriac to their horror they met the big British Flag ship the Royal George (100 guns) coming into the Bay round the Plateau du Four shoals and were again engaged, suffering considerable damage and more losses. Low tide again claimed victims as one French and two British vessels were lost on the Plateau du Four reef, off Croisic. As night fell and the storm moderated, many of the residues of both fleets anchored between Pirriac and the Ile Dumet and along the shore towards Le Croisic. Only as dawn broke did the French realise their peril and in the scramble to cut anchor and get away, the French Flag ship, Soliel Royal, was lost. In all some eleven major French vessels were captured or totally destroyed and two British ships were lost.

I have seen no record of the lives lost but the total French numbers have been put at 7,100 seamen, 1,500 marines and 2,700 coastguards (pressed or volunteered). On nine of the lost vessels they were said to carry some 4975 sailors. In both fleets skin colour would have shown the multi-racial nature of the men who handled the big guns or hauled on the yard arms; men whose differences paled in death. The human casualties from both sides would have run to thousands. The Bay must have been littered with the floating wreckage of vessels. The shores would have been scattered for months with the sad remains of ships and sailors. The sea bed must still carry the heavy guns and shot of fierce engagement.

The defeat of the French fleet destroyed French plans to invade England or, as a second best, to invade Scotland or Ireland. The disputed control of the seas fell clearly to Britain, significantly damaging the French economy and severely limiting French global colonial ambitions for years.

* * *

But back to us. The fresh Westerly made the 25 miles to Crouesty rather tedious but we got there in the end. Once into Croesty we could relax, make contacts, freeze down the freezer, walk the headland towards Navalo and call in the weather forecasts.

Our next preferred destination was Haliguen on the Quiberon as a launch pad for Belle Ile. It was no more than 12 miles; but dead into a freshening westerly gusting 6 and not a lot of fun. We opted for good old Plan B – often a popular choice. The Navalo Channel into the Little Sea at full flood is always entertaining and reputed to touch 8 knots. The (revised) objective was an old favourite – pontoons at Ile aux Moins. There are not many of the 60-odd Morbihan islands on which you can readily land, but Ile aux Moins has a small indigenous population, a little village and frequent mainland ferries. That was for us. But first we had to skate down the Navalo narrows, past Navalo with a fresh five on our tail and a good tidal push. In two places south of the Ile au Longue the current prescribed a very visible and complete whirlpool in mid channel - a disturbance that our big headsail drove us through at great speed.

In short time we were powering up between the little, wooded Iles de la Gezek and Creizig and into the gap between aux Moines and the mainland. At the north end of Moines there are the two previously visited and fully serviced but freestanding pontoons linked to the land by a frequent rib ferry service. This is a welcoming and beautiful island and we always enjoy cross-island walking and the many good views over the Morbihan.

So we spent our two nights and moved on. In the past, as I have described, we have picked up a mooring off Lamor-Barden and seen a short distance away the sandy fringes of the Ile de Gavrinis with small craft lying off. The chart shows a small anchor off Gavrinis so that was an invitation to take root after a short but enjoyable sail through the Port Blanc narrows. We picked up a professional looking buoy and the dinghy landed us on the foreshore at the top of which were steps leading to a small open gate.

Alice-in-Wonderland could not have resisted such an invitation and we knew that the far end of the island held a major Neolithic burial mound. Well, hey! There are plenty of these around so 'no big deal' but perhaps worth an explore. So 'though the looking glass' we stepped. Beyond we found no walls not broken down, or fences not holed, or gates not penetrated or pasture fields not abandoned. A very cheerful looking cat peered down from a leafy tree.
" I think he needs help getting down. Shall I call the 'Pompiers'?"
"Just help me over this broken down wall and stop being very, very silly." Beyond two eight foot high white rabbits (it's all true) we come across an abandoned farm buildings turned into (empty) education 'field centres'. And so to the mound.

Of the many such mounds you might see, this one is pretty impressive, perhaps 5000 years old, with a clear masonry structure and deeply incised stone markings. An ambitious archaeological investigation and restoration has been made in recent years and interpretation is available to organised groups arriving by their own special (paid-for) ferry. What we got was a good telling off from a pointy-nosed White Queen-of-Hearts and a reminder that the Morbihan islands are mostly private even when in public ownership. Whoops! Haven't been told off like that in forty years (except by my wife, Jacky reminds me). Seemed to be time to abandon Alice and return to the safer Yellow Brick Road. We scurried back to *Wise One* and the welcoming cockpit.

As we settled into the cockpit and the evening sun we saw the small tourist ferry heading round the end of the island for the mainland after its Neolithic trip. Seeing us it changed course and came across, clearly for a 'word'. We waited with a little foreboding, thinking perhaps we were on his mooring and this was a half hour warning to relinquish. Fair enough, it happens. When he arrived the skipper addressed us at some length, probably with a pronounced Breton accent. Good news: it was clearly not about the mooring. Beyond that we were uncertain but thought it was something like: "I say fellows, a Breton chap has to earn a crust, you know, and chaps slipping in round the back not paying don't help". We did pick up one or two repeated words which the dictionary told us were 'expli. delet' whatever that meant. Anyway the tourist cargo seemed amused so we smiled and waved (good news about the mooring) and he got redder (the effects of the evening sun, probably), spun his wheel and throttled to the mainland leaving us bobbing in his wake.

We slept well and securely as the owls called over the woods. For them, I guess, sex is a hoot but all the noise must disturb the hunting. Like the rest of us, I suppose.

* * *

The wind and tide were fair and we moved on. - out of the Morbihan, out through the Navalo Channel, headed out with a free force four across the Baie to the 1000 berth Haliguen. The marina is just a modern marina but it has beach and cliff walks and a very pleasant town centre some 15 minutes away by folding bike. We had our two nights and, again, moved on.

Our next destination was Sauzon on Belle Ile. The route to Belle Ile is straight forward in reasonable weather. The big Teignhouse light is easy to pick up and the passage through the reefs is well marked. However the tidal currents can run hard through the passage and the reefs are not a place to mess with in strong westerlies.

Belle Ile, is the largest of the south Brittany Islands at 17.5 km long and 9.5 km wide and rising to some 55 m above sea level. It has two ports in le Palais and Sauzon. The primary port, Le Palais, lies some 20 km from the Port Haliguen on the Presque Ile de Quiberon and 55 km from the lock at the Arzal Barrage. But our destination was Sauzon which is a little closer and which we had not before visited and of which we had only heard good things.

You can lie outside Sauzon on visitors' moorings or on your own anchor. You can enter the main harbour and lie to fore-and-aft deep water buoys which you might share with four or five other vessels (to each buoy). Or you can go beyond the main harbour to an inner, drying harbour where you lie to fore-and-aft buoys which you share with nobody. Not knowing the state of the seabed in the drying harbour and not wanting particularly to lie outside, we went in past vessels of all sizes lying out and picked up harbour deepwater buoys – and were in due course sandwiched between four other vessels just on 'our' buoy in a potential nightmare of a cat's cradle of lines. At about half flood tide a procession of vessels entered, passed beyond us and took the drying berths. As the tide fell so they settled on to firm and reasonably clean sandy/gravel. (But of course you have to cope with a dry loo).

If you can take the ground and the half-tide constraint is not a problem, then that could well be the thing to do. In fact we enjoyed the community atmosphere of the shared buoys and eventually released ourselves with no great problem and a certain amount of community aid.

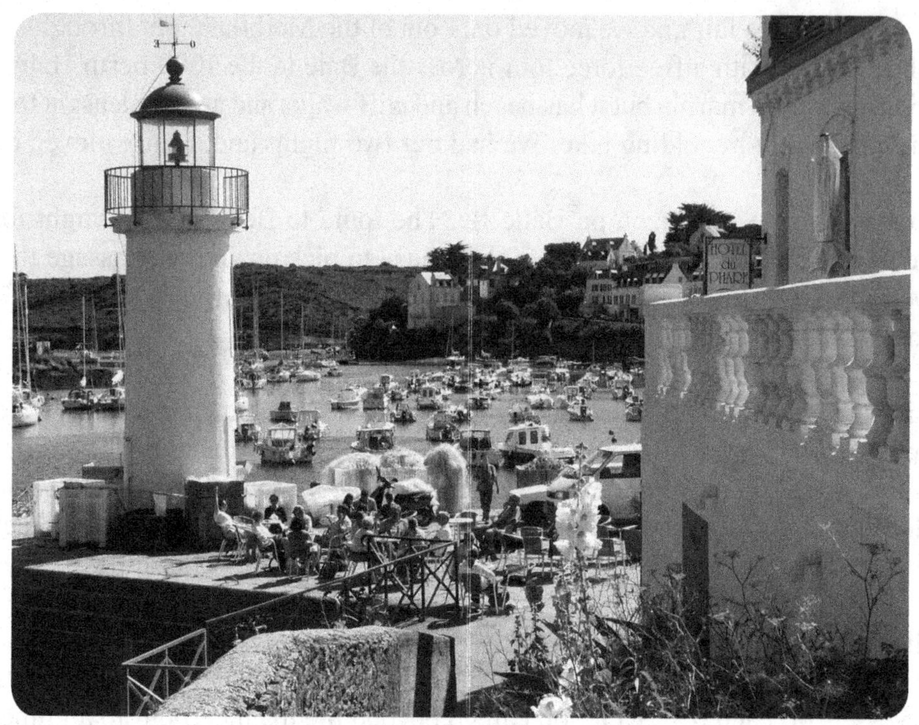

Sauzon, Belle Ile.

Sauzon is a delightful little port; clean, colourful, well loved and busy. Locally caught and landed fish can be bought from a quayside stall every day and we spent an enjoyable evening prizing meat from a couple of large spider crabs. Well we enjoyed it but perhaps the crabs didn't. Killing the crab is always a bit controversial; we took the line that if immersed in lukewarm water and slowly brought to the boil, the crab concerned would be lulled to sleep and subside almost without knowing it. The saucepan was a bit small and the crab only just fitted in with the lid on. A spooky moment for us was when the crab concerned stretched out an arm during the process and removed the lid clearly in an attempt to make a run for it.

For sure the deep water harbour buoys can be congested, but for once we simply enjoyed company and the occasion.

We day-walked across the western end of the island to explore the rocky Ster-Vraz inlet, clearly a favourite place with the local boats (but not a favourite with the pilot book.) Ster-Vraz is a deep, narrow inlet with a westerly-facing mouth that gulps the prevailing swell. Within the inlet there is a smaller, narrower, deep water branch to starboard, Ster Wenn, in which local boats make a fair-weather stop lying to anchor and shore lines. At the end of this branch are several permanent shore lines to which very small boats might tie. The end of the main inlet is fine shingle and families gather there to sea and sun bathe. A pleasant walk from Sauzon, for sure. If you go on your own keel be ready to leave if the westerly freshens since even the very sheltered Ster Wenn gets uncomfortable..

Ster Wenn

From *Belle Ile* it had been our intention to visit and explore the islands of Houat and Hoedic which lie between Le Palais and the return track to either Croesty or the Vilaine. They are said to be a delightful destination but are also said to have very limited real shelter or permanent moorings. Most craft lie off (either island) and over night can be uncomfortably exposed.
We were faced with several problems. Our starter motor chose this moment to pack up and Belle Ile is not the best place for spares. We had a family visit to us in the Vilaine pending and faced the unknown mechanical problem. The engine started easily by hand, but a better solution called for a return to Crouesty for advice. Finally conditions were not ideal for the small islands so, not for the first time, they were aborted.

A four gusting five on the beam gave us a great sail back to Crouesty. British engineer Graham was working in Crouesty that very day and came to call. After sustained attempts to effect a revival, the starter motor was pronounced 'dead'. Its replacement with a reconditioned one was promised in Roche Bernard within a couple of days, so back we scooted to the lock at Arzal and the short sail up stream to Roche Bernard. The starter motor was replaced the next day. Thank you Graham.

* * *

On the 27th July Anna, Daz, Amelia (7) and Elliot (2) arrived to camp on the site adjoining the Roche Bernard river moorings. Since the start of our project we had been joined by the Oldham Family Branch before but small Elliot (ambition; like his dad to be a lead vocalist in a heavy Mancunian Rock Group) was a new-comer to *Wise One*; so welcome aboard Elliot!

Mind you, a small boat not defensively organised for an active and curious two-year old is a dangerous place with not one surface not stacked with books, bottles, navigation gear, food, pencils, hand bearing compasses, cleaning gear; not to mention Stanley knives and dividers. It was fortunate that there were several adults on board..

Space on board, however, is a bit limited for two grandparents and a family of four, so parallel camping and boating works quite well. Space on board might be limited but there had to be a boat trip. We had an appointment to pick up son-Alex from Nantes rail station. However that did gave us time for a short, pre-Alex family voyage and so on the 29th we embarked up-stream toward the little wayside stop at Rieux.

Once again we appreciated the sheltered waters of the Vilaine, ideal for a very young crew. And from Roche Bernard we again passed under the sky-high Roche Bernard and Morbihan Bridges. Both link the wooded and rising banks which crowd the river on either side. Prevailing winds are a fluky westerly (sometimes quite fresh) so a headsail-alone rig is a bit lazy but certainly effective.

After five winding and forested miles we reached Foleux with its two marina facilities on either side. This time we continued our gentle pace past Foleux where the woodland falls away and the river opens up to fields and more distant prospects. After a further seven miles we arrived at the turning bridge at Cran and two miles on to the gentle rural stop at Rieux. The dinghy was inflated, life jackets donned, skills of rowing and swimming explored. A watch was kept for dangerous 'logadiles', frequently seen skulking in these waters. Food was carried ashore to the generous green picnic area and the family generally spread themselves around this green and pleasant 'stop'.

Two days later we returned to Roche Bernard. We have a summer-only pontoon arrangement in LRB which gives us a certainty of a space in la Roche and a 'passport' which gives a credit in other nearby named ports, but we don't have a single dedicated space in Roche. However our VHF call established that a space was available in the Old Port.

It happened that close to our pontoon berth there lay against the old stone quay a 34-footish, 1950's wooden motor-sailer. A nice traditional craft, probably quite roomy below because it had a large harp and an elegant harpist on board. She would set up her instrument on deck and play to a dreamy, drifting crowd on the tree-shaded quay. Her music spread like ripples on the surface of a still pond, embracing the port and its old stones. You can't organise these moments; they just happen.

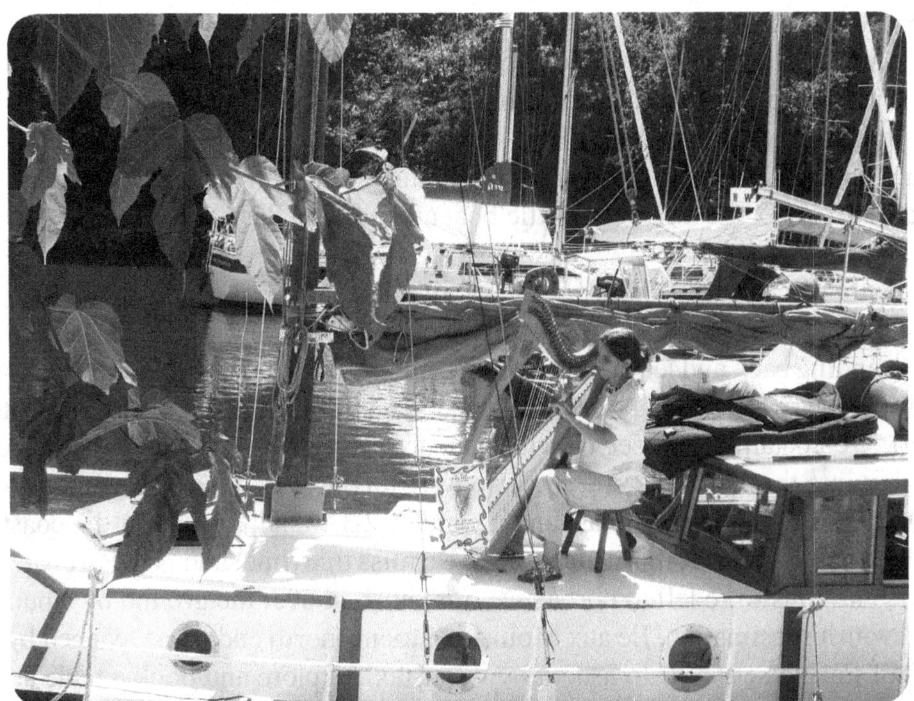

Harpist in the Old Port

In due course Alex joined us, this became our base for several days of drawing, beaching and sea swimming. There are good beaches to be found, particularly at Penestan. Of course it was popular and busy. I was sure I saw a flash of a red dress and heard a clear voice calling "Beignet; ChouChou; Glaces".

"You're imagining things again" said Jacky "Silly old fart." (I think she meant me, not the Red Dress.)

Visiting the Vannes aquarium and butterfly centres were a well spent rainy day and showed, again, the value of having a car with us. We then returned to the UK for a couple of weeks of grandparent duties. You've got to do it.

* * *

On the 16th August we returned to LRB and on the 19th were joined by Linda and Graham for a few sailing days. These are again old friends from Lyndhurst. Linda takes daily yoga classes when not exercising her cuisine craft. Graham is a retired solicitor, pianist, philosopher and yachtsman a little older than I but in quite good nick considering. At 6' 6" Graham is challenged lengthwise when it comes to berths; and altitude-challenged when it comes to cabin head room. He managed. With great philosophic good humour Linda puts up with Graham (as far as we could tell). Both now work in the B & B biz. In addition they have just bought a Moody 33 in Turkey which "needs a little work".

We have known Linda and Graham for some thirty years in the New Forest, Lyndhurst area. No New Year's Eve is complete without Graham and Linda (or Pete and Kate) (or Bill and Vicky). Curiously we discovered that Graham and I had both owned very small 17' boats (a veritable shoe box for Graham) which we had both sailed in North Wales at about the same time. In fact Graham had used a mooring in the Manai Straits on the Anglesey side quite close to the small Port Dinorwic where our little boat and holiday flat were.

Of course with sailing guests on board the Morbihan again beckoned, the weather was fine and after a brief settling-in we left for Arzal. The next day target was the 0800 hrs lock but, in politely standing back and letting the queue-jumping rivals have space, we found ourselves excluded from a very full lock. (The skipper's judgement was under question but sentence was suspended). We containing ourselves with patience which was rewarded when the eclusier waved us first into the 0900 lock and soon we were on our way down the estuary to the open Baie de Quiberon. With a hint of east and a gentle f 2-3 we slipped down the coast, turning into the Morbihan past Crouesty (which we gave a miss this time) and past Port Navalo. Ile de Longue and Gavrinis were left to port as we were hurried over the ground by a punchy flood tide. Our favourite destination, Ile aux Moins' pontoons (north end), was reached by 1600 hrs with loads of time to settle in, go ashore by water taxi, explore and book a table again at the 'Chez Charlemagne.

Unfortunately Linda and Graham had not much time to cruise the Morbihan, but we were able to spend the next night in the little bay east of the Point de Penhap at the south end of the Ile aux Moins; initially lying to our anchor and later picking up a fixed buoy. A small dinghy expedition ashore was launched and a walk along the headland path through the bracken and gorse, under the shading trees that reach down to the water's fringe. These gentle walks give a special view of the Little Sea. I find that, in general, photographing the Morbihan works much better from a shore location than from the deck of a small boat. The waterways, other nearby islands and boats can still be captured, but they can be framed by tree foliage. The foreground of pasture or rough shingle beach and mussel beds provides a context which is much more difficult to grab when on the water.

It was a still and quiet night. The wind had gone down with the sun and only the occasional owl called across the tree-clad islands.

The final Morbihan day was spent making the short trip back to Crouesty and enjoying the 5-7 knot current (10.5 knots over the ground !) on the way. On the previous day Jacky had commented:

"Look across at that undergrowth at the top of the beach. There are twin hulls peeping out that really look just like seaplane floats". Graham and I conferred:

"No, no. Sea-planes simply aren't that small. That's clearly just a small sailing cat, there are a lot of them around".

From Ile aux Moins, Morbihan.

We did notice that on the chart a mid-channel aircraft reservation strip was indicated which, we imagined, was available for fire fighting water collection. However now we were amazed (but not Jacky) to witness what looked like a micro-light, about the size of a very small dinghy with floats, taxi out from the shore, take off and head for the horizon. Jacky's rapidly taken photo provides the evidence supporting her judgement in case Graham or I deny it (which we wouldn't).

"Told you!" she said.
Actually the photo's a bit fuzzy but I suppose it is undeniable.

The final return to Arzal and LRB was with the benefit of a WSW but, sadly, not the promised force 4. A bit of motoring was done and I was reminded of how shallow the Vilaine estuary entrance can get at bottom tide.

So farewell to Linda and Graham and thanks for your company. We were now approaching the end of our five-year '*Yellow Brick Road*', French circumnavigation. It really didn't seem so very long since we entered France at Honfleur – perhaps we should have stayed longer in the South after all. However, this was now our long-awaited Dumet, Hoedic and Houat islands slot, so "let's go for it !"

These three small islands do present a problem. From Arzal, Houat is some 24 miles; from Crouesty and Piriac about 16 miles. You can't really go there without exploring ashore for which you also need time. The local advice warns that the little harbours in Hoedic and the slightly large one in Houat are unlikely to have any spare space. The alternative is to anchor off in open waters that can be subject to swell. Two-in-the-morning scenes are painted of minimal clad figures rushing around deck tackling anchor drag (theirs or someone else's) with gunnels rolling under. Fifteen to twenty miles is not exactly a remote destination; but an awful nuisance if you don't like your mooring at two in the morning.

But we had a settled forecast, a usable angle of wind promised to take us there and a 180 degree shift to bring us back. We chose to go via Piriac so as we left the Vilaine estuary we took a southerly turn and, after an enjoyable f3-4 on the beam, spent the night in Piriac. This stretch of water lived up to its fecund reputation and gave us a nice medium sized bass on the line which we enjoyed that evening.

Just a note on Piriac: as mentioned earlier, it has a rising and falling sill which has a minimum 1.4m into the marina when dropped. The Pilot suggests that the marina is open from about half tide; but of course every tide is different and the maximum time the marina is open on any one day can only be found from a comprehensive table which is published or, of course, calling them on the VHF. If in doubt I would certainly recommend the latter before arriving at the marina entrance when exactly how much water is available becomes apparent. We arrived on a rare day when, to our confusion, the neap tide gave us free flow all day.

The next day a gentle 2-3 delivered us to Ile Dumet and, subsequently, Port St Gildas on Houat. Dumet is a delightful rock of something like 500 x 50 metres. Or there abouts. At high water. It rises modestly from the sea some three-and-a-half miles from the harbour entrance to Piriac. On a settled day its white beaches draw yachts and small motor boats to drop a hook or beach for a swim. It is a nature reserve but we could walk the salt-spring grass and tough scrub with care. There are two stone forts described officially as C18th (the round one) and C19th (the square, block house one). The latter is called Fort Vauban – a little odd since he died many years before it was built. Possibly it was one of very many he designed but not built in his lifetime. Anyway it illustrates the way in which the French would put heavy guns on almost any piece of rock where fire cover could be obtained for a nearby port.

The two islands of Hoedic and Houat lie some 3 miles apart. Both have small permanent communities (Houat is said to be some 320) whilst host to a major influx of summer time and weekend visitors. Both have small harbours whose major functions are to contain the small local fishing fleets and accommodate the frequent passenger ferries from ports including the Quiberon, Trinite, Vannes and Navalo. Houat is 5 km long, 1 km wide and the architecture is white-painted vernacular. Houat's Port St Gildas (some 10 miles from le Palais on Belle Ile) has a number of sheltered moorings in the form of three large buoys linked with a stainless steel rod to which you tie alongside. You then reach the granite quay using your own dinghy.

The pilot advises that yachts over 10 m are unlikely to find a berth. The conventional wisdom is that 'in season' visiting leisure boats cannot expect to get in simply because of the pressure for sheltered space.

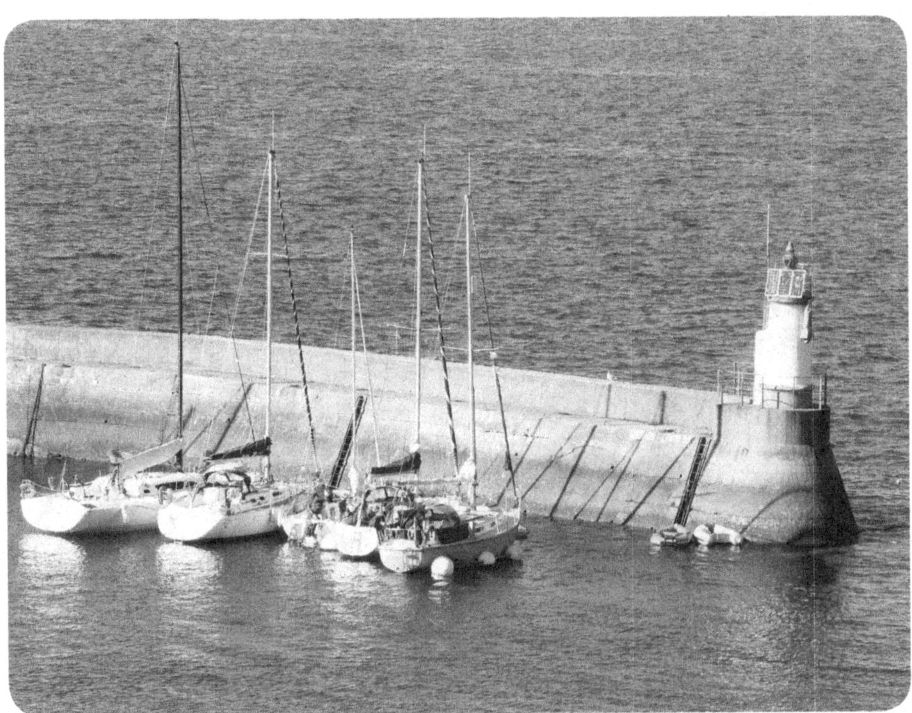

Port St Gildas, Ils de Houat.

Outside the harbour there is an area where anchoring is possible although it is now substantially laid to permanent buoys available (we understand) to visitors. Our visit was on the last weekend of August and many French boats were running home with their holidays over. When we arrived at Port St. Gildas, the little harbour was pretty full but, despite predictions, we still found one berth just inside the harbour mole. For a couple of nights it could hardly have been better.

The alternative popular anchorage is in the Treac'h er Beniguest bay and its spectacular white curving beach lying just to the east of Port St Gilda. Walking from the Port westwards the path leads along a small cliff which falls to a series of discrete sandy bays the first of which is only reached by a fixed rope abseil. It quite took us back to our distant flirtation with rock climbing in Derbyshire. Over the years we seemed to have lost our elegant touch; particular on our return upwards.

So walking the island is a must and enjoying the gentle network of informal footpaths, (motorised vehicles forbidden), headlands, open sea views, beaches, and wild flowers. And we did with great pleasure.

On return from one expedition we found a smaller boat (the *Saphyre,* said to be an ex-Glanan vessel*)* lying along side. Two French guys (older Phillippe-with-the-dreadlocks and younger Richard) on board seemed to live in some informality, surviving off the products of sea and shore and day-expired baguettes.

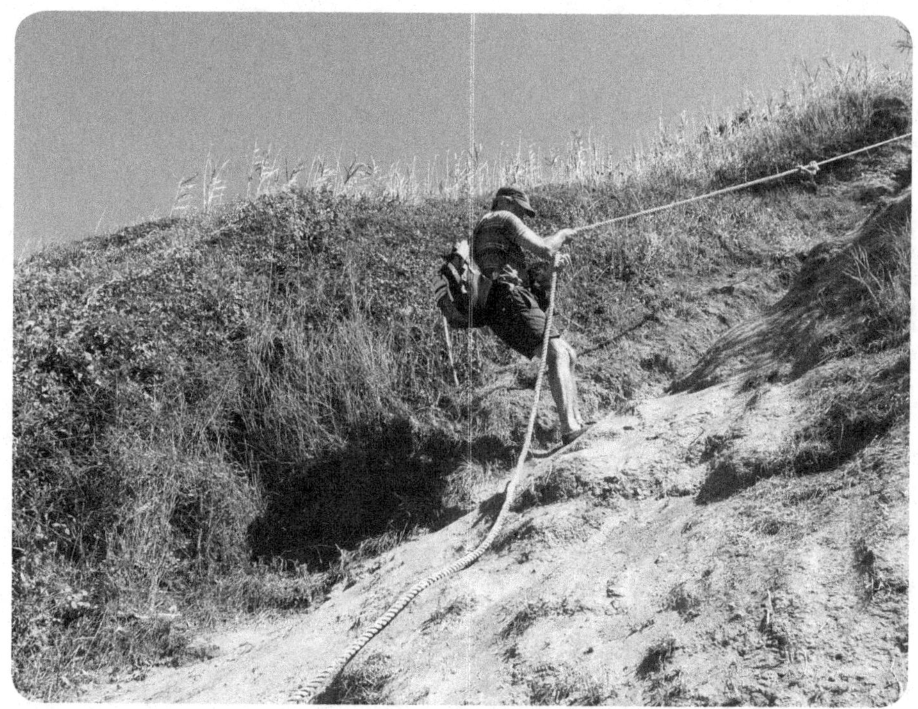

Elegant descent to the beach

When we arrived on board, they had a dinghy in which they went ashore for provisions. A little later they hailed us from the mole for a lift back on board. Whose dinghy they started with was not at all clear. So our initial contact with these two sea gypsies was a little cautious. However come evening time, and after we had shared a couple of glasses of red, Philippe produced his violin and played music from the Celtic nations. Breton dances, Irish jigs and Scottish love songs entertained us for an hour at the end of which applause echoed across the harbour moorings.

The next morning when we spotted the Harbour Masters launch coming round for fees, we rattled on their roof in warning. They had no engine and there was no wind, but within a few minutes they had sails up and were off the mooring. Unfortunately the Harbour Master had to pluck them off the harbour mole where they had drifted and set them on their proper track. I don't think any fee was collected ("Mooring? What mooring?") but I think that an elderly pain-au-chocolat exchanged hands. Everyone seemed satisfied.

Life in the round continued in this small community. Whilst we were there a wedding took place (the French make sure you know about these things). Now the only effective way the guests and the departing couple could leave was by ferry which, as it happened, passed our stern on its way out by a matter of yards to turn the mole and head for the mainland. It was clear that the bride's young drinking friends (mostly female) had decided to see off every relevant ferry by taking station at the end of the mole and howl, cheer, mock, screech and, finally, coordinate a grand mooning at the departing vessel. We cheered and applauded and the girls took a finale bow to us.

You just can't plan these things. But it was now time to complete that Circumnavigation.

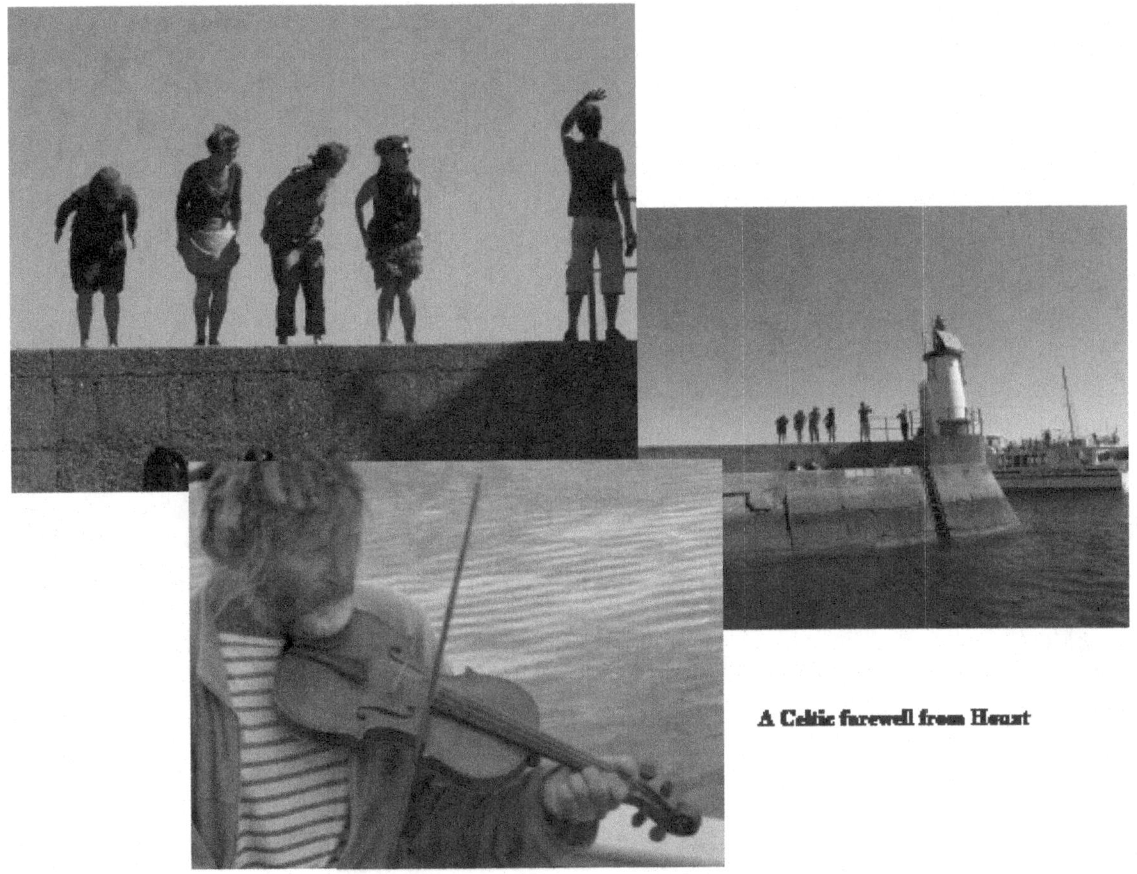

A Celtic farewell from Houat

New Moon over Houat

Chapter 21

'Stamping on Shadows'.

We are now coming to the end of our travels. Our final return to Le Palais will be our 'Emerald City', our end of the Yellow Brick Road and our Circumnavigation of France.

So finally we managed to make le Palais. We last visited this port about thirty two years ago and it was at that time our southerly most point from our home base in the Solent. Getting here via Paris and the Mediterranean Port Camargue was our own Circumnavigation of France; well more or less anyway. The port hasn't changed. On entering this principle harbour of Belle Ile, leisure yachts vie with commercial space for the few fore-and-aft moorings on the starboard hand against the quay. Just as we moored all those years ago. You can go through a lock and into a small wet basin but I confess that we did not find it terribly attractive or welcoming.

It is a busy old commercial town with deep historic roots and is dominated by the great *Vauban Citadelle*. This huge and intimidating fort was built by the ever-energetic Sabastian Vauban for Louis XIV in 1683 and designed to keep the Brits out. Actually they did occupy the fort in 1761 and Belle Ile was then exchanged by France for Nova Scotia in 1763.

* * *

Le Palais, Belle Ile equals. 'Circumnavigation done', 'Emerald City' discovered and mission accomplished.

As we approached the old port, from a distance the island rose above the huge 17th Century grey fortress which dominates the harbour. With increasing anticipation we approached the great masonry projecting arms of the harbour which slowly grew from the foreground until they stood tall above us. A number of small boats gathered at the entry and several came towards us, waving as trippers do. We could see now that the walls were topped by crowds promenading and enjoying the July sun. There seemed some excitement with a pointing of arms and a waving of coloured flags. As we passed through the high harbour entrance, triumph and astonishment combined. From the battlements of the high Vauban Citadel six huge 17th Century cannon roared a fire-spitting welcome that echoed from the low hills and momentarily killed the cheers of thousands. The sky was split again by rockets launching their own white trailed suns. In a flash Jacky leapt to the fore-deck, a red flare held high in each hand.

And the people. Momentarily we caught sight of Anna and Alex and Peta with families small and large. Surely there was Anna and Harro from Mettmann. And beyond Morton and Eva from Denmark with Scottish Bill and Marie; Ann and Bill, Chris and Sue from Indaloo were there; and Mike and Barbara; and Swiss Nicholas. And somewhere in between the flash of a red dress. ("When I close my eyes, you are everywhere").

But other faces appeared on the battlements; there were the Veneti and the Amoricans backed by Roman centurions respectfully acknowledging the 'Triumph'. Bretons, Moors, Hollanders, perfidious English (even 'Blondie' Hasler), a sharp-nosed White Queen and plotting Spaniards. Admiral Zheng-He looked down with inscrutable benevolence, his open hand holding a tiny Magellan. A blooded Pope 'Innocent' 3rd was seen eternally washing his hands, the faint whiff of burning heretics on his pure white vestments; his shoulders were bowed with the weight of the church militant. Entrez chien et loup. There, surely, was the tall, gaunt and mournful man with a scythe from whom, amidst the clamour, came a Churchillian growl "Can hardly walk; can't fuck. All in all I'm buggered up!" (Winston circa 1938). Quite good news for us the un-dead. But behind all stood the distant, grey shadows of long drowned sailors and heretical ghosts.

To the faint air of 'Goodbye Yellow brick Road', a gilded barge with smartly sweeping oars drove towards us with the great, silk-clad Monsignor Nicolas Fouquet waving a plumed hat to assure us that little had changed for centuries and, essentially, nothing for ever. A shaft of sunlight caught on the highest battlement the figures of Paul and Sabastian (one person or two ?); the creative wizards of this story. Ghosts, heroes, villains, tin men, giants, witches and wizards were all there to welcome us to the Emerald City.

Actually it was rather quiet that day as we dropped into the same berth occupied by us more than 30 years ago. So that's what's at the end of the *Yellow Brick Road.* It seemed at least a tidy moment and

" *I just couldn't have liked it more . . . . . .*"

'A quiet sleep and a sweet dream when the long trick's over....'

(Thanks to JM)

Finale

But the time came to leave. We had a cross-Channel ferry booked from Le Havre and a boat to strip and lift ashore. A WSW was promised and we took off for Arzal and LRB. The return was lively but started with a f 1-2 over the stern and motoring for home. The wind slowly filled in and soon we were goose-winged under full main and big headsail. Six knots is a good speed for us and was soon regularly exceeded. A following swell was building and a 'preventer' rigged on the boom. When we surfed down a wave at 7.5 knots we knew it was time to get things under control. However with a well reefed main and several rolls in the headsail we continued in more comfort but still exceeding 6 knots. Great stuff. My only small anxiety (again !) was not to get into the Vilaine estuary too early; it can be very rough with fresh westerlies. I couldn't forget that a thousand dead sailors' hands waved from the shoaling sand to catch our shallow keels…. ('In Domina Patrie, et Felis et Spiritus Santis'). All however went well; we passed the estuary bar, slipped quietly up stream to the lock which, when not active, lies open to vessels arriving from down stream. For the next hour the lock slowly packed with arriving yachts until eventually we were ejected through and on our way to our final night in LRB.

The next day I took Wise One up-stream to Foleux where Jacky met me by car. (In the end you've got to get both vehicles in the same place !). Bill and Ann joined us for a meal on board that evening. The next day we stripped the boat; the crane lifted us out and we headed off for a final couple of days relaxing over our 44th wedding anniversary in our delightful French starting port of Honfleur. We even ate where we did five years ago in our favourite restaurant, l'Homme de Bois. Just seemed a good way to complete the circle.

Verdict

Did Dorothy 'find herself' (and her way home) and the Scarecrow get some brains ? Sailing puts a great perspective on life so we all find ourselves a little. That was OK then. And the brains ? Well perhaps we are both a little the wiser. But to make any real improvement I guess we will just to have to keep on sailing….. Where will we sail next year? You'll have to ask Jacky that one, she's the boss.

Wise One away

Post Script message to you, the Reader:

come and talk to us on www.locksandtides.com
We'd love to hear from you.

Appendix 1

Locks on the French Inland Waterways. 2005-2007 (A sort of Appendix to our first two years)

Over the previous seasons 'Wise One' has passed through 408 French locks and this is a brief account of that experience. They varied largely (you might imagine) in age, size, purpose and workings. Let's just divide them into big, medium and small.

The big ones were in the working rivers of the Seine, the Soane, the Yonne, and the Rhone. They were mostly twentieth century construction and of mixed commercial and leisure use. They were managed remotely from high glass boxes and typically communicated by disembodied loud hailer and traffic lights to control movements. In our very first lock (on the Seine) the 'eclusier' (i.e. lock keeper) beckoned us up to his eyrie where he looked at all our documentation and asked us our intentions. He was the only one who did but we became aware that the information followed us right down to the Med.. The system seemed to know at all times where we were.

Commercial traffic always had the priority and was generally composed of freight barges (think 1000 + tonne barges and 4500 tonne push-pull tows) and 110 m long cruising hotels. Generally this mix was not a great problem to us although one lock on the Seine took two hours to get through. If the 'eclusier' allowed we could share a lock with big barges (if we were quick) and were sometimes offered help by the bargees to fall alongside them for the big lift (or drop). There is one barge that no one may share a lock with. That is the dangerous freight barge; i.e. petroleum cargo or similar. Shapes, lights and signals give you the warning so you have got to learn them or be shouted at by the 'eclusier' !

The lock rise and fall in the Seine was typically 5-8 m. However on the Rhone the great Ballene and Mondragon locks are a huge 22 m.. Life jackets are advisory everywhere but are compulsory through the Pouilly Tunnel and on the Rhone. These heights are too great for throwing ropes or even scrambling up ladders with rope in teeth. (Assuming your teeth can stand the strain). No problem. On the Rhone you expect to find a big floating bollard at deck level which takes you up (or down). Easy peasy. On the other main rivers typically there will be continuous vertical steel rails up which your mooring line will slide. Generally water turbulence is very controlled – until your high powered fellow occupants leave with great clouds of exhaust and backward directed water jets.

A big one on the Rhone

All major locks have a river overflow system to bypass the lock when closed. In the smaller locks this will take the form of an enclosed water gully run-off around the lock. On the bigger locks this might be a weir which itself can be a source of danger and concern. (Keep well clear!). On the Rhone this is typically used for hydro-electrical generation, sometimes paired with a land-based powered generator (gas, oil or even nuclear). The Rhone system generates some 7.5 % of the county's electrical power so it is no small business. VHF communication with the 'eclusier' is always useful – if only to thank him on departure. A big lock on the Rhone is not difficult to pass through, but can be a big complex of heavy industrial construction.

Medium sized locks. In the upper reaches of the rivers and in the more recent and larger canals these locks have typically a rise and fall of some 4-6 m. They have mostly been built in the late 19th century. They will have mixed commercial and leisure use with leisure perhaps being the majority and the declining commercial sector being mostly cruising hotels. Commercial craft still take priority. Locks will all be staffed with the 'eclusier' using a mixture of traffic lights and voice to control the entry. The quayside bollard will be accessible by ladder and or rope hurled to an accomplice.

As you enter the lock, be sure that you know where the ladder is; there might be only one. The lock gate normally has ladder rungs up it and I have been known to scale the gate as the last option left. Sometimes (but not often) the 'eclusier' will take a line; sometimes there are helpful by-standers who will join in. Whether or not they know what to do with the line is another matter.

Medium -to-small sized, with battered sides. So, imagine you are entering a lock and, as you go in, you find that the sides slope away from you. If you are going down, you might not even realise. But as the water falls, so you scrape and bump your way down the rough masonry slope until you find some way of holding your self off (boat hook, oars). If you enter to go up, at best you are faced with a slimy ladder that slopes away from you which you climb holding the fore and aft lines while fellow crew member keeps the delicate hull off the sloping wall. At worst there's not even a ladder.

The flight at Fonserannes

The design logic totally escapes me except but I believe these were very early locks and were easier to build that way. Also in those days there was no such thing as a gel coat ….. . Help however is at hand. Having negotiated several such nightmares, we then came across several where a floating pontoon is attached to sloping rails and climbs the wall as the water rises. The nastiest and most difficult of locks was charmed into being the easiest of all. You enter, fall alongside the pontoon which then looks after you (up or down).

Small, old and manual. Throughout the Canal de Bourgogne (central France) and generally along the line of the Midi (and linking canals) we were in canals built in the 17th and 18th centuries. Nowhere were they as small as the oldest English canals. We met English narrow boats (no, don't cross the Channel in one!) and they really look extraordinarily small and thin even on the oldest of the French canals. This group of canals typically have a rise and fall of about 2-3 m. and they are nearly all staffed.

The Canal de Bourgogne locks are typically managed by summer-holiday-youngsters. All jolly, energetic, chatty and helpful but not necessarily very wise in the way of locks and boats. Over one section we (and several other boats) were given a small team who managed perhaps six locks and rushed between them on buzz bikes; before handing you on to the next team.

Small lock on the Midi

To help prepare the next lock I would often see Jacky away from the last one, cycle ahead and get the next one moving and cycle back to meet Jacky plus 'Wise One' and signal the state of preparation. ("Hold back, it's still filling" or "Bash on, it's waiting for you"). Many locks still had their old fashioned 'eclusier' living with family in the lock house. They help you through as well as clearing the unmentionable, inflated, furry corpse from the gates. Important job. He/

she would have fresh fruit and veg for sale as well as some local wine for your delight. And was always happy to do a deal. (But do get there well before the published closing times).

Small, old and automatic. Finally the Canal du Midi and the Lateral de la Gironne held two surprises. Unique (as far as I can gather) these canals have water overflows that fall directly over the closed gates instead of being directed around the lock by a sluice. Secondly, some locks are unmanned. A hanging white and red pole over the canal before you reached the lock had to be grabbed and twisted. This started the lock process and a traffic light told you whether to advance or hold back. Once in the lock a set of buttons pressed in the right sequence operated the lock and released you. With these it was often a good plan to drop a member of crew at the waiting pontoon who would trot ahead to receive the boat as it entered the lock. (All quite energetic).

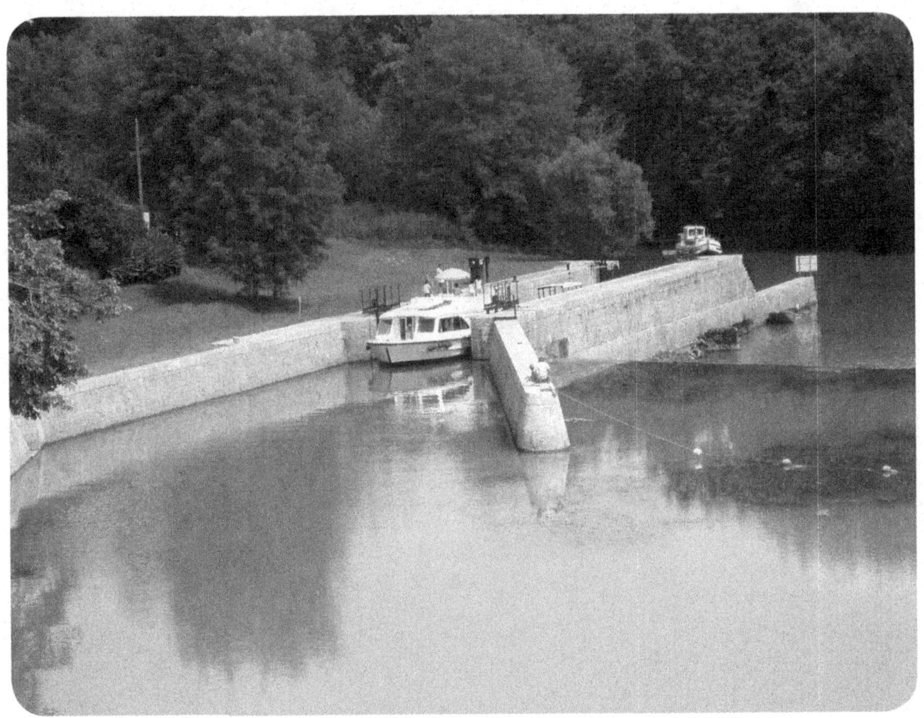

73 Junction between Midi and Baise

In summary It would be impossible to manage the system single handed without the help of very sympathetic fellow travellers. Three people on board are good. Two pensioners managed perfectly well (and got fitter and leaner). The boat has to be well protected from casual damage but our Snapdragon 890 survived happily with four car tyres (bagged fetchingly in blue polythene), eight large fenders, four tarpaulin skirts, and two long softwood planks. And, occasionally, some language. NB Car tyres are officially discouraged because if they are lost in the canal they sink and can cause problems. However they are widely used to protect hulls. If you must, make sure they are well secured. But don't be daunted.

Go and do it.

Appendix 2

Many references have been made to Sebastian Vauban and his contribution to the shape of these cruising coastal towns, that it seemed appropriate to give some account of him.

Sebastian Vauban 1633-1707 'Ingenieur extraordinaire'.

The medieval European castle of children's book tradition is based on the bow and arrow followed by the introduction of the light musket. With the advent of mobile heavy cannon, siege warfare changed radically. The massive castellated masonry curtain walls of tradition were now rapidly breached by heavy cannon ball. The renaissance, star shaped earthwork defences of the 16th to 18th centuries were developed and sophisticated by the iconic siege engineer Vauban. Of course masonry was still used but was protected by earthworks and designed to deflect rather than stop cannon fire. Earth embankments absorbed cannon shot; but did give an attacking force a possible scalable hill to ascend into the citadel. Vauban went much further than most of his predecessors in developing theory and practice of defence and attack. More than others he shaped those defences into elaborate geometric form which not only absorbed artillery impact but also drew the attacking troops into killing traps.

Sebastian Vauban was born in 1633 in the small town now called St. Leger-Vauban. His father had a military background. His parents died when he was young and he was brought up in poverty but usefully educated by the Priory of the local church, proving to be a gifted mathematician. He entered the army at the age of 17 and soon started to work within military engineering. The army engineers had many duties of logistics, mechanical construction and building works. They were also prominent in the field of siege engineering; both in defence and attack. The senior army officer engineers would substantially take charge of a siege on both sides. Vauban's talents became recognised at an early stage and he rapidly rose in the service of Louis XIV. Vauban's life almost exactly matched that of the 'sun' king who lived from 1638 until 1715.

Over this period France was asserting herself in Europe; establishing her own borders and increasing in wealth and power. However in doing so she had to resist the similar ambitions of Spain, the Netherlands and Britain. The king became aware of the need to establish his southern boundaries and strengthen his defences in northern and southern France and along the Atlantic seaboard. Throughout his early years as a middle ranking army engineer, Vauban had repeatedly distinguished himself and was rewarded by advancement. During his active military life he was involved in 140 battle actions, 50 sieges and was wounded seriously 8 times.

Belle Ile

In 1677 he was appointed 'Commissionaire General des Fortifications'. He was now in a position to implement his theories of an integrated plan to fortify France's shores and borders. These plans involved double lines of forts, particularly in the north. They involved the development of a powerful naval Atlantic port in Brest and Rochfort (and others). These were accompanied by fortifications in depth making the breaching of these ports very difficult and risky. Part of the process was at last to deny to the British any occupation of off-shore islands from which an attack might be launched. (The original Atlantic Wall).

Vauban remodelled many existing forts as well as constructing totally new ones. He was noted for not applying a standard solution to all sites, but for designing around the local constraints and needs. The modest little-island fort might be not much more than an artillery terrace whilst the great citadel in la Palais was a vast and complicated military base defended by great and extensive engineering works. Many are still very visible today and explain the shape of some of the ports that yachtsmen will visit on the Atlantic coast.

Belle Ile

Belle Ile

The list includes:

Le chateau d'Oleron
Ile d'Aix - Fort de la Rade
Ile de Ré - Fort du Martray, St Martin and Fort de la Pree.
Belle Ile - La Citadelle (See chapter 21)
Ile d'Hoedic - tour d'Hoedic
Ile d'Houat - tour d'Houat
La Rochelle - Fort de chef de Bai
Rochefort - Brouage, Fort Lapin, Fort de Fouras and Fort du Chapus

In addition there are three forts on the approaches to Bordeaux and three on the approaches to Bayonne. Brest and Cameret are defended by six forts and St Malo by a further six. Of all these works, some have now vanished and some remain in a good state of preservation. Some are simple walled emplacements; some are very sophisticated and complex citadels.

Appendix 3
George's view

The following is a brief book review which seemed just appropriate as a sort of Appendix to Part 4 of this book.

The Oyster River
By George Millar
published by the Dovecote Press in 1963. Reprinted in 2003.

While cruising in the Golfe du Morbihan this summer, I was several times recommended to read 'The Oyster River' by George Millar

The author had spent a period of the war as a POW in Germany. He escaped back to the UK but returned to work with the French Resistance Movement. His war-time experience (captured in a subsequent book by him) did not extend to Southern Brittany, but his resultant friendships included links into the Morbihan area. Those links both enriched his summer and the reader of this delightful book.

George and Isabel Millar had owned a series of vessels in the 40 to 50 foot range over a period of years. Central to this book is their pride and joy, the photogenic and classic 50 ft yawl, Amokura. They had sailed widely but not previously in South Brittany so in 1963 this was their project.

The Oyster River is the author's name for the River Auray although their cruise covers the whole of the Golfe and touches on the adjacent Vilaine River as far as La Roche Bernard. The special Golfe experience is beautifully captured by George Millar. The myriad of green and wooded islands; the powerfully tidal waterways and narrows; the gentle sheltered backwaters all appear on the page and before your thoughtful eyes. The book makes an entertaining and revealing entrance into French life around the islands at all social levels, ways of life which I am sure substantially no longer exist. Although visiting yachts were becoming an increasingly common sight in south Brittany, the great Plastic Armada had yet to arrive. The Amokura soon became a recognised 'friend' beating between the islands or foaming down 'the Gut' on a big tide.

The book is beautifully and observantly written but seems quaintly old fashioned, even for 1963. It does speak of an earlier age as we find Vannes waterfront deserted of boats (and no mention of a locked entrance). The Vilaine River has no barrage and is therefore still vigorously tidal. Their ambition to sail up to Redon is thwarted by the temporary post-war floating causeway up-stream of Roche Bernard. The causeway replaces the destroyed suspension bridge while its permanent replacement is under construction. (The occupying Germans had mined the previous bridge and a lightening strike had triggered the explosion).

But we know from The Riddle of the Sands that no good story is complete without a sinister and unexplained foreign threat. The huge bulk of the twin six cylinder 72 hp Gardiner-engined motor yacht Ric-Rac provided threats of danger, violence, sabotage and international intrigue. That threat could only be outwitted by superior (and British) boat handling in difficult waters; and, of course, it was. And none of it fiction, I am sure.

Our heroes mixed with farming peasants, fishermen, countesses, Directors of Gendarmerie, international 'something' runners, gales, tidal rips and all with good humour and a ready glass of pernod or whisky. As you do when sailing the Golfe. And all of it absolutely true; read for yourself !

Appendix 4
Bibliography Charts and Pilots

Guide Fluvial NaviCarte
(www.guide-fluvial.com)

Caneaux du Centre No. 6
La Saone No. 10
Rhone No.16

Guide Fluvial
Bourgogne Franche-Comte No. 3
Midi Camargue Aquitaine No. 7
Champagne Ile de France No. 11

Guide Vagnon de Tourism Fluvial
Caneaux de Midi

And

Inland Waterways of France by David Edward-May
Waterway Routes Through France (Map) Jane Cumberlidge
Map of the Inland Waterways of France K. Nussbaum

And

North Biscay Pilot Imray
Carte Marine Officielle, Golf du Morbihan
Imray Noth Biscay Charts – C39,C40,C41,C42
West France, Cruising Companion. Neville Featherstone

And

The Battle of Quiberon Bay 1759 - Nicholas Tracy
The Vauban Fortifications of France - Paddy Griffiths
Holy Warriors - Jonathan Phillips
The Oyster River - George Millar
Wikipedia

INDEX

NB Numbers represent chapters not pages.